BEYOND THE HYPE

BEYOND THE HYPE

REDISCOVERING

THE ESSENCE

OF MANAGEMENT

Robert G. Eccles
and Nitin Nohria

with James D. Berkley

**HARVARD BUSINESS SCHOOL
PRESS**

© 1992 by the President and Fellows of Harvard College
All rights reserved
Printed in the United States of America
97 96 95 94 93   5 4 3 2 (hc)

97 96 95 94 93   5 4 3 2 1 (pb)

Library of Congress Cataloging-in-Publication Data

Eccles, Robert G.
    Beyond the hype : rediscovering the essence of management / Robert G. Eccles and Nitin Nohria with James D. Berkley.
        p.   cm.
    Includes bibliographical references and index.
    ISBN 0-87584-331-X (hard: alk. paper)—ISBN 0-87584-506-1 (pkb: alk. paper)
    1. Management.   I. Nohria, Nitin, 1962–   II. Berkley, James D., 1968–
III. Title.
HD31.E27   1992
658—dc20   92-18707
                                                                            CIP

The paper used in this publication meets the requirements of the American National Standard for Permanence of Paper for Printed Library Materials Z39.49-1984.

CONTENTS

PREFACE

We did not plan to write this book. In fact, we started with a different and quite opposite objective—to write a book on our own version of the "new organization." As two business school professors (Bob and Nitin) joined by a research associate (Jim), we were quite aware of the intense interest among managers, consultants, and academic colleagues in the development of a new organizational form that might transcend the limitations of the unfashionable bureaucratic hierarchy. Like many others before us, we saw writing such a book as an opportunity to contribute both to our profession and to our professional identities.

We also had reason to believe that such a form might someday exist. During the late 1980s, before Jim's arrival, we had undertaken a field-based research project with the awkward title of "The Management of Knowledge-Intensive Organizations." Because many arguments about the need for a new type of organization were based on claims about a shift from an industrial to an information society, we reasoned that any new paradigm would most likely arise in a "knowledge-intensive" industry. We were convinced that by studying such industries we would surely find the leading-edge companies pioneering the organizational forms of the future.

The problem, of course, was deciding what counted as knowledge-intensive. In mid-1989, we cast our nets wide and began conducting interviews in a variety of firms: in biotechnology, machine tools, footwear, law, consulting, advertising, computers, software, entertainment, health care, financial services—in short, in anything we could see possible reason to accord the label "knowledge-intensive." In all of the companies we visited, we were looking for evidence of a new organizational type, or at least for a transformation toward it. At the same time, we began an equally intensive case-writing effort for a new required first-year MBA course called Information, Organization, and Control. A central message of the course was how information technology made possible management practices that had heretofore been impossible to achieve—how it permitted new approaches to individual work, organizational structure, and management control systems. We wrote a number of case studies in some of the above industries, as well as others in a range of manufacturing and service businesses. When Jim joined us in 1990, he became a part of this effort as well.

In January 1991, our attempts to figure out exactly what we had been seeing in the companies we studied culminated in a working paper entitled "The Post-Structuralist Organization." (Because so many labels for the new organization had already been suggested—including post-industrial, post-bureaucratic, and post-entrepreneurial—some effort was involved in finding a label of our own. Admittedly, the one we chose was not exactly zippy.) Our paper was very much in keeping with contemporary excitement about the emergence of radically different approaches to management. While we had not been able to find full-blown examples of a new management paradigm, we nonetheless tried to cobble one together from what we had seen—or what we believed we had seen—in a number of different organizations.[1]

Yet sometime between January and May 1991, our thinking took an unanticipated turn. Put simply, we began to doubt the very premise that a new organizational form was destined to emerge in the first place. At the same time, we became increasingly convinced of the value of the perspective from which the post-structuralist paper had been written—that action rather than design was the best way to think about the task of management. As we confusedly pondered our dilemma, we began to think about our research in a new light. Certain events and conversations—including some we had originally supposed to be minor—began to come to the fore, and new meanings began to crystallize around them.

We recalled for instance a conversation we had with a manager at Reebok named Angel Martinez who was trained in classical rhetorical theory. We had a long discussion with him in Los Angeles on a day we will always remember as magical—August 14, 1990. He was the first manager to pose clearly for us the central role that rhetoric plays in the practice and study of management, although we did not understand the full import of his words at the time.

We also began to see how our perspective had changed through ongoing conversations with Jim, who had come to us fresh from studying literature and philosophy at Williams College. Jim had been slowly introducing us to a whole range of literatures and to cultural movements such as post-modernism—ideas with which Nitin had a passing acquaintance and Bob had almost no acquaintance at all. Jim's training in the humanities had brought a distinctly different and complementary perspective to Bob and Nitin's respective undergraduate backgrounds in mathematics and engineering and their graduate training in the social sciences.

The result of these fortuitous developments was that, slowly and steadily, we had begun to question what lay behind the words we heard in the companies we were researching. Not surprisingly, given the hub-bub over the emerging new management paradigm, many of the people we talked to were themselves anxious to discover its elements or to claim that they were already practicing it, at least in part. But we had begun to feel that the connection between this impassioned rhetoric and real, nitty-gritty organizational action was more complicated than we had been ready to concede.

Our attitude shifted further as we reflected upon our field research at Giddings & Lewis, a factory automation and machine tool company in rural Fond du Lac, Wisconsin, sixty miles north of Milwaukee. Founded in 1859, the company was originally a proprietorship which produced, repaired, and serviced machines for lumber and flour mills. During the final decades of the nineteenth century, the company diversified into a foundry and into the manufacture and installation of industrial steam engines. Its entry into machine tools began in 1902. In 1982, the company was acquired by a Canadian conglomerate, AMCA International, which then sold it in a public offering in 1989. This company of 2,250 people worldwide and sales of $243 million in 1990 was (and is) for us a microcosm of the great changes that have taken place in America's industrial landscape over the past 150 years.

Giddings & Lewis was also one of the few American machine tool companies that had been successfully competing with the Japanese and Germans, as described in a 1990 *Fortune* article that prominently featured a picture of CEO Bill Fife on its cover. During a year when orders for American tools dropped 22%, Giddings & Lewis's sales had risen 38%, outpacing the growth of even the Japanese tool firms.[2] *Fortune* lavished praise on the company's management and manufacturing systems in terms that made the company seem like some other "leading-edge" companies we had observed in action.

Yet Giddings & Lewis was puzzling. Throughout our field research, the company had always appeared to be an outlier. Despite the fact that it competed in an environment said by many to have the preconditions forcing the emergence of the new organization—a highly competitive global market with demanding customers, rapidly changing technologies, and great pressures for organizational flexibility and responsiveness—managers often described the company in decidedly traditional terms. For example, Fife himself would speak enthusiastically about the advantages of centralization and a well-defined hierarchy. At the same time, some of Giddings & Lewis's management practices—such as ignoring the hierarchy when communicating on important issues, constant and rapid organizational change, and linking compensation to performance rather than to seniority or hierarchical position—were consistent with the new management paradigm we thought we had uncovered, although nobody in the company made a very big deal about them.

The more we thought about it, the clearer it seemed to us that the reason Giddings & Lewis was an outlier was not that its management practices were different from those we observed elsewhere. Rather, the *language* used to describe them was simply different from the language used in other companies. The location of the company and the backgrounds of its employees put it outside of the mainstream of contemporary management discourse. Yet by any measure, the company was extremely well managed and very successful in a highly competitive industry. Giddings & Lewis's managers acted in much the same way as managers in other effective companies facing similar challenges, but they spoke about their actions quite differently.

On reflection, it became apparent to us that the "newer age" companies in our research and case writing projects also contained many "older" management practices as well. In these companies, of course, there was a tendency not to discuss these old practices, or, at the very least, to treat them as transitory to the arrival of the transformed organization. We concluded that while there was indeed variation across companies, and while some management practices appeared to be more effective than others in certain circumstances, the presumption that a radically new type of organization was just around the corner was simply unsupported by the empirical evidence we had gathered.

From here our attention was redirected to the problem of understanding the relationship between language and action in management, a task to which we soon added the concept of identity in order to emphasize the role of individuals in the organizations we had studied. We decided to end our search for the new, or knowledge-intensive organization and turn our attention to the triadic relation of rhetoric, action, and identity in managerial practice.

SOME NOTES CONCERNING OUR AUDIENCE

This book is addressed to the thoughtful manager. In our research, course development, and teaching activities we have met many such managers with whom we have had very productive discussions about the issues addressed in the pages that follow. We think of them as thoughtful because although they are eager for and open to new ideas, they also have a healthy skepticism about the latest sure-fire solutions to what they realize are eternal problems that must be *constantly* managed. This group of managers—and we suspect their legions are large—will hopefully appreciate an effort that suggests we step back and take a constructively critical look at how management is being practiced and studied today.

Managers who are still looking for the silver bullet will be disappointed in this book. We have none to offer. And while we have made every effort to avoid academic jargon in order to make this book as accessible and relevant as possible, it is not like most of the management books that have proven to have popular appeal. Instead, we are offering a perspective—one that good managers may already implicitly have—rather than guaranteed solutions to today's management problems.

We also hope that this book will be of interest to students of management—to academics, consultants, and so forth—and even to laypeople interested in the ideas we explore. Based upon feedback we have received on earlier drafts of this book from such people, we expect this book to strike a number of responsive chords. Of course, nobody will agree with everything we say—we would be disappointed if everyone did. What we are trying to do is present another point of view, a kind of enlightened skepticism that challenges many of our received ideas about how organizations work. Our goal is to generate debate by challenging prevailing modes of thinking in a way that will make all of us concerned with effective management more thoughtful.

The reader will soon discover that we have used the feminine pronoun throughout the book. It is necessary to explain why three men would choose to do so. One reason is quite natural: some of the managers who had the most impact on our research were women, and our thoughts frequently turned to these women as we put our ideas into words. Of course, some male managers were equally important, and we soon found ourselves in something of a quandary. In a time when identity is a sensitive issue, any choice of pronoun construction has its critics: *he* for being sexist (despite the usual footnotes explaining that it is meant to refer to both men and women), *he* or *she* or *s/he* for being awkward, and *she* for being reverse sexist or even disorienting. Authors have to resolve this issue in their own ways. Our personal decision was to choose the underused feminine pronoun—perhaps as our own minor demonstration of the importance of words.

ACKNOWLEDGMENTS

We have learned a great deal from the many managers who so graciously took time from their busy days to talk with us. We have benefited enormously from our conversations with them: to say that this book would not have been possible without them is trite, but true. Although too numerous to name, we would like first to thank all of them for their contributions.

We are also grateful for the time and effort expended by the numerous people who carefully read previous drafts and gave us blunt and constructive criticisms, often under severe time pressures. In particular, we would like to thank the following readers: managers Melissa Beach, Stew Dougherty, Ellie Luce, Vicki Sato, and K. K. Nohria (Nitin's father); consultants Bob Berkman, Vince Di Bianca, Amit Chandra, Tom Davenport, Chuck Gibson, Linda Gioja, Keiron Hylton, Eileen Shapiro, and Joel Uchenick; and academics Joe Bower, Wally Gilbert, Richard Hackman, Paul Lawrence, Warren McFarlan, Leslie Perlow, Michael Piore, Joshua Smith, Bob Sutton, and Harrison White. We, of course, are solely responsible for what appears here.

Our wonderful editor, Carol Franco, has shown us how valuable an editor can be. She deserves recognition and sympathy for weathering our "fast-cycle-time" approach to writing and revision, and for putting up with our occasional antics with tolerance and good humor. Natalie Greenberg, also of the Harvard Business School Press, provided invaluable suggestions for slashing our original "final" manuscript down to a more readable and manageable form.

We would also like to thank Dean John McArthur and Senior Associate Dean Warren McFarlan for providing intellectual encouragement and financial support through the Division of Research at the Harvard Business School. In particular, we acknowledge the high-quality and timely research assistance provided by Mike Stevenson, Chris Allen, Sarah Collins, and Phil Hamilton, all of Baker Library Research Services at the Harvard Business School. Last, but certainly not least, we extend our appreciation to Hilary Gallagher and Rita Perloff, our secretaries who provided untiring assistance at every turn.

As often happens, this book was an obsession for us from the first draft begun in June 1991 to its final one at the end of April 1992. Friends and family have tolerated this with good humor. Since we had each other to talk to, they were usually spared excessive conversations about "the book." Bob's wife, Anne, and children, Charlotte, Philippa, Isabelle, and Gordon, Nitin's wife, Monica, and Jim's entire family are all owed time we plan to repay. These commitments give us an opportunity to demonstrate that we can match action to words ourselves.

1

INTRODUCTION: GETTING BEYOND

MANAGEMENT HYPE

Overture

Globalization. Information technology. Total quality. Benchmarking. Best practices. Customer focused. Micromarketing. Flexible manufacturing. Value creation. Core competence. Competitive advantage. Strategic intent. Strategic alliances. Partnering. Outsourcing. Networks. Time-based competition. Continuous improvement. Concurrent engineering. Computer-aided design. Computer-aided engineering. Computer-aided manufacturing. Computer-integrated manufacturing. Cross-functional teams. Downsizing. Rightsizing. Flattening. Delayering. Information. Revitalization. Restructuring. Reengineering. Organizational transformation. Business process redesign. Mission statements. Organizations as orchestras. The new organization. The information-based organization. The knowledge-intensive organization. The learning organization. The network organization. The shamrock organization. The self-designing organization. The informated organization. The cluster organization. The adaptive organization. The hybrid organization. The post-entrepreneurial organization. The post-industrial organization. The transnational organization. Knowledge workers. Empowerment. Pay-for-performance. Diversity. Entrepreneurs. Intrapreneurs.

Words may come and go, but *action* is always the managerial imperative. While this claim may at first seem rather obvious, it is surprising how few writers currently mention it in their attempts to advise people how they should think about their jobs. In recent years, there has been an amazing amount of verbiage instructing managers on how to become "leading-edge," "excellent," or "innovative"—yet little of it attends to the practical questions of how to actually get things done in organizations. To be sure, there has been a lot of hoopla about the 1990s heralding a new era of progressive, nonbureaucratic organizations, but these New Age ideas are often propounded in such a way as to make their translation into action frustrating or even impossible.

This book puts action back at the center of managerial practice by proposing a way of thinking about management that runs directly counter to most of the frameworks, models, and buzzwords advocated today. Instead of focusing on abstract panaceas for organizational revitalization, we will focus instead on the very root of what goes on in organizations. Clearly, this root has everything to do with action. But while action is always the goal, it is not the whole story. In developing an action perspective on management, we will also examine two other themes which, broad and obvious as they are, have been neglected by many commentators: language and people—or as we will come to call them in this book, rhetoric and identity. By meshing these three themes together, this book aims to give a fresh account of what managers really do—and in some cases, what they really should do—with their time.

By introducing words like rhetoric and identity, we do not intend to make managers think more like academics. In fact, one of the prime lessons of this book is that, if anything, the reverse would be infinitely more desirable. This being the case, our task in this first chapter will be to explain these concepts in as plain a language as possible, and to build a case for why we think managers need, especially now, to adopt the perspective that we are advocating.

DESPERATELY SEEKING NEWNESS

As we approach the twenty-first century, a host of academics, consultants, practitioners, and journalists have produced and disseminated new concepts for the manager to use. The range of these "new ideas" spans the entire breadth of what organizations do, from strategy to organizational design to performance measurement to manufacturing. Many of these new ideas become widely popular among managers, even if only for a short period of time. For example, many if not most managers today will have heard trendy terms such as *empowerment* or *core competence*—a fact that shows just how quickly certain kinds of management language can become universal.

What is fueling this desperate quest for new approaches to management? Certainly, concern about America's competitive decline in the global economy—especially vis-à-vis the Japanese and now even the European Community—is one of the driving forces behind this trend. Far-reaching economic and social changes have been proposed: new technologies, new expectations from customers, new social patterns, and so on. Taken together, these forces signal that we live in a time of rapid and discontinuous change, an "age of unreason" unparalleled in the course of human history.[1]

Such views are standard doctrine in the management literature today—so much so that, to many, the arrival of the new has begun to sound a little like old news. Nevertheless, it will be helpful to review some of the features usually associated with this massive environmental change:

● *The global economy.* At the head of almost every list of changes is the emergence of a truly global economy in which U.S. firms no longer enjoy an unquestioned competitive advantage. More and more, it is argued, the world economy centers on competition among multinational companies, which account for an increasing share of the output of global products and services. Competitive statistics reveal the emergence and rise of new players in the world economy such as Japan, Korea, Singapore, and Taiwan; the list of the top ten companies in various industries is no longer dominated by the United States and Europe, but by Japan. The collapse of the Soviet bloc and the rise of the European common market are interpreted as further steps toward the creation of a truly global economy.[2]

● *The post-industrial economy.* Several observers see this new globalism in the context of a wider transition, one often described as a transition from an industrial to a post-industrial economy.[3] The primary distinguishing feature of this post-industrial world—which is not, as we will see, an exactly new idea—is postulated as the shift from material resources to information and intellectual resources as the basis of the economy, a trend resulting in the growth of a highly educated, "knowledge-based" service sector. New information technologies occupy a pivotal role in almost all conceptions of the post-industrial society, and thus have found their way into many models of the new organization.

● *An accelerated pace of change.* Another standard motif in arguments for management's unique historical situation is the claim of a radical acceleration in the pace of change. Typically, writers make this claim by tying the knowledge- and information-intensive character of the post-industrial economy to the observation that we are witnessing the emergence of new products and technologies at a greater rate than ever before. Product and technology life cycles, it is argued, are getting shorter, and windows of economic opportunity open and close more rapidly. As the common wisdom has it, this situation creates early-mover advantages and makes time-based competition more important than it ever was during the more stable days of managerial capitalism.

● *New demographics.* Recent demographic trends are also seen as motivating changes in organizations. In America, the much publicized *Workforce 2000* report highlighted the changes that will be required as women, minorities, and the elderly become a larger proportion of the work-force.[4] The very definition of the term *career* has also been challenged by a new focus on job mobility rather than on the traditional pattern of lifelong affiliation.

● *Turnover in corporate control.* The emergence of an active market for corporate control—a development that led some observers to call the 1980s the "Age of Takeovers"—has been cited as a turning point in managerial capitalism, reversing the progressive separation of ownership and control underway since the 1930s. The rise of leveraged buyouts and other forms of governance are seen as creating enormous pressures for organizations to transform themselves by becoming more efficient in their use of resources through downsizing, delayering, focusing, and consolidating. Although relatively quiescent in the last few years, the market for corporate control has even invited predictions of the eclipse of the public corporation.[5]

Exploring the Obsession with Newness

The lesson of all these environmental changes has been surprisingly clear. As leading management guru Tom Peters bluntly put it, the answer for organizations is simple: "Get innovative or get dead."[6] For managers who have taken his message at face value, the quest for new organizational practices—for new words, new structures, new designs, new systems, and new strategies—has become a rather frenzied pursuit.

We certainly *do* believe that change and innovation are important. Yet our experience and research has also led us to the conclusion that a certain skepticism of newness is necessary—that the constant talk about "new practices for a new age" is shortsighted and may lead us both to misunderstand the past and to ignore what is really important in organizations. As we will see, much of the new thinking is basically old wine in new bottles, and many progressive management concepts have been articulated in some fashion or another for quite some time. This is not to say that some are not useful, only that it is not always useful to think of them as new. And while we wholeheartedly agree that stressing change and newness has an undeniable rhetorical power in certain situations, we fear that many managers are actually unsure of how to harness this power effectively.

Stereotypes of the past tend to obscure the fact that, recent hype aside, effective management actually has little to do with the newness of one's conceptual arsenal. A good illustration of this is in the work of Mary Parker Follett, one of the early so-called administrative theorists, writing almost seventy years ago.[7] The stereotypic view of this seemingly ancient time is that business organizations were unenlightened bureaucratic machines where people were told what to do and then did it, or else. Yet what Follett actually learned by observing business practices in the 1920s was quite similar to the kinds of lessons that are today packaged as "cutting-edge." One such lesson, discussed at length in a 1926 talk, was that authority and responsibility in organizations actually has little to do with one's position in a formal hierarchy.[8] Referring to a conversation she had with a superintendent of a multidepartment division in an industrial plant, Follett makes the passing comment that the superintendent recognized "that authority should go with knowledge and experience; that that is where obedience is due, no matter whether it is up the line or down the line."[9] Similarly, Follett called for an emphasis on "cross-functioning"—on the replacement of "vertical authority" with "horizontal authority"—in order to promote the exchange of knowledge in organizations.[10]

Follett's relative de-emphasis of hierarchy is echoed in much contemporary writing about the need for new organizations and empowered workers. And just as current management prescriptions emphasize the need for decentralizing authority and responsibility, Follett too noted that "the tendency today is to decentralize."[11] Of course, whenever authority and responsibility are decentralized, there emerges the problem of coordination: How can autonomous parts be made to work together to produce what is best for the whole? This dilemma, which has been central to management from the very beginning, was reflected on by Follett at great length and with great erudition.

The decentralization of authority is only one example of a "new" management theme that turns out to have been quite common throughout this century. Others include producing quality products, providing responsive customer service, formulating strategy in a way that takes into account distinctive internal capabilities, rewarding performance fairly, and running a socially responsible enterprise. Who could argue with such advice? When did managers think—let alone say—they were doing otherwise?

Even a casual reading of the management literature over the past seventy-five years, both popular and academic, shows that every age "discovers" these principles anew. From such reading, one thing becomes especially clear: even as the fundamental themes of management remain the same, the words used to express them constantly portray them as new. What are we to make of this? Of course, to a large extent, there is a sense in which we all (Americans perhaps most strongly) have an underlying need to believe that the world is more challenging and volatile than it was in the past.[12] Even beyond this, a natural social dynamic might also be seen at work. It is some people's *job* to think up new ways of managing, and people everywhere seek to establish their professional reputations and identities through the words and concepts they introduce. To an extent, innovation of this kind is natural—it is simply the way the world works.

Understanding Today's Hysteria

Even to the manager most frustrated with the situation we have described, our message may initially seem somewhat cynical. Yet this is certainly not our intention, since we firmly believe that there is value to be found in the careful and skillful use of words. There *is* something to be said for each age creating new words that best express some obvious truths in a way that will be most meaningful to people at the time. But there is also something to be said for raising a cautionary voice that says that the strength of these new words does not lie in their containing superior solutions to eternal problems. Our position is that *understanding* the way words are used and re-used is perhaps the most vital aspect of management—and certainly more important than grasping at every new program and buzzword that comes along as if it were the managerial equivalent of the Holy Grail.

As we have mentioned, there are certain historical forces that might be driving the present frenzied search for new and better management practices. On the one hand, there is genuine concern about America's uncertain position in the world economy. On the other, there has been a dramatic increase in institutionalized knowledge about management and, during the 1980s, a revived interest in business often associated with the Reagan presidency. Paradoxically, then, the last decade has been one of both boom and malaise, a "business decade" that was nonetheless marked by real and mounting anxieties about the future of America's global economic role.[13]

Despite management's emergence as a hot topic, doubts about America's future have indeed increased in recent years. A growing trade deficit, a decline in the value of the dollar relative to other major currencies, loss of world market share in some key industries such as automobiles and semiconductors, acquisitions of American companies and real estate by foreign companies, the decline of the manufacturing sector relative to the service sector, debates about the value of a national industrial policy, a burgeoning national deficit—these trends have created the resigned belief that American companies are not as well managed as some foreign ones. This is particularly true when Japanese companies are used as the basis of comparison—not surprising in light of the fact that much of America's competitive decline has been at the hands of the Japanese.[14]

Even now that the Japanese economy has tasted setbacks of its own, the extent to which Japan is seen as the source of good management continues to be captured by one Harvard MBA student who summarized the lesson of his first year simply as "Japan does it better."[15]

Such concerns about American management are in vivid contrast to the more optimistic 1950s and 1960s, even though (as we will discuss in Chapter 2) the optimism of those times was not always universal either. During this period the key economic challenge was a more domestic one: namely, managing the large and diversified companies that were both a cause and an effect of America's economic prosperity, establishing their legitimacy in society, and using this legitimacy as an ideological weapon in the Manichean struggle against the dark forces of Soviet communism. Such dramatic differences in national mood between then and now make the underlying similarity of prescriptions about good management all the more striking.

The Contemporary Diffusion of "New" Ideas

Although a sense of urgency about the need for good management has existed throughout this century, institutional mechanisms for creating and transmitting this knowledge have grown dramatically. Increases in the number of business schools and MBA graduates, in the number of executive training programs (by business schools, training firms, and companies themselves), in the size of the consulting industry, and in the number and circulation of business books and periodicals (more than 1,600 new books in 1990 alone) have all contributed to a greater awareness and more rapid dissemination of the latest, most up-to-date management practices.[16] Given the temporal correlation between our competitive decline and the growth in institutionalized knowledge about management, one can only hope that this correlation does not represent a causal relationship.

The desperate search for quick solutions to eternal management challenges—combined with the opportunities this has created for managers, academics, consultants, and journalists who proffer solutions to these problems—has resulted in an impressive proliferation of nostrums, techniques, and philosophies of management. Typically, these "new" ideas are presented as universally applicable quick-fix solutions—along with the obligatory and explicit caution that their recommendations are *not* quick fixes and will require substantial management understanding and commitment. As many managers will attest, the result has been a dazzling array of what are often perceived as management fads—fads that frequently become discredited soon after they have been widely propagated.

A good example of one such fad is the recent "empowerment" movement, in many ways a contemporary version of the participative management trend of the 1950s and 1960s. While the vague goal of empowerment is something most people are for, many managers today cannot use the word without simultaneously expressing discomfort and cynicism with its current popularity. Their unease is legitimate, and echoes the unease many felt earlier toward participative management programs, which even a 1950 *Fortune* article bluntly described as "programs [which] have been little more than well-meant fictions designed to give the worker a 'feeling' of belonging and very little else."[17]

FROM NEWNESS TO USEFULNESS

We suggest it is time for a change of attitude. The time has come to get off the verbal merry-go-round which the search for the newest management ideas has become. The search is only taking us in circles, and the accumulation of words and theories is making us dizzy rather than clear-headed in our attempts to develop organizations that foster the kinds of action needed to survive and compete in today's business environment. Instead, we advocate a return to the true elements of effective management: rhetoric, action, and identity. Combined, we will refer to these three elements as providing an "action perspective" on management, a perspective we ask the reader to judge by the criterion of usefulness rather than novelty. While these three concepts are simple ones, each has a very particular meaning, elaborated in Part I of this book. Here we present an overview of each and how they are related to one another.

Using and Understanding Rhetoric

As shown in the first section of this chapter, management has a lot to do with the use of language, both in the sense of how language is used *in* organizations and in the sense of how it is used in ways—such as business books and journalism—that *span* organizations. Unfortunately, the use of language is such an everyday activity that it tends to be almost invisible. A manager may spend the better part of her day talking to people or deciding how to talk about certain actions in her organization, yet she may nonetheless be unaware of the extent to which language creates the context for everything she does. Similarly, managers may read and hear all kinds of arguments about new practices or changing times, yet be unaware of how the authors of these arguments actively use and abuse language to try to provide a certain picture of the world.

In a nutshell, managers live in a rhetorical universe—a universe where language is constantly used not only to communicate but also to *persuade,* and even to *create.* The first step in taking a fresh perspective toward management is to take language, and hence *rhetoric,* seriously—to understand rhetoric as a powerful force always at work in our understanding of organizations. In Chapter 2, we therefore take a close look at rhetoric and the different roles it plays in the manager's world.

In its traditional meaning, rhetoric refers to the formal field of study that examines how language is used to shape the way people think and act—a study that needs to be properly understood as one of the central concerns of effective management. In his translation of Aristotle's *On Rhetoric* (a book that has more than passing relevance for today's manager despite the two millennia that have elapsed since its writing), George Kennedy defines rhetoric as "the energy inherent in emotion and thought, transmitted through a system of signs, including language, . . . to influence [people's] decisions or actions."[18] By this definition, almost every situation that a manager faces has something to do with rhetoric: one-on-one conversations, small group discussions, presentations to large audiences, written documents and memos, articles in newsletters, project proposals, capital appropriation requests, management information reports, committee proposals, strategic plans, vision statements, magazine articles, best-selling management books—all are examples of situations where managers must actively wrestle with language in the service of decision and action.

We suspect that, to some readers, our use of the term *rhetoric* is something of a red flag. After all, most of us are accustomed to thinking of rhetoric in a negative sense, often as verbal trickery that blurs the distinction between words and reality. Yet it is partially for this reason that we have chosen to use this term in the first place. True, most of us today have a negative connotation of the word *rhetoric,* as exemplified in such phrases as "mere rhetoric" and "inflammatory rhetoric." But rhetoric has a positive component as well, as in the "powerful" or "moving" rhetoric that can force us to see the world in new and enlightening ways. This understanding of rhetoric is usually confined to the world of politics—for example, it is often associated with leaders such as Mahatma Gandhi, Martin Luther King, John F. Kennedy, Margaret Thatcher, and Winston Churchill. When we agree with the message, the effective use of rhetoric can profoundly influence how we lead our lives. And even when we do not, we are forced to acknowledge the impact that rhetoric can have in shaping the actions of others.

While this latter example is closer to what we mean by the term, our position on rhetoric goes even further. Taking our cue from a variety of recent writers, we argue that rhetoric is not the kind of thing one can be for or against—it is simply the way of the world, the way human beings interact and get things done.[19] It exists everywhere and on many different levels—from individual conversations to entire systems of thinking and speaking. Rhetoric is something that can be used and abused, but it *cannot* be avoided. Rather, it constantly serves to frame the way we see the world. In our view, rhetoric is used well when it mobilizes actions of individuals in a way that contributes both to the individuals as people and to the performance of organizations as a whole. It is abused when it remains unconnected to action or when it leads to actions that are detrimental to individuals and the organization.[20]

To see this distinction more concretely, take the example of the way one kind of rhetoric—corporate vision statements, say—is received in different organizations. Clearly, in some companies the distribution of a corporate vision statement by senior management is seen as a very positive gesture which influences people's actions and the way in which they think and talk about the organization. In other companies—perhaps the majority, we are afraid—the distribution of such a statement is seen simply as a meaningless exercise, one that merely promotes trite phrases indistinguishable from those found in similar statements in other companies. Clearly, the particular words chosen to express the corporate vision can make a difference—often a significant one. But given the similarity in many of the statements we have seen ("produce high-quality products," "pay attention to customers," "treat employees fairly," "provide a good return to shareholders," and so forth), it cannot be merely the words alone that explain these differences.

Taking Action

Whether words and the concepts they represent are old or new, their efficacy is judged by how well they are used to generate *action*. The fundamental problem with the "flavor of the month" phenomenon so common in many American companies today—e.g., "If it's March, it must be 'Vision 2000' "—is that words are used carelessly without ever being connected to action. In organizations, words without deeds are less than empty since they can potentially undermine the power of all the words that follow them.

As we will stress repeatedly, action is always the final test. But there are many kinds of action, and simply to urge action is futile and meaningless. *How*, for example, should managers think about action? What kinds of guidelines can help the manager take action and make decisions day by day? In Chapter 3 we argue that managers should be taking a particular kind of action, which we call *robust action*. Simply stated, robust action is action that accomplishes short-term objectives while preserving long-term flexibility. Because future problems and opportunities are always uncertain, present actions should not constrict a manager's ability to adapt to new situations as they evolve.

Robust action depends upon the timing of making—and *not* making—decisions. Harvard Business School's Dean, John McArthur, once brought to our attention an insight Chester Barnard made over sixty years ago, one that corresponds perfectly to our notion of robust action. "The fine art of executive decision," Barnard instructed, "consists in not deciding questions that are not now pertinent, in not deciding prematurely, in not making decisions that cannot be made effective, and in not making decisions that others should make."[21] And as we will see, rhetoric is crucial to robust action at every stage in the game.

But how does a manager *know* what questions are pertinent and what times are right? In the end, we believe, robust action fundamentally depends upon the exercise of judgment: each manager must eventually decide for herself what needs to be done. Like everything else in management, robust action is about finding out what works in particular contexts and situations—it is about the pragmatic know-how gleaned from actual experience. In light of the fact that companies differ in terms of size, industry, strategy, culture, geographical location, people, and history, this advice may seem obvious—though not exactly comforting. Nevertheless, much contemporary writing about management does little to qualify the circumstances under which its principles apply. Excellent companies, Japanese companies, and leading-edge companies are all championed as if they somehow hold the keys to competitive success. This dubious proposition is especially questionable if one asks how unique competitive advantage could be obtained if the trick were ever as simple as to mimic what other companies were doing.

Of course, most managers know better than this, as expressed in the common observation that "our situation here at FAD Corporation, Inc. is unique." In some sense this is always true. No two situations are exactly the same, if for no other reason than spatial separation and the passage of time. But it *is* possible to find lessons or practices that are applicable across a number of situations. Managers are aware of this and are therefore constantly searching for universal principles, which consultants and academics are only too eager to provide. Yet as soon as a manager has been given a general model, if she is reflective she immediately sets to thinking about how it needs to be qualified for her particular situation.

Ultimately, it is the manager on the line who is in the best position to decide if something makes sense in her particular situation. In doing so, she needs to be aware of and resist the pressures to adopt an action based on the perceived expertise of the person who is advocating it. Put frankly, there is no escaping the need to exercise judgment at every turn. And in this there are no easy guidelines. Judgment comes from experience, wisdom, and a willingness to admit mistakes.

Recognizing Individual Identities

The final component of our action perspective on management is the importance of individual *identity*. As every manager soon learns, taking effective action requires understanding the unique identities of the people with whom one deals. Regardless of the issue at hand, treating individuals simply as an "organizational resource" ignores many of the important specifics that must be taken into account for action to happen.

Of course, a concern for individuals is not new—and it is a quality that most managers are quick to claim. An action perspective, however, means more than simply taking individuals into account. It means considering how identities get built and maintained in organizations, and how the quest for personal identity—in contemporary society perhaps more than ever—is an inseparable aspect of everything that occurs within them. Indeed, throughout this book we will have many opportunities to discuss the ways in which both identity and its pursuit play a central role in management issues—strategy and structure, for example—that might at first seem to be detachable from them.

In the sense we are using the term, identity is not to be confused with the narrower notion of self-interest. Our notion of identity is broader and more robust insofar as it stresses that human action takes place along multiple, often vaguely defined dimensions. Since identity is something that must be understood and managed in the particular, the question of "what motivates people" must always be grounded in specific contexts. While general models of human behavior can provide useful orienting frameworks, each person in an organization is truly unique and must be dealt with as such. Robust action, which takes account of situational specifics, requires a robust concept of human behavior based on identity, which takes account of individual specifics. And as we suggest in Chapter 4, adopting such a view may actually require moving away from the idea that "motivation" is the proper way to frame the issue in the first place.

LESSONS FROM THIS BOOK

While the first part of this book sets up an alternative way of thinking about management, the rest applies our perspective to familiar concepts in the world of the manager. In Part II we apply the insights of the first section to the traditional organizational trio of strategy, structure, and performance measurement. The shared goal in these chapters is to approach old concepts in a new light—to ask the question "What are strategy, structure, and performance measurement really all about anyway?" Similarly, in Part III, we turn our attention to some broader themes—knowledge, change, and finally, individual practice. In these chapters, the goal is the same: to give managers a fresh way of thinking about their situation in general, and to suggest how certain issues might be approached differently.

Taking a Rhetorical Stance

As should be clear by now, our perspective on management—based as it is on the themes of rhetoric, action, and identity—is an *action perspective*. We intend it to be understood as a kind of wide-angle view of management, one that might allow the reader to start thinking differently about what the dynamics of successful managing really are. Basically, the action perspective sees the reality of management as a matter of *actions* and *processes*—rather than as a matter of things, states, structures, or, in a term we will often use, *designs*.

Sadly, we feel that most of the ideas pitched at managers today tend to distract managers from the importance of the action perspective. Instead, much of the current management discourse lends itself to the frenzied adoption of designs. The appeal of these designs lies in their broad generality and in the fact that designs are generally much easier to put into words than processes and actions. Designs are static snapshots and thus easier to capture than dynamic actions which unfold in unanticipated ways over time.

All the same, it is important to point out that we are not hostile toward design when used effectively as a management tool. To the contrary, designs are necessary. After all, it is hard to conceive of any organization that could survive without the use of certain structures or systems that were perceived as fixed, however momentarily. What is harmful, however, is when designs are understood as an end in themselves rather than as a means of encouraging and facilitating action. Sometimes designs work; other times they don't—and when they don't, new ones can always be tried. While some designs may have a certain rhetorical efficacy, the manager should not be seduced into thinking that any one word or phrase perfectly captures the realities of management.

As we have mentioned, this kind of perspective has been advocated before. But we think it is time to add our voice to the numerous others (such as Follett and Barnard) who have advocated a similar perspective on organizations.[22] In particular, the action perspective—with its emphasis on managerial judgment and the particular nature of managerial situations—can serve as a partial antidote to the contemporary search for a managerial elixir. It recognizes that the challenges of management are never resolved permanently, but only day by day. In the end, we argue that what is most important is that managers adopt a *rhetorical stance* in their activities—a constructively skeptical attitude that appreciates language's immense power as a form of action in its own right. After all, words are too important to remain only words.

PART I

BUILDING AN ACTION PERSPECTIVE

2

RHETORIC: THE WORK OF WORDS

"Words, words, words . . ."

—William Shakespeare, *Hamlet*

Try an experiment: imagine an organization—a company, a school, anything—but imagine it without language. The very idea may strike one as absurd. Indeed, in the manager's world, language is everywhere. Every action a manager undertakes is somehow connected to its use, from devising an organizational chart to energizing a colleague, from writing a report to reading a book. Of course, most managers don't usually think of their jobs this way. Usually, words go relatively ignored—they are seen as the mere background noise of an organization. But they are always more than background, and thinking about the way that words are really *used* in organizations is the inevitable first step in understanding the manager's job from an action perspective.

EXAMINING TODAY'S MANAGEMENT RHETORIC

Taking a closer look at how language works in management is especially crucial today. As we mentioned in Chapter 1, there is a contemporary fervor for new and better ways of managing, and an awe-inspiring flood of words—not all of them useful—about a coming age of enlightened organizations. A 1991 article in *Fortune* magazine captures this verbal giddiness remarkably well:

> If you were to ask a CEO in the year 2000 to take out his Montblanc and draw the organization chart of his company, what he'd sketch would bear little resemblance to even the trendiest flattened pyramid around today. Yes, the corporation of the future will still retain some vestiges of the old hierarchy and maybe a few traditional departments to take care of the boringly rote. But spinning around the straight lines will be a vertiginous pattern of constantly changing teams, task forces,

partnerships, and other informal structures. Picture one of those overhead camera shots in a Busby Berkeley musical: Dozens of leggy dancers form a flower on stage, disband into chaos, and then regroup to
form a flag or a fluegelhorn. Like the dancers, in tomorrow's corporation teams variously composed of shop floor workers, managers,
technical experts, suppliers, and customers will join together to do a
job and then disband, with everyone going off to the next assignment.
Call this new model the adaptive organization.[1]

Read by many thousands of people, this *Fortune* article provides a pleth-
ora of new words and concepts meant to challenge the "old way" of
thinking about organizations and management. In it we find a vision of
a swirling and exciting "adaptive organization," an organization con-
sisting of an harmonious orchestration of cross-functional, cross-level,
and cross-organizational teams that come and go, a vision compared
explicitly with the staid and boring hierarchy of yesterday.[2] *Fortune* even
uses the millennium effect, invoking the year 2000 to argue that even in
1991 "you ain't seen nothing yet."

Clichés of the New Organization

At first, such messages are certainly exciting. Unfortunately, for many
managers, all this excitement can (and has) become rather tiresome. For
years, various theorists and gurus have been predicting an impending
revolution and offering their various models, concepts, and frameworks
to cope with it. We have found five basic principles that, taken together,
form the new gospel being preached to managers:

1. *Smaller is better than larger.* Smallness is achieved by eliminating staff,
reducing managerial layers, and outsourcing certain functions and services. (Admittedly, this principle is somewhat ironic in light of the fact
that the Japanese and German companies held up as paragons of excellent management are typically *very* large bureaucracies in a classical sense.)

2. *Less diversification is better than more.* Much of the focus of recent restructuring activities has been on selling off assets in order to decrease
the extent of a company's diversification. To the extent a company needs
capabilities beyond its basic business, "soft-contracting" alternatives such
as partnering, joint ventures, and strategic alliances are advocated over
acquisitions and vertical integration.

3. *Competition must be replaced by collaboration.* Barriers between companies, it is argued, must fall. U.S. regulatory policies that inhibit the

formation of company relationships are seen as interfering with the ability of American companies to become truly world-class competitors. More generally, networks of relationships which ignore typical organizational boundaries are promoted as a way of enabling people to work together better in order to identify and pursue their common interests.

4. *Formal authority must be diminished.* With the rise of collaboration also comes the call for a decrease in "command-and-control" styles of management. In the visions of the new organization put forth, formal authority will diminish and perhaps even disappear as widely available information and dense networks of relationships weaken the authority of office.

5 *Time cycles must become shorter.* As mentioned, product development cycles, product life cycles, technologies, and windows of market opportunity are all seen to be shrinking. These shorter time frames call for organizations that are more flexible, responsible, and adaptive than the traditional hierarchy permits. (Never mind that this conclusion co-exists somewhat uneasily with the concern that American business already places *too much* emphasis on short-term results.)

Most popular writing about management presents various combinations and permutations of these five basic principles, none of which are very revolutionary in their own right. To be fair, they are appealing on a psychological level. They appeal to traditional understandings of what organizations are and how they work. Furthermore, and just as important, they appeal to our deep-seated desire to believe we are living through a unique period in the history of management, that the rules of the game are changing, and that rapid adaptation is necessary. This is all very exciting for managers and academics alike, but a quick look at the "old" rhetoric will lead us to question how much this kind of thinking really makes sense.

RETHINKING THE OLD RHETORIC

Are we living in a period that is truly in transition from the Industrial to the Information Age? Are we moving from one historical epoch to another, during which radical and fundamental changes are taking place in organization and work? Are we witnessing the demise of one of the most successful social inventions in human history—the bureaucratic (in the nonpejorative sense, if that is still possible) organization? Or are all these revolutionary claims "mere rhetoric"?

The answers to these questions are obviously complex, and we must be excused if we seem reluctant to try to answer them directly. It is perhaps more worthwhile to focus first on the historical stereotypes on which discussions of the new organization typically depend. Contemporary management discourse relies on a clever and not uncommon rhetorical strategy: the past is depicted as a more placid and less competitive age in which hierarchies were able to prosper, and the brief period of American economic hegemony is described in near-Utopian terms when contrasted with the current global dog-eat-dog world.

Was the Golden Age Golden?

Admittedly, the one historical period that is most often evoked to contrast the changing present with the stable past is post–World War II 1940s through the late 1960s. This was indeed a period of great American optimism, of the building of large corporations, and of William H. Whyte's "organization man."[3] From the present, it is perceived as a period of remarkable stability in which American economic hegemony reached its peak. And it was a time in which a number of management practices presumed to be the cause of our current competitive woes were developed and elaborated.

Obviously, the world is a different place today than it was during the 1950s. Yet how did the world appear to people at the time? Interestingly, when one looks back at the same sources that have so much rhetorical currency today—magazines such as *Fortune* and the CEOs of highly visible companies—one receives much the same impression of change and dynamism that is supposedly unique to our own era. When one examines the historical literature, one is surprised to find that change—indeed, transformative change—has *always* been a common theme, as has been the call for management practices that elude bureaucratic stereotypes.

Stereotypes of a stable, bureaucratic past are the very lifeblood of current management discourse—yet they are often inaccurate. In fact, as early as the 1940s, authors spoke of a thunderous change sweeping through society that would deliver us into a so-called post-industrial age characterized by new lifestyles and massive decentralization.[4] Similarly, competition and rapid technological change have *always* been issues of great importance to managers, even if the nature of such issues has changed appreciably with the development of information technology and global markets. The fact remains: the basic managerial concerns of the 1950s were remarkably similar to those of today. The almost exponential growth of available products, the pressures on product development times, the need for strict quality control—such are the concerns one finds throughout the 1950s, often framed with great urgency.[5]

There was also the belief (surprise!) that the changing times required an entirely new approach to management. In 1955, *Fortune* featured a twelve-part series of articles on "The New Management." In one of them, author Perrin Stryker took a look at the growing trend toward decentralized authority in organizations.[6] While he warned that such "revolutionary" concepts were difficult to apply in practice, Stryker nonetheless concluded that "the arguments in favor of delegating decisions are persuasively logical."[7] The more complex a company became, Stryker reasoned, the more it made sense for top executives to relinquish their control over the decision-making process of the firm. The consequences were seen as major: "Such delegation," he reported, "could develop the decision-making powers of executives below the top echelon; speed and improve decisions because those deciding are close to the problem; reduce friction among executives and increase their desire to do a better job; . . . and relieve top executives of supervision so they can spend more time planning and thinking out better decisions."[8]

While 1950s decentralization is usually not thought of in such terms today, Stryker's description is quite similar to what today goes under the label of "empowerment." Then as now, the goal was simple: to make companies "less authoritarian and less arbitrary" so that they might "harmonize better with this country's democratic tradition."[9]

General Electric in the 1950s

These exciting new practices of the 1950s were not celebrated solely by journalists and academics. As is the case today, they were espoused directly by companies themselves and by some of the most respected managers of the time. Consider for example the speeches delivered in 1956 by Ralph J. Cordiner, who was then president of the General Electric Corporation.[10] Cordiner had been the architect of GE's massive reorganization during the early 1950s, a job that, according to current management guru and long-time GE consultant Peter Drucker, "perfected the model most big businesses around the world (including Japanese organizations) still follow."[11] (The Japanese have also been far less frenzied about finding a new model.) Presumably, Cordiner's rhetoric would reflect the very mind-set that contemporary observers—including Drucker—are busy protesting against.

Yet many of Cordiner's speeches and writings give a quite different picture. In the first place, Cordiner clearly perceived the 1950s to be as challenging and dynamic a time as any other. Among the imperatives for change at GE, he cites the dynamic pace of technological progress, the rise of research and innovation in all fields of functional work, and the need to push responsibility downward in organizations. "Very few substantial businesses today," he proclaimed, "can expect to survive and grow without a dynamic plan for continuous innovation in products, processes, facilities, methods, organization, leadership, and all other aspects of the business. These innovations require early major investments in projects whose commercial maturity may not be reached for ten years or longer."[12]

The dynamic pace of technological change. The need for continuous innovation. The need to make long-term R&D investments. Which of these issues aren't perceived to be important today? And where in Cordiner's words is the sense of relative stability that firms were presumed to have in the 1950s, stability permitting business as usual from one day to the next?

Today's managerial concerns were hardly unknown to Cordiner. In addition to his emphasis on how GE takes a long-term perspective and that GE cares about its customers ("General Electric is a customer-focused Company. We earnestly believe that."[13]), Cordiner devoted an entire speech to the theme "Decentralization: A Managerial Philosophy." Like many of his counterparts today, Cordiner essentially understood decentralization as a way of bringing the benefits of smallness to a large company: "Decentralization," he proclaimed, "is a way of preserving and enhancing [the] contributions of the large enterprise, and at the same time achieving the flexibility and the 'human touch' that are popularly associated with—though not always attained by—small organizations."[14] By putting "responsibility for making business decisions not with a few top executives, but with the individual managerial and functional employees who have the most immediately applicable information required to make sound decisions and to take prompt action," the result was that "each individual in the Company has a challenging and dignified position which will bring out his full resources and enthusiastic cooperation."[15]

General Electric: Then versus Now

What would current CEO Jack Welch—who has seen GE through another successful transformation in the 1980s and the 1990s—have to say about Cordiner's principles? One would expect Welch's rhetoric to be very different from Cordiner's, as the Cordiner model of organization is ostensibly the very model that needs to be overthrown. But listen closely. Here for example is Jack Welch in 1988 reflecting eloquently on the "new" transformation at GE, in a speech entitled "Management for the Nineties":

> At the beginning of the decade, we saw two challenges ahead of us, one external and one internal. Externally, we faced a world economy

that would be characterized by slower growth with stronger global competitors going after a smaller pie. . . . Internally, our challenge was even bigger. We had to find a way to combine the power, resources and reach of a big company with the hunger, the agility, the spirit, and the fire of a small one. . . . So we reduced the number of management layers in the company to get closer to the individual—the source of that creative energy we needed. . . . We found that the leaders—people with a vision and a passion—soon began to stand out. And, when they did, we found our own self-confidence growing to the point that we began to delegate authority further and further down in the company. . . . We know where competitiveness comes from. It comes from people—but only from people who are free to dream, to risk, free to act. Liberating those people, every one of them, is the great challenge we've been grappling with all over this company."[16]

Notice the commonalities between Welch and Cordiner. While the language is somewhat different—Welch strikes us as more charismatic, less businesslike—both talk about the need for change, both articulate the importance of finding a way to combine the strengths of a large enterprise with those of a small enterprise, both espouse the merits of delegating authority down to the lowest levels of the firm so that the individual can make important decisions and be responsible for the future of the company.

There are, of course, important differences between them that deserve to be stressed. Welch explicitly rejects Cordiner's emphasis on formal planning, for example, which is probably for the better.[17] Despite such exceptions, however, both Welch and Cordiner are essentially engaged in the same project: applying timeless common sense to organizations and cloaking it in an energizing rhetoric of historical necessity and innovation.

THE RHETORIC OF REVOLUTIONARY CHANGE

As the language of Cordiner and Welch shows, management language has certain persistent themes—although the words and labels are often transient—and other themes that are more short-lived. Perhaps the most persistent rhetorical theme—and one that has reached the most giddy heights today—is that the business environment is changing now like never before, that previous management practices are no longer tenable, and that a new management paradigm and a new organization must be created. (During the 1960s, in particular, there was no shortage of discussions about how conventional ways of thinking about organizations were obsolete.[18]) Perhaps the most vivid example of this theme's persistence is to be found in the work of Peter Drucker, who—through incarnations as journalist, philosopher, consultant, and academic—has become one of the most widely read management gurus of the century.

Peter Drucker's New Organization

In 1988, for example, Drucker wrote an article in the *Harvard Business Review* called "The Coming of the New Organization," which subsequently became one of the most widely reprinted articles in the magazine's history. In it he argues that since the turn of the century there have been two major changes in the "concept and structure" of modern business enterprises, the first separating management from ownership and the second introducing the various command-and-control mechanisms of the traditional multidivisional firm. Yet now, argues Drucker, "We are entering a third period of change: the shift from the command-and-control organization . . . to the organization of knowledge specialists." From here, he goes on to predict that the typical large business twenty years from now "will bear little resemblance to the typical manufacturing company, circa 1950, which our textbooks still consider the norm."[19]

Drucker's article masterfully espouses the ideas—many of them empirically based—that have so captivated the current management discourse: in particular, the elimination of middle management and the rise of knowledge-based work. Yet Drucker's version of history also raises some vexing questions: stereotypes to the side, it is doubtful that command-and-control management was ever as highly regarded as he claims, and it is unclear just how great a distinction should really be made between management practices of the present and past.

These doubts are confirmed when one examines Drucker's writings from the earlier periods he claims to be characterizing. What one finds is both surprising and enlightening, since Drucker was proclaiming the advent of a radically new organization at that time as well! For example, in an article written in 1959, Drucker described the form of a new organization which is remarkably similar to today's "information-based organization." At that time, he wrote:

> The business enterprise of today is no longer an organization in which there are a handful of bosses at the top who make all the decisions while the workers carry out the orders. It is primarily an organization of professionals of highly specialized knowledge exercising autonomous, responsible judgement. And every one of them—whether

manager or individual expert contributor—constantly makes truly entrepreneurial decisions, that is, decisions which affect the economic characteristics and risks of the entire enterprise.[20]

In fact, regardless of when Drucker is writing (and this is not to deny that his work has contained some very valuable insights), the present is *always* an exciting, challenging time to be contrasted with a stable past. These same stirring announcements of impending change can be found repeated in nearly all of his writings from the 1950s to the present.[21] While one would be hard-pressed to deny that certain changes *have* indeed been occurring in organizations and society at large (and, indeed, we will come to consider them in due time), the obsessiveness with which this idea of revolutionary newness is invoked can swiftly become meaningless. One might characterize the basic idea as "Here Comes the New Organization! Really!"

The Cycles of Management Rhetoric

As Drucker's work illustrates, every generation of management discourse portrays the present as especially challenging, stereotypes the past, and then paints a vision of the future that is sharply contrasted with it. Every generation believes itself to be on the forefront of a new managerial frontier and posits the coming of a new organization that will revolutionize the way people work and interact.

Although different constellations of terms have been used to describe the ideal future organization, it has for some time now been cast as an alternative to bureaucracy. The "network" organization, today's leading image of the future organization, bears striking resemblance to the "integrative" organization proposed by Rosabeth Moss Kanter in 1983, which in turn is similar to the "organic" organization proposed by Burns and Stalker in 1961—and that model too was apparently identified by the German sociologist Pieper as early as 1931.[22] Similarly, contemporary excitement about "knowledge workers" can be traced back to Drucker's own writings in the 1950s, and even (as Drucker himself has argued) to Frederick Taylor's earlier Scientific Management.[23] And as we have noted, arguments for the empowerment of employees are as evident in Mary Parker Follett's influential (but now largely ignored) writings of the 1920s as they are in the contemporary business media.[24]

Alternative ways of thinking about organization have been with us for as long as people have thought about management itself—which is to say, at least a few millennia. At the heart of all these anti- or post-bureaucratic models of organization is an emphasis on the decentralization of authority and spontaneous organic coordination. Again, though the labels change over time, the rhetorical message is persistent: we must push decision-making authority down to the level of each individual in the organization and tap their specific skills and knowledge for the future success of the organization. In this sense, today's knowledge worker is a timeless ideal. Equally, "autonomous management," "commitment-based management," and the currently fashionable "team-based management" are all recurring visions of an alternative to command-and-control based coordination, even though contemporary accounts usually try to paint a clear historical progression from the latter to the former.[25]

Throughout history, this rather cutting-edge vision of the organization of the future has been balanced by visions that seem more conservative and traditional. At various points and in various ways, hierarchies and strict control *have* been praised, and some continue to praise them.[26] Similarly, there has always been, and will always continue to be, rhetoric whose purpose it is to legitimate managerial authority, whether by vaunting the "professionalism" of managers or, alternatively, by cleverly reconstruing management as "leadership," a strategy heavily favored during the past decade.[27]

Same As It Ever Was?

Although the claim may seem heretical in the age of managerial hype, it is nonetheless crucial: when it comes to the basics of management, there is little new under the sun. Indeed, different ways of thinking about management have come and gone; sometimes they have returned; sometimes contradictory rhetorics have even appeared at the same time, much to the confusion of later historians. The words, the trends, the theories change—yet the underlying tensions and themes of management remain the same. This observation about the development of management concepts has been made even by the change-obsessed Peter Drucker, who once wrote that: "In the ten years between 1910 and 1920 . . . every single one of the great themes of management is struck. . . . And almost everything that we have done since then, in theory as well as in practice, is only a variation and extension of the themes first heard during that decade."[28]

Faced with the sober recognition that there is very little that is really new in the modern-day claim about the transition to a new management paradigm, we have to return to the original question: *Is* something really fundamental going on, or does today's craze for newness simply point to our willingness, perhaps even our need, to indulge in the excitement of imaginary revolutions?[29] Are recent writings guides to a brave new world or are they a form of hysteria, one which will probably grow because of the millennium effect of the approaching year 2000?

There are several ways in which one might begin to answer these questions. One would be to say: history will tell. By this token, only after some time had gone by, and perhaps a lot of it, could we even hope to have anything approaching a consensus on whether the 1980s and 1990s was truly a time of organizational transformation and discontinuous change in the world. Future business historians may be in a better position to make this assessment than are any contemporary writers. When one is immersed in the present it is hard to know what is fleeting, what is idiosyncratic, and what is a part of more permanent and systemic change.

A second, only slightly more satisfying answer would be to take a cynical stance and conclude that today's rhetoric of overwhelming change is no different from that of the past. Indeed, there is something to be said for taking such a position. Over a century ago, after all, did not Karl Marx—to deliberately cite someone who has gone out of fashion—proclaim that constant change was the very determining feature of the modern world, and in particular of the managerial elite? For the Marx who wrote the *Communist Manifesto,* sweeping and constant change was at the very heart of capitalism: "All fixed, fast-frozen relations . . . are swept away," he announced, and "all new-formed ones become antiquated before they can ossify. All that is solid melts into air, all that is holy is profaned."[30]

While this historical attitude has a certain appeal, we concede that it remains ultimately unsatisfying when applied to the question of managerial change.[31] The temptation is thus to try a third approach: getting to the "facts" of the situation. By looking at the empirical facts, one might argue, it would be easy to tell when the rhetoric of change was false rhetoric and when it was true rhetoric.

Unfortunately, however, little comprehensive evidence is provided by those who claim that these are truly revolutionary times. Instead, their facts are typically anecdotal, often referring to contemporary events that are the focus of a great deal of interest and uncertainty. The empirical evidence, when collectable, is rather slippery. For every graph that can be used to suggest that we are in a unique moment of total upheaval, there is another, equally persuasive one that suggests the world is practically steady-state. For example, Figure 2-1 shows the U.S. deficit and debt over the past thirty years. From it we might deduce that since the mid-1970s our economy has undergone a profound and radical change—which perhaps it has. Figure 2-2 shows the very different statistic of patents issued in the United States, a figure we might expect to be growing exponentially due to the presumed "knowledge explosion"

Figure 2-1: U.S. Deficit and Total Debt, 1960–1990 (in $ billions)

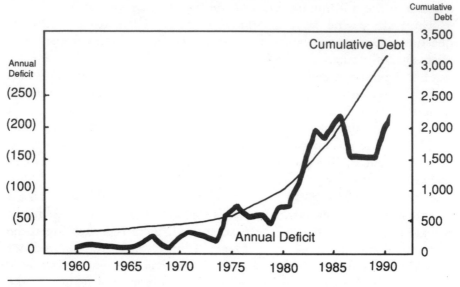

Source: U.S. Department of Commerce, *Statistical Abstract.*

Figure 2-2: Patents Issued (per million population)

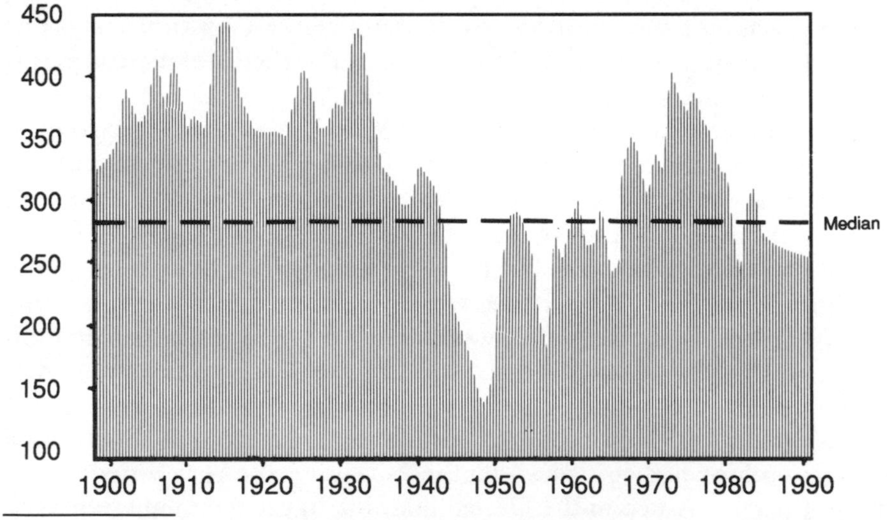

Source: U.S. Department of Commerce, *Statistical Abstract.*

in our society. In this case, however, the data are much more fuzzy—there is no simple historical trend to this statistic at all. In the end, all attempts to measure change empirically prove naive. Since they always depend on exactly *what* one measures, we are always plunged back into the very same uncertainty we were trying to escape.

How then might we begin to make sense of all this? A fourth view—and the one that we advocate here—is that to see these claims about revolutionary newness only in regard to an underlying truth or falsehood is ultimately to miss the point. What is more important to understand is the *rhetorical* nature of management discourse and practice—now and then. To view management from a rhetorical perspective is to recognize that *the way people talk about the world has everything to do with the way the world is ultimately understood and acted in, and that the concept of revolutionary change depends to a great extent on how the world is framed by our language.* Viewing management in this way is also to realize that the primary concern of managers—as well as other players in the field of management—is, or at least should be, mobilizing action among individuals rather than endless quibbling about "the way the world really is."

The rhetorical stance entails understanding, as the literary and legal scholar Stanley Fish has written, "that the givens of any field of activity—including the facts it commands, the procedures it trusts in, and the values it expresses and extends—are socially and politically constructed, are fashioned by man rather than delivered by God or nature."[32] A rhetorical view of management, it must be stressed, does not absurdly deny the existence of facts. It merely asserts that whatever these facts are, their importance and meaning are only established through language. And as any manager intuitively knows, it is language, not facts, that ultimately shapes the way we see things. Rhetoric can certainly be used to deceive or manipulate, but it can equally be used for more positive and productive ends.

TAKING RHETORIC SERIOUSLY

A rhetorical stance toward management correctly points out that the primary task of managerial language has always been to persuade individuals to put forth their best efforts in a collective enterprise with other men and women. Indeed, much of the current hysteria over labels such as "the new organization" and "empowerment" can be seen as an attempt to lend new energy to the collective enterprises that have recently found themselves in a period of doubt and realignment. In their daily practice, individual managers *use* such labels and concepts as they see fit, as part of their ongoing use of language to coax, inspire, demand, or otherwise produce action in their organizations.[33] And as we have seen so far in this chapter, sometimes this use of language coalesces into whole systems of thinking and acting, into general *rhetorics* that may come to dominate an organization or even an entire age. At every level, language has a rhetorical function—in the words of management theorist Jay Conger, it constantly "frames" the way we understand the world.[34] Language's framing role in management has also been recently stressed by Stanford's Jeffrey Pfeffer, who writes that "We perceive things according to how they are described in conversation and debate."[35] Pfeffer even goes on to cite the story of Confucius—who when asked what he would do if he were chosen to lead a country, responded that the first thing he would do is "fix the language."[36]

Language Systems in and of Management

Just as much of what managers say is intended to persuade others to accept a certain view of the world, we have seen that such is also the purpose of those who communicate *to* managers. This is certainly what books and articles written for managers are intended to do: to persuade them that certain kinds of actions are required—such as "empowering your employees," "getting close to your customers," or "eliminating the hierarchy and creating a network organization." These same messages are also delivered in live speeches and training sessions and in audio- and videotapes. By this token, Tom Peters—co-author of *In Search of Excellence* and author of *Thriving on Chaos*—is probably among the most effective rhetoricians in the business world today. Through his books, syndicated columns, television shows, magazine and journal articles, and live appearances, Peters has succeeded in building a rhetorical empire that suffuses management practices all over the world.

Managers take these messages from Peters and other rhetoricians and use them to persuade others in their organizations to act in certain ways. Yet because these messages are typically very general, managers have a lot of leeway in interpreting them. After all, how *does* one empower an employee, get close to a customer, or create a network organization? Those attempting to take actions based on such rhetoric have to exercise judgment in deciding what these words mean for them in their particular circumstances. Meaning is not intrinsic in these phrases. It must be actively created by managers who choose to *use* them (or twist them) for their own particular purposes.[37]

The world of management is therefore a complex social system that involves a network of managers, academics, consultants, and journalists playing many overlapping roles in complicated and surprising ways. Far from being neutral or objective, the words and concepts that they disseminate are always embedded in specific "language systems"—systems of talking about the world that vary over time and from organization to organization. The *Fortune* "Bureaucracy Busters" article mentioned earlier provides a vivid illustration of how these language systems work through a complicated interweaving of the views of these different players into a single "objective" statement about management. To the extent that managers who read this article take actions and cause others to take actions that make their organizations more effective, it has played a useful role.

Yet as the *Fortune* example highlights, it is impossible to understand the practice of management without understanding the broader language systems within which it is embedded. In contrast to atomic particles which are presumably indifferent to the theories used to explain their properties, people in organizations are increasingly aware of theories that exist about their behavior and how organizations function. They actively seek out this knowledge in order to use it. And as this knowledge is disseminated it becomes part of the lexicon of managers—a shared vocabulary comes to exist within and among industries. Concepts and ideas such as "get close to your customer," "stick to your knitting," "empower your workers," "create cross-functional teams," "delegate decision-making authority," and "manage for total quality" become commonplace. New vocabularies cycle quickly through the elaborate social system of management discourse—adopted under the promise of change and innovation, discarded when they are no longer able to inspire and mobilize action.

Powerful Rhetoric versus Mere Rhetoric

Management is about rhetoric, that much is clear. But what is it that makes certain rhetorical strategies—certain kinds of "speech acts"—more stirring than others? What rhetorical strategies are likely to inspire an audience to act rather than contribute to a growing sense of management hyperbole? To see, we might contrast the rhetoric of Jack Welch at General Electric with the rhetoric of his contemporary Roger Smith at General Motors. Both of these highly visible CEOs took charge of their firms in 1981 and tried to champion change, to lead their firms into the 1990s in a transformed state. To contrast their rhetoric is instructive, because by most counts, Welch's rhetoric has been far more successful at mobilizing action than Smith's.

Both Jack Welch and Roger Smith were concerned with transforming their companies, and both relied heavily on promoting their "visions" of what such a transformation would entail. Only Welch, however, was an expert at this game. Only Welch seemed to realize that any effort to mobilize change, let alone the more lofty ambition of transformation, requires more than simply invoking "newness." Welch's rhetoric has shown the understanding that this effort typically requires a deft combination of several elements: an imaginative vision of the future, a realistic portrayal of the present, and a selective depiction of the past which can serve as a contrast to the future.[38] A vision statement, for example, must first and foremost appeal to the desires and emotions of the audience, and must unleash in them a picture of a future that is radically better than the present. In the words of Peter Senge, there must be a "creative tension" between reality and vision that inspires people personally to take up the challenge of transformation.[39]

In his public speeches and writings, Roger Smith always tried admirably to portray GM as transforming itself to become the American exemplar of the "21st Century Corporation." Unfortunately, his vision of the 21st Century Corporation was almost never spelled out in meaningful detail, and it hence remained uninspiring in the extreme. The concept was a vague, futuristic label that did little to spur the imagination because it had few hooks that tugged at the emotions of the audience. Even more damaging, Smith refused to face the realities of GM during the 1980s, often making the counterproductive claim (found consistently in the company's annual reports) that the company's transformation had already occurred. Maryann Keller, who chronicled the Smith years in a recent book, pointed out the basic problem: "Smith is brilliant, but he often lacks both the charisma and sensitivity to motivate others to see his vision through to completion, or to understand when the vision is flawed. He is like a cook who gathered all the ingredients for making a cake, then just tossed them in the oven randomly, thinking they would come together on their own."[40]

Typically, Smith externalized GM's problems—disappointments were because of "a dramatic shift in customer demand," "high interest rates," "a deteriorating economy," or "excessive and costly government regulations."[41] Only rarely were the challenges seen as *internal:* in most places, GM's past is portrayed as great, the present as great, and the future as great—and yet Smith spoke about a transformation being underway. It was never clear from his statements what this transformation was, where it was headed, or what specific progress had been made. As a result, there was little creative tension to be found in Smith's rhetoric. Consider, for example, the following prognosis of GM's condition that he offered in 1987, a year in which GM stock sharply lagged the S&P 500 and in which GM lost market share:

> GM today is the leading car manufacturer in the world by a wide margin. We build and sell nearly one out of every five cars purchased

in the entire free world. Precisely because of our great organizational and financial strengths, we have been able over recent years to transform GM into a 21st Century corporation, so that we can be expected to grow even stronger and more profitable in the years ahead.[42]

Made at a time when GM was actually in deep trouble, the irony in this passage would be laughable were it not so sad. From the mistaken equation of bigness with greatness to the unsubstantiated optimism of its predictions, Smith's rhetoric appears as only so much hot air.

Unlike Smith, Jack Welch knows how to cook—and the recipe is rhetoric. Consider his vision for the GE of the 1990s, a vision that he describes as the "boundaryless company." In his words:

> "Boundaryless" is an uncommon word—perhaps even an awkward one—but it has become a word we use constantly, one that describes a whole set of behaviors we believe are necessary. . . . In a boundaryless company, suppliers aren't "outsiders.". . . Customers are seen for what they are—the lifeblood of the company. . . . In a boundaryless company, internal functions begin to blur. . . . Even the barriers between GE work life and community life have come down.[43]

Here we see a vision that effectively spurs the imagination. Despite its awkward label, the vision is imaginative and coherent. The deceptively short statement discloses several layers of emotional appeal: a genuine feeling of goodwill, a Utopian blurring of work and community, supplier and customer, employer and employee. As opposed to Smith's picture—which can hardly be called vision—Welch's vision is explicitly geared to arouse the emotions of his employees. It is a vision that invites the employees at GE to imagine a new set of possibilities, and encourages them to take actions that they believe would be in keeping with this vision. One would never see the following in a GM report:

> We want GE to become a company where people come to work every day in a rush to try something they woke up thinking about the night before. We want them to go home from work wanting to talk about what they did that day, rather than try and forget about it. We want factories where the whistle blows and everyone wonders where the time went, and someone suddenly wonders aloud why we need a whistle.[44]

Admittedly, such language can seem calculating, especially when it comes from someone whose propensity for *downsizing* (a dubious rhetorical term if ever there was one) has earned him the nickname of "Neutron Jack." Nevertheless, there are indications that much of Welch's rhetoric has increasingly found itself translated into practice at GE, and it is clear that GE's performance as a company has lived up to it. In any case, Welch's rhetoric is certainly preferable to the defeatist, adversarial views on labor relations that came from Roger Smith who in an early shareholder message simply wrote: "Without question, noncompetitive labor costs represent the single biggest disadvantage we must overcome. No company can compete for long, and no jobs are safe for long, with that kind of disadvantage."[45]

The Devices of Powerful Rhetoric

Powerful rhetoric such as Welch's involves the use of a variety of devices. Metaphors and analogies, stories and myths, slogans and maxims—all can play important roles in making action happen. These rhetorical devices are often more persuasive than numerical data, analytical models, and formal reasoning, especially if they are combined with a powerful delivery style.

Metaphors and analogies work by drawing parallels between two things whose relationship is not immediately apparent. Their power comes from their ability to stimulate the imagination and "from their ability to capture and illustrate an experience of reality by appealing simultaneously to the various senses of the listener."[46] Welch frequently employs powerful metaphors and analogies to communicate his vision. Here, for example, he masterfully mixes analogy and metaphor to describe vividly his attempts to dismantle the old GE management system:

> We have been pulling the dandelions of bureaucracy for a decade, but they don't come up easily and they'll be back next week if you don't keep after them. Yes, we've taken out lots of structure—staff, span-breakers, planners, checkers, approvers—and yet we have by no means removed them all. Those who have cleaned out an attic and returned a year later are often shocked to see what they left as "essential"—the pairs of old pants that would never be worn for the painting that would never be done, the boxes of moldy National Geographics that would never again be read. I feel the same way every time we revisit our management system—our processes—and see the barriers that insulate us from each other and from our only reason for existence as an institution—serving customers and winning in the marketplace.[47]

Organizational myths, legends, and sagas employ a different rhetorical technique.[48] Here, events are drawn from an organization's history and typically involve the firm's employees; the function, broadly speaking, is to tie an organization's past to its present and to create a legitimacy for current action and rhetoric.[49] Organizational stories have been found to be particularly effective at communicating policy changes and in generating commitment to organizational objectives. A *Harvard Business Review* interview with Welch nicely illustrates the power of a story to communicate a desired change and to generate commitment toward it. In it, Welch speaks of his concept of "Work-Out," the GE "town-meetings" introduced to overcome the rigidity of organizational life:

> It's not going to be easy to get the spirit and intent of Work-Out clear throughout the company. I had a technician at my house to install some appliances recently. He said, "I saw your videotape on Work-Out. The guys at my level understand what you're talking about: we'll be free to enjoy our work more, not just do more work, and do more work on our own. But do you know how our supervisors interpreted it? They pointed to the screen and said, "You see what he's saying. You guys better start busting your butts." We have a long way to go![50]

Slogans, maxims, and declarations—such as Ford's "Quality Is Job 1," GE's "#1 or #2 in every business we are in," Cray Computer's "We build the fastest computers in the world," and Reebok's "We make a difference"—are all examples of how rhetorical devices can be used to communicate and anchor an organization's strategy, priorities, and policies. The power of such statements lies in their directness and simplicity—and just as important, in their ambiguity. (What *kind* of difference do we make? How do we *define* being one or two?) They are particularly effective at establishing a clear purpose in the midst of uncertainty and in providing a focus that can serve as a strategic umbrella for a diverse set of activities.

Finding Clarity in Ambiguity

What is said above applies in general: effective rhetoric aims to be clear, but never *too* clear. It aims to be robust across as many different situations as possible, and to be flexible enough to incorporate the different meanings, emphases, and interpretations that different people will inevitably give to it.[51] (People are quite adept at using and interpreting rhetoric in innovative ways, a fact of human behavior that is better anticipated than ignored.) The concept of robustness also implies that the rhetorical strategy should be dynamic, adjusting over time to evolving contingencies.

In this arena, one can again refer to Jack Welch. Throughout his tenure, he has employed robust neologisms such as the Boundaryless Corporation, Work-Out, and Integrated Diversity—concepts that, like his predecessors' preferred term, *decentralization,* are all evocative but ambiguous. These ideals serve as broad rubrics under which Welch has been able to launch a series of specific initiatives and spin a variety of moving stories. In doing so, Welch has succeeded in transmitting a common message to a large number of people, while being able to impart specific meanings and interpretations to these ideas depending on the situation at hand.

The robustness of rhetoric often depends upon how well it succeeds at being inclusive of others. As Jeffrey Pfeffer has recently pointed out, often this can be simply a matter of what pronoun is used in framing a message.[52] Using the language of "we" rather than of "I" immediately connects rhetoric to collective action, even if it leaves the details of this action up to the audience itself. Welch, of course, has proven to be a master of this approach. Another example of this skill can also be found in a statement from a videotaped address that Vaughn Bryson, the CEO of Eli Lilly, made to his company:

> We have our work cut out for us. Therefore, we must emphasize openness throughout the company. We must *all* know where the company is going. We must *all* contribute to identifying the issues impacting our business. We must *all* work for ways to improve our operations. We must *all* overcome the goblins of routine. As baseball immortal Satchel Paige once said: "None of us is as smart as all of us."[53]

Note how these comments, made just after Bryson's succession to CEO, are evocative and inspiring even in their intentional vagueness. Precisely how they are to be interpreted is left up to the listeners, who have been explicitly let in on the action by the new CEO's repeated use of the plural "we." The evocative term "goblins of routine" could refer to anything—yet every Lilly employee will probably immediately think about what they are and how they can be eliminated. And the concluding baseball reference, far from being arbitrary, functions to ground the entire statement in Bryson's specific personal identity—that of a renowned ex–baseball player.

RHETORIC, ACTION, AND DESIGN

Clearly, rhetoric is a double-edged sword. As powerful as it can be, one must always remember that its real purpose—clearly seen in the Eli Lilly example—is to get action. Words are important, but ultimately they must produce action: new products and services must be initiated, produced, and delivered in a competitive marketplace. All too often, rhetoric that does not produce action leads to disillusionment. Change programs are started, new organizations are designed, new mission statements are forged, new strategies are formulated—but it can all be empty rhetoric. It is hard to find a company today that has not launched some initiative such as a total quality program or customer satisfaction program or time-to-market program. But only in a small minority of these companies have these programs resulted in any real action or change.

Why does the new rhetoric—which often seems so stirring, so revolutionary—so often fail to produce change? The answer may consist in looking at the ways the new rhetoric *fails* to be revolutionary. All too frequently, this new rhetoric remains on the level of simply promoting new designs—new rational management concepts that are taken at face value rather than seen through the proper rhetorical stance. Of course, it is tempting to believe that organizational effectiveness can be achieved simply by adopting and implementing new structures, strategies, and systems. And all too often these new designs are appealingly presented as packaged solutions. They offer neat, rational explanations that are as attractive to academics as they are to many managers. By adopting these solutions, managers often feel that they will be perceived as progressive. As a result, there is sometimes an almost faddish rush to adopt the latest designs—as if the adoption of certain concepts would by necessity bring an organization closer to some ideal state.

Yet very rarely does change result merely from design—while designs will always play an important managerial role, real change depends fundamentally upon new ways of acting accompanied by new ways of talking. The basic task of management, if we may state it so boldly, is to mobilize action by using language creatively to appeal to the self- and collective identities of individuals. (As Lawrence Miller nicely puts it, "Achieving return on equity does not, as a goal, mobilize the most noble forces of our soul."[54]) Seeing matters in this light helps explain why the rhetoric of the coming of the new organization has been so persistent over time. After all, it would hardly appeal to people's sense of self to be told that their times were boring, dull, and routine; that change was not in the air; and that they were not pioneers of a new world but instead dinosaurs of the past. Yet unless language is mobilized in such a way as to create the possibility for action—the theme to which we now turn— it remains just so many words.

3

ACTION: THE REALITIES

OF MANAGING

"To action alone have you a right, and never at all to its fruits. Let not the fruits of action be your motive; neither let there be in you any attachment to inaction."

—Bhagavad Gita

Management was, is, and always will be the same thing: the art of getting things done. And to get things done, managers must act themselves and mobilize collective action on the part of others.[1]

Unfortunately, the importance of individual and collective action is often obscured in our everyday language in which organizations, not people, are seen to act. For instance, we typically say that so-and-so organization launched a new product, laid off so many workers, sponsored some event, hired one of our friends, made so much profit, announced a bold new strategy, and so on. Generally, the traditional rhetoric about management makes matters worse by focusing on rules, principles, and frameworks that contribute to this perspective rather than help us move beyond it. On one level, ascribing actions to an organization as if it were a purposeful system in its own right is a convenient and helpful convention. But it runs the risk of making organized action appear automatic. And it glosses over the fact that behind every organizational act are the actions of specific people.

IN SEARCH OF EFFECTIVE ACTION

Any organizational action is the result of the actions and conversations of some individual or collection of individuals. The eminent scholar of organizations Karl Weick urges that we need to learn to "translate" organizational action into the language of individuals: "Any assertion that an organization acts," he explains, "can be decomposed into some set of interact(ion)s among individuals so that if these people had not generated and meshed a specific set of their actions, . . . then the organization would not have performed the act attributed to it."[2]

The ability to see beyond organizations to people and actions is a crucial aspect of effective management. After all, it is the quality of the actions of the people in an organization that adds up to determine the effectiveness of the organization. At the same time, so-called conventional wisdom can often lead us to downplay the importance of individual action and, especially, to downplay language's role as a form of action itself. Our purpose in this chapter is to provide a different way of thinking about action—one that addresses these deficiencies and causes us to rethink what it means to be a manager.

Making Action Robust

For us, effective action is best understood as *robust action*, a concept that was introduced by Eric Leifer in his study of chess masters.[3] Imagine a game of chess: at any moment, a player has several possible courses of action, which can multiply into millions of possibilities in only a few turns. A common view held about chess masters is that their superior ability lies in their capacity to plan moves and countermoves many turns into the future—that they are constantly envisioning and evaluating the different future scenarios that might be produced and that they choose their moves accordingly.

Leifer, however, has convincingly shown that this is not true.[4] Leifer actually found little difference between skilled chess players and novices in terms of how many moves they planned ahead. What distinguished skilled chess players from novices was that the former knew how to make moves that preserved their flexibility, that were "robust" to whatever moves their opponent might make in response since these countermoves could never be predicted with much certainty. Only when the time was right and the opportunity existed to consolidate gains or win the game completely did these players make moves that eliminated flexibility by eliminating uncertainty.

Our observations of skilled managers suggest that they are very similar to Leifer's chess masters. Like skilled chess players, managers who are able to "make things happen" or "get things done" act according to the following seven principles of robust action:

1. *Acting without certitude:* Managers skilled in robust action recognize that in most situations it is impossible to act only when one has full

information. They display a high tolerance for uncertainty and ambiguity. And they are willing to act without fully knowing the consequences of their actions. Indeed, many of the actions taken by a skilled manager are intended to actively uncover additional information that can be used to guide her further actions.

Of course, to act without certitude does not mean to act blindly in every situation. There may be times when the best action is to do nothing. But as the Nobel prize–winning economist Kenneth Arrow observes, sometimes "We simply must act, fully knowing our ignorance of possible consequences. . . . We must sustain the burden of action without certitude, and we must always keep open the possibility of recognizing past errors and changing course."[5]

2. *Constantly preserving flexibility:* Robust action involves an ongoing effort on the part of a manager to increase or at least preserve her degrees of freedom. At any point in time, actions are taken that are likely to increase her options for different actions in the future. Skilled managers are acutely aware of the dangers of painting themselves into a corner or of showing their hand too soon. Like chess masters, they carefully manage their position to permit a variety of countermoves, depending on what the opposition does. As Scott Newquist, head of Investment Banking at Kidder Peabody, told us: "You must always act to increase your options. Every time you walk through one door, you must make sure that you open some others through which you can exit if and when you need to."

Preserving flexibility does not imply that able managers don't commit themselves to any course of action. They proactively adopt those courses of action that they believe will help them to accomplish what they want to get done, while leaving room for them to change course in the face of unexpected events or other contingencies. They always act with a view to move forward as expeditiously as possible, recognizing that the best path may not always be a straight line.

3. *Being politically savvy:* Skillful managers understand that getting things done entails a sequence of actions that must interlock with the actions of others. As a result they pay enormous attention to the manner in which their own actions are ordered and especially how their actions are related to the parallel or sequential activities of others. Effective managers stay informed about the actions of others that interlock with their own, and they act accordingly. By being savvy about the agendas and actions of others, skillful managers can act to preempt actions that can block their own efforts or to co-opt actions that help them further their own efforts.

Such savvy behavior often results in managers being labeled as "political," in the pejorative connotation of the word. Nevertheless, these
political skills are a key reason why these managers are able to get things
done. In our view, this pejorative connotation is only warranted when
this savvy is used for selfish ends: when such political skills are deployed
in the service of the organization, however, they must be acknowledged
as a vital and most desirable component of effective action.

4. *Having a keen sense of timing:* Managers adept at robust action are most
notable for their keen sense of timing. They have an uncanny ability to
judge when to engage, when to disengage, when to do nothing, when
to act, when to react, when to delay, and in what order to take action.
Good timing, as we have all experienced, can have an enormous effect
on the success of our actions. Well-timed actions can succeed, but the
same action, if taken at the wrong time, may have no chance of success.
For instance, there are times when there are enormous first-mover advantages in acting before anyone else does. This is widely believed to
be the case in the personal computer business. But even in such situations, one can always act too early and introduce a product before the
market is ready and unnecessarily cannibalize the sales of an earlier-
generation product. As Rod Canion—the former CEO of Compaq
Computers who built the company to more than $3 billion dollars in
sales—told us, timing is "always a game of inches."[6]

5. *Judging the situation at hand:* Good timing can often depend on being
able to judge the situation at hand: Is it an opportunity or a threat? A
moment of weakness or strength? A moment of crisis or hope? Based
on the assessment of the situation one must also exercise judgment about
the appropriate actions to take and the way in which rhetoric is used to
mobilize or explain the actions taken.
     Actions and rhetoric based on poor judgment of the situation can fail
miserably. For example, we know a marketing manager at a large computer company who responded to the pressures placed on her by the
three internal business units to whom she provided services by initiating
a formal planning exercise to come up with a way of being more responsive to their demands. Her judgment of the situation was that what
it required was a refocusing of the activities of her group. What she
misjudged was that the situation had already reached a crisis stage. The
result was that while she was engaged in planning, the business groups
maneuvered to break up her group and redistribute its marketing people
among themselves, leaving her with a much smaller group of support
services.
     We have also seen examples where managers have accurately assessed

the situation at hand and taken advantage of it. Paul Fireman, the CEO of Reebok, provides one of the best examples of such judgment. At a show of shoe manufacturers in Europe in 1989, Fireman remembers walking around and being unimpressed with most of the merchandise displayed. In conversations with the members of the trade press who were covering the show, he got the sense that they too were unenthused and were "looking for a story; for something that they could get excited about." At that moment he recognized that if he could come up with something exciting he could generate some of the best publicity possible. Based on his judgment of the situation, he made the spontaneous decision to create an aura of mystery around Reebok's "Pump" shoe, which was still in its early stages of development. The Pump shoe featured an innovative inflatable technology that could give the wearer a close personal fit. Its innovative features had all the makings of a great story. In another situation, the project could have gotten bad press for being introduced prematurely. But in an atmosphere where the press was looking for a story, it turned out to be a great hit. These early rave reviews, according to Fireman, not only created market anticipation for the shoe, but also helped "light a fire inside the company to get the product developed and released quickly." By taking a risky rhetorical stand by promising the shoe faster than Reebok had expected to deliver it, Fireman not only judged the situation accurately, he also displayed a great sense of timing.

6. *Using rhetoric effectively:* As the Fireman example shows, not only is all action dressed in rhetoric, but *rhetoric itself is a kind of action.* Managers use words to get others to act and to paint a picture of the world that is in line with other actions both taken and foreseen. For robust action, the rhetoric managers employ must on the one hand be "local"—it must pay attention to the particulars of the situation and the identities of the participants. On the other hand, the rhetoric managers use must be ambiguous and general enough to allow for flexibility and adjustment. They must spin a story that can evolve and yet retain its general integrity.

Managers skilled in robust action are inevitably skilled rhetoricians also. Like Jack Welch, they masterfully weave myths, stories, metaphors, analogies, and other rhetorical devices to give meaning to their actions and to persuade others to take action. Through rhetoric they are able to build momentum for the actions they desire and opposition for the actions they wish to block. Moreover, they constantly adapt their rhetoric to keep it fresh and relevant. These skills contribute a great deal to their ability to get things done.

7. *Working multiple agendas:* To take robust action, a manager should try as often as possible to "kill two or more birds with one stone." If the same action can help advance multiple agendas, then it has a greater chance of being supported and effective over time.

For example, when Sealed Air Corporation—a specialty packaging company whose products include the packaging bubbles everybody loves to pop—undertook a leveraged recapitalization in 1989, it enabled the firm to pursue multiple agendas relative to the leveraged buyout that was its other option. Through the leveraged recapitalization, the company's top managers felt they could simultaneously get rid of excess cash, make themselves less vulnerable to a takeover, satisfy their shareholders, put pressure on the organization's employees to shake off their complacency and strive for additional revenues through world-class manufacturing, leave enough slack to pursue growth through an acquisition strategy, and keep the governance of the company in their own hands. The ability to "work so many agendas at the same time" was, according to Sealed Air's CEO, one of the main reasons why the leveraged recapitalization turned out to be so effective.[7]

The Example of Ellie Luce

The best managers we have encountered exemplify almost all the principles of robust action we have been describing. In September 1990, for example, we began research at a major telecommunications company, where a manager named Ellie Luce was championing the introduction of a distributed computer system to manage the engineering of circuits in the company's vast telecommunications network. While we thought we were in for a standard field research experience, we were wrong. From her director-level position, Luce was working to introduce an untraditional way of using computer technology that could ultimately affect the entire company—a way that was practical rather than rational, or in her terms, "business-oriented" rather than "systems-oriented." At the same time, Luce was also using brilliant management techniques that could not be accounted for in most standard theories of what management was. In retrospect, we came to understand that Luce was (and is) an intuitive practitioner of robust action.

The most striking thing about Luce's approach was her predisposition to act, even when she was not exactly sure what the results of her actions would be. She had come to her position only three months earlier, and had immediately begun to champion an ambitious project: to make a radical transition from mainframe computers to workstations in the engineering function and to cut the development time for MIS projects from years down to months or even weeks. Although her position was not a natural one from which to try to launch the revolution she foresaw—there already were people whose job it was to think about such things—this did not stop her. She used her involvement in the workstation project as a way of actively creating new possibilities and coalitions, and of experimenting with many different options to see how she could move the project forward. Like the chess player who has no choice but to make a move, Luce refused to be merely contemplative—her role as a manager was to *act*. One of her associates in the project explained: "We like change, so our goal is to always be moving forward. For people like Ellie and me, staying the same is boredom, and boredom is a fate worse than death."

Over time, the plans for the engineering workstation project changed significantly, but the rhetoric surrounding the project was so flexible— it came to be called simply "Business View"—that such changes could happen without adverse effects. Since her emphasis was on results rather than planning, she freely allowed, and even encouraged, this evolution. While a basic rhetorical overview of the project was kept in place (for example, a variety of different stories about the need for a transition from a systems view to a business view), Luce stressed that the final end-product of the undertaking could *not* be predicted. To the contrary, what she held to be most important was simply to be able to master the present situation and leave enough options open for future actions. At one point, she bluntly explained to us: "We know that the workstation project will never go exactly where we think it's going, so we try not to get too hung up about planning exactly what's going to happen. On the other hand, we won't get anywhere if we think for a minute that where we are today is the right place to be."

At carefully considered points, Luce created visibility for the project by enlisting the support of others outside her organizational vicinity, both her superiors and employees in other departments. (We suspect that her eagerness to serve as a field site for our research fit in quite nicely with her need to build this visibility!) Her basic goal, however— in terms of both her management style and the fast-paced MIS paradigm she was championing—was to get results as quickly as possible, and to have those results make immediate positive contributions to the business.

Key to Ellie Luce's ability to launch this project from a director position more than a thousand miles from the firm's headquarters was a finely tuned sense of just how important her use of language was. Using the right language allowed her to preserve a fruitful ambiguity about the project, and to sell the idea to people in the organization with diverse goals and interests. Depending on whom she was selling the project to, Luce would adopt quite different "styles," emphasizing different benefits and employing different kinds of language, from the minutely technical to the broadly entrepreneurial. In fact, one thing that struck us was that everyone on the periphery of the project had a radically different sense of what the Business View project really was, even as support for it began to snowball—everyone had learned to frame it in a different way. Although the cultivation of such an attitude may be seen as calculating by people who have learned to disparage rhetoric, we would argue that what separated Luce from other managers was her awareness of how consensus is really built in organizations, and her ability to apply this awareness to her own practice as a manager. Over dinner one evening, she explained to us: "I pay attention to every single bit of what I say to people. Only very rarely do I just 'talk.' In most cases, I'm trying very hard to understand where the other person is coming from. I try to get an understanding of what *their* agenda is and what I can say or do to allow some sort of synergistic movement."

For most people, Ellie Luce is an unlikely role model. Even in her own firm, while she is acknowledged by almost everyone as effective, she is open to criticism because she does not fit the typical model of an effective manager. A rational approach to management would have us believe that the process of management involves planning, organizing, staffing, directing, coordinating, reporting, and budgeting.[8] Yet the robust actions of managers like Ellie Luce don't conform to this rational view—a view revealed in the enormous value typically placed in management education on action planning, a wonderful oxymoron when one thinks about it. Only in the simplest of circumstances is it possible to "plan" actions in the sense that if x happens I will do y. In most circumstances action is a constant response to unanticipated events, and the world does not afford us the opportunity to disengage ourselves to become either rational or objective.[9] And even if we could step back in such a fashion, it is unclear how useful our efforts would prove in a constantly evolving situation.

Nevertheless, the prevailing view in management—supported by a dominant, if waning, rhetoric in academia and the press[10]—continues to be that actions are rationally planned before they are taken, rather than allowing that plans are often just rhetorical tools or *ex-post* sense-making of what has already transpired. This view inhibits managers from admitting that they often take action just to see what happens, to stir things up, to create opportunities, or simply because "it felt right." To admit this, especially to others in their organization, would be to appear capricious, unsophisticated, and reckless. The result is that managers often profess a rationality that does not actually exist at the time actions are taken.

WHAT DO MANAGERS DO ALL DAY?

Observing managers in action reveals that even though they may describe their work in rational terms, they spend very little of their time explicitly engaged in planning, organizing, staffing, directing, coordinating, reporting, and budgeting. These activities, as Jane Hannaway found in her study of managers at work, "do not in fact describe what managers do."[11] At best they describe vague objectives for managers which they are constantly trying to accomplish in a far more messy and hectic stream of ongoing activity.

The Manager at Work

Managers are in constant action. Virtually every study of managers in action has found that they "switch frequently from task to task, changing their focus of attention to respond to issues as they arise, and engaging in a large volume of tasks of short duration."[12] For instance, while observing five CEOs in action, Henry Mintzberg found that they averaged thirty-six written and sixteen verbal contacts per day, almost every one of them dealing with a distinct issue. Most of these activities were brief, lasting less than nine minutes.[13] The same picture of hectic activity emerges from studies of middle managers as well as managers in different settings.

Managers also spend little time by themselves. They rarely spend time alone drawing up plans or brooding over critical decisions. Instead, they spend most of their time interacting with others—both inside and outside the organization. Including casual interactions in hallways, phone conversations, one-on-one meetings, and larger group meetings, it is estimated that managers spend about two-thirds of their time with others. As Mintzberg has pointed out: "Unlike other workers, the manager does not leave the telephone or the meeting to get back to work. Rather, these contacts *are* his work."[14]

The interactive nature of management means that most management work is conversational.[15] When managers are in action, they are talking and listening. Studies on the nature of managerial work indicate that managers spend about two-thirds to three-fourths of their time in verbal activity.[16] These verbal conversations are the means by which managers gather information, stay on top of things, identify problems, negotiate

shared meanings, develop plans, put things in motion, give orders, assert authority, develop relationships, spread gossip—in short, they are
what the manager's daily practice is all about. Through other forms of
talk such as speeches and presentations, managers establish definitions
and meanings for their own actions and give others a sense of what the
organization is about, where it is at, and what it is up to.

Reebok's Paul Fireman thinks of action in his organization as a large
"network of conversations." "If you want to find out what's going on
in the organization," he says, "all you have to do is listen to the conversations in the hallways. That will tell you more than any report or
formal control system can." He even believes that by "listening to conversations in the air" one can also find out better than any market research study how the firm is doing in the marketplace. As a result, he
and several of the firm's marketing executives often spend weekends in
the neighborhood mall or at high school sporting events, and hang out
with teenagers to listen to their conversations about "what's hot and
what's not." In keeping with this view of action as a network of conversations, Fireman also believes that the only way to get real change
in an organization is "to go out there and start having a new kind of
conversation. . . . And you have to keep doing it until you start hearing
a different kind of talk. Then you know you have managed to get real
change."

Events and Problems

Events—expected and unexpected, planned and unplanned—play an especially significant role in the otherwise constant flow of actions and
conversations that define the nature of managerial work. Like punctuation marks, events give shape and form to the ongoing flow of actions
and words in an organization. Events such as a product launch, a budget
review meeting, an off-site strategy-planning exercise, an annual performance appraisal, a strike, a product announcement by a competitor,
a collapse in the financial markets—these are all occasions that serve to
focus and crystallize meanings in organizations. These events also serve
as focal points for the different streams of ongoing activity in the organization. Although they may often only be ceremonial and not be
remembered as events of any significance, they serve as moments to
take stock of ongoing actions, to spin new stories, to set in motion
future actions, to formally announce beginnings, milestones, and ends,
to trigger a change of course, or just to touch base and reaffirm individual and organizational identities.

If events give shape and form to the ongoing actions of managers,
problems provide the continuous stimulus. Managers spend most of

their time solving problems. As we have indicated, few of these problems are what could be considered engineering or design problems. Most managers spend little time drawing up new organizational designs or formulating new strategies. Instead, they are constantly trying to fight fires and solve local problems. Making sure that an irate customer gets an order fulfilled, that Joe is no longer depressed about having his budget cut, that Jane the wonderful job candidate can be persuaded to take the job, that John gets the message that he has been goofing off for too long, that Mary modifies a presentation she is going to make, and that Susan can be counted on to be on the same side during an upcoming meeting—these are the kinds of everyday problems that consume most of the time, attention, and efforts of managers. Moreover, most of the problems that managers work on are not initiated by them but are triggered by demands and requests from others. One manager we met put it perfectly bluntly: "You come in to work, and it's one damn problem after the other. You have barely had time to attend to one thing, when someone asks you to attend to another. Before you know it, the day's gone!"

Managing in Situations

The picture of management we have been painting will doubtless strike many as unconventional or unflattering. We grant that many people will believe that rational choice is still the most desirable way for managers to act. Indeed, if managers could, many probably would act in this way. But most of the time, this model is an unattainable fiction given the situations that managers commonly face.

The limitations of rational choice models of managerial action can be brought into sharp focus by considering the following scenario suggested by Terry Winograd and Fernando Flores, authors of a groundbreaking book called *Understanding Computers and Cognition*. In their book, which attends to the problem of creating computer systems that work the way effective managers do, they ask the reader to imagine "chairing a meeting of fifteen or so people at which [an] important and controversial issue is to be decided." Winograd and Flores outline several interesting conditions that arise in this common managerial situation, conditions that we paraphrase here:[17]

1. *As a manager, you "cannot avoid acting."* At each moment of the meeting you are acting. Even letting things go constitutes an action, with effects you may or may not want. So, you are always "thrown into action, independent of your will."

2. *"You cannot step back and reflect on your actions."* You have to rely on your instincts to react and act in real time, even though you may reflect on the meeting later on and realize or wish that you had done things differently.

3. *"The effect of your actions cannot be predicted."* There are too many paths that any action could lead to, so you cannot always depend on rational planning to find steps that will achieve your goals. Instead, you have no choice but to "flow with the situation."

4. *"You do not have a stable representation of the situation."* Things in the meeting evolve continuously. At any moment, you only see fragmentary pieces. The overall pattern of the meeting is only discernible after it is over.

5. *"Every representation is an interpretation."* Even after the meeting is over, your description of what transpired at the meeting will never be the only one. Someone else will read the meeting differently and so the facts will always be elusive—what one must work with is opinions and interpretations.

6. *"Language is action."* Every time you speak, you are not merely stating the facts, you are acting. You are actively shaping and constructing a definition of the situation and trying to persuade others of the facts as you see them and the actions that you believe must be taken.[18] The rhetorical nature of managerial action cannot be escaped and must be constantly attended to.

Winograd and Flores sum up the manager's situation perfectly. Problems rarely come to managers in well-defined ways. Most of the time, the problems managers must solve are poorly defined and have fuzzy boundaries. Organizational theorists Peter Keen and Michael Scott-Morton frame the matter nicely: "Most, if not all, of . . . managers' key decisions tend to be fuzzy problems, not well understood by them or the organization, and their personal judgement is essential."[19] Indeed, managers spend a great deal of their time just trying to better understand the nature of the problem they are confronted with. For instance, a manager may have an irate employee come and vent her frustration over one thing and later discover that the real problem was something quite different—or even that the problem didn't have any clear bounds at all.

Fuzzy managerial problems are made even trickier by the absence of universal models for formulating solutions. In the case of the irate employee, it is hard to know if the right action for the manager is to take serious notice of the employee's frustration or just to let it pass. Managers have few well-defined guidelines by which they can make these decisions and inevitably have to rely on their own judgment. Even learning-by-doing is not easy because it is hard to say that a particular action led to a particular effect. If for example a manager did nothing in the above situation and found that the problem went away, it in no way implies that the manager can assuredly act in the same manner the next time and expect the same result.

In the manager's world—which is really the world of all human action—problems are always inextricably connected with the situation or the context in which they occur. And no two contexts are really the same. The people involved, the particulars of the circumstances, even the words chosen to describe the circumstances all shape the way the problem is understood, and all can have an enormous bearing on the course of action that is most likely to be taken and the one that is most likely to succeed. Most of the time, people are simply engaged in the question of "what to do next."[20]

Acting Pragmatically

As the above scenarios show, managers have no choice but to take a pragmatic approach toward solving problems. The renowned organizational theorist Philip Selznick has framed this lesson even more explicitly by urging a return to the action perspective of nineteenth-century pragmatist philosophy. "Our institutions," he wrote in 1983, "would be better served if the lessons of that peculiarly American philosophy, the pragmatism of William James and John Dewey, were better understood. In that perspective, practical judgement must always be tied to the here-and-now; it must be rooted in genuine problems; it must be tested by experienced pain and satisfaction." Pragmatism, Selznick concludes, does not entail "a flight from principle." Rather, "it is an argument for discovering principles and for making them relevant to everyday life."[21]

Managers must apply this same pragmatism to daily practice by basing their actions not so much on what is rationally *known* but rather on what might be expected to *work*. If a manager waits until she has enough information and knowledge to reduce uncertainty, she will end up doing nothing at all unless there are specified routines for her to engage in. Taking action—robust action—requires intuitively acting *as if* one could predict the effects of one's actions, while being willing to revise one's fuzzy "as-if" models when subsequent events suggest otherwise. Those who are unable to generate this pragmatic knowledge either fail to act

or act in the same way every time. They shuttle between the extremes
of total ignorance and total knowledge.

As-if models are never perfect, but managers usually have little else
to go on. And that is why judgment is so crucial for effective managerial
action. In order to act effectively, managers have to exercise their judgment in choosing among different models based on the particular situation at hand. They also need to exercise continuing judgment to modify,
abandon, or apply new models as the situation unfolds. In the end,
judgment and flexibility are the manager's most important tools for
achieving robust action.

The Rhetoric of Rationalization

Most of the effective managers we have met acknowledge that the models
or knowledge on which their actions are based are far from being scientific or rational. They also admit that their personal biases and judgments greatly influence their actions. Yet these same managers will
sometimes publicly explain their actions as if they were based on rational
calculation. For instance, they might explain structural changes that were
made to get around the problem of an ineffective manager as having
been motivated by a search for business efficiencies or a better way of
meeting the needs of customers. Strategic changes may similarly be rationalized as based on careful competitive analysis, even if they were
triggered by a particular problem with a customer or a product.

Cloaking actions with the rhetoric of rationality is a way for managers to build legitimacy for their actions. The objective, unbiased, im-
personal, and logical nature of rational reasoning makes it more palatable
to others and more persuasive. Since managers must inevitably persuade
others to act collectively to get things done, a great deal of their rhetoric
has a rational character. Even though she does not *act* that way, a manager may portray herself as being engaged primarily in planning, organizing, staffing, directing, coordinating, reporting, and budgeting.

In fact, most organizations reveal what initially seem to be two entirely different ways of describing their actions and activities: one that
stresses the practical requirements of action, and another that stresses
rationality, logic, and predictability. In Ellie Luce's company for example, Ellie and those around her were quite frank in discussing the
way their company existed in a state of productive chaos, while more
senior-level people adopted the language of rationality to demonstrate
that the company was not chaotic but controlled, understandable, and
predictable.

The co-existence of two different rhetorics in the same company can
initially seem confusing. One is tempted to ask: "Who is right?"

Admittedly, this is the attitude we often took during the early stages of our research. During extensive study at Amgen, the enormously successful biotechnology company headquartered outside of Los Angeles, we became confused at the entirely different ways people in the company discussed the role of planning in the company. In a business that was uncertain at best, top executives boasted of the importance of the company's long-range plans and spoke as if the success of the company had been rationally engineered from the start. Others, however, stressed the entirely *un*-plannable nature of the business that they were in, gleefully explaining the way day-to-day developments in science and the industry at large made rational planning obsolete almost as quickly as it could be done.[22]

At first, we decided to take what the executives had said with a grain of salt. As we thought the situation through, however, we realized that we had written off this rational "design perspective" too quickly. We realized that even if the company's formal planning wasn't really usable in a traditional sense—and middle-level employees stressed that it usually wasn't—it served a number of extremely important rhetorical functions in the company. It communicated to the external environment (investors, analysts, other companies, and the scientific community) that the company was in full control of its very complicated situation. Even more important, *it gave people in the company a framework for thinking about the activities they were engaged in, and a sense of mastery over these activities.* In essence, we found that the rhetoric of rationality was crucial in the way it allowed people to get a grasp on an uncertain and constantly changing environment.

What was most important, however, was that this rhetoric of rationality did *not* interfere with the way managers really acted. The plans were sufficiently flexible in and of themselves that they were not seen as overly constraining to managers. Moreover, Amgen's very attitude toward planning created additional flexibility: that is, scientists and managers in the company never took the planning rhetoric as gospel. The plans served as guidelines to action rather than as objective descriptions of the company's reality. Planning was a tool for getting things done— no more, no less. While most found the exercise of developing plans extremely useful in helping them understand their situation, these same people often claimed that they never looked at a plan once it had been drawn up. In contrast to many companies, the language of rationality here functioned as a rhetorical tool that actually contributed to, rather than hindered, robust action.

BALANCING ACTION AND DESIGN

As the Amgen example illustrates, the apparent schizophrenia between the pragmatics of action and the rational rhetoric of action does not necessarily represent a contradiction. Effective managers recognize and know the difference between the two modes of management and act accordingly. There are, however, some dangers that must be avoided. Managers must remember that their ultimate aim is to get things done, not to devise elegant designs. Designs must properly be seen as the means to an end, as opposed to an end in themselves. Losing sight of that can be particularly insidious if managers begin to believe that there is a rational solution to their problems and become preoccupied with designing the perfect organization structure, the perfect strategy, or the perfect control system.

The Allure of Design

The tensions we have been describing in this chapter—between organizations and individuals, between rational planning and robust action, and on a slightly deeper level, between objectivity and rhetoric—have brought us back to a consideration of the relative importance of action and design. Ever since the turn of the century when Frederick Taylor sought to apply industrial engineering techniques to redesign work and make it more efficient, there has been a quest to scientifically "engineer" organizations through the right combination of rules, structures, and practices. Science, it was felt, was capable of producing a universal, rational theory of management design that might eliminate the sloppiness and ambiguity of managerial work.[23] But as we have seen, this is clearly not possible, since this sloppiness and ambiguity are part of what *defines* managerial work in the first place.

Old habits die hard. Even now that the specifics of Taylor's program have fallen from favor, there is still the tendency to give priority to rational design. Today's talk is no longer of engineering companies but of "reengineering" them.[24] For the most part, the emphasis continues to be on how managers can design new organizations, new strategies, and new systems that will be most effective in the emerging new world.

Design from an Action Perspective

Granted, a manager may sometimes *need* to act as rational designer and architect—but this attitude never captures the essence of what the manager does. For this reason, the action perspective focuses its attention on management as process, and on the pragmatics of effective individual and collective action. The action perspective more accurately portrays the manager as a pragmatic actor, responding to a barrage of demands and problems to get things done.

We are certainly advocates of the action perspective. But, as we will continue to insist, *we are not opponents of design.* Designs can be very useful because they allow the manager to form solid pictures of new possibilities and to discern new relationships. Models of organizational structures such as the matrix and network organizations, new analytic frameworks such as BCG's growth/share matrix, Michael Porter's five-forces model, and McKinsey's 7-S model can be helpful in expanding the repertoire of as-if models and the knowledge that managers use to take action. These new models of action can help galvanize managers into launching new initiatives and trying new experiments. They are effective rhetorical tools that managers can use to persuade others to take action and to create legitimacy for actions that they have already taken or wish to take.

Yet while certainly useful for envisioning new possibilities and for creating rhetorical appeal, a reliance on management by design poses perils for action. For one, the inherent bias of all designs toward form and structure often gives short shrift to the ongoing activity in an organization, sometimes almost suggesting that this activity doesn't exist at all. Designs tend to "thingify" organizational action, and lead one to forget that organizations are really grounded in a network of ongoing conversations. By relying on designs, the emphasis is one of constantly re-charting strategy on different matrices, drawing abstract new organizational charts in order to "nail down" the firm's structure, or coming up with arcane sets of performance measures to discover the "true" performance of the firm. Little attention is paid to how these symbolic designs are filled in with human action.

Focusing on design separates conception from execution and formulation from implementation. Designs are supposed to be drawn up and then translated into practice, with the emphasis often more on formulation than on implementation. Yet as we have seen, such a separation is not really practical nor possible. An action perspective emphasizes that it is *impossible* to separate conception from execution or formulation from implementation. Moreover, from an action perspective, though coming up with a bright idea is certainly important, getting things done or translating ideas into practice is always the more significant management challenge. In firm after firm, we have seen all sorts of plans, blueprints, and white papers that outline wonderful designs for new organizational practices gather dust on the bookshelves of managers. The ideas were great but they could never be translated into action.

Models and principles are inevitably at a level of generality that does not take into account the nuances of the particular situation that the manager must confront. Effective managers recognize the necessarily abstract character of most designs and use their judgment to modify them to suit their unique circumstances. They don't worry about getting things exactly right. Like Ellie Luce, they are willing to work with "kludges" and imperfections as long as they support robust action. We know of other managers who obsess so much about perfecting design that they create elegant designs that aren't geared to their particular situation at all.

FROM DESIGNS TO INDIVIDUALS

Managers must constantly remember that however innovative and perfect it may appear today, no new strategy, structure, or system is going to guarantee success tomorrow. Failing to take this attitude is what breeds complacency far more often than designs themselves. The real challenge of management goes beyond design; it consists of mobilizing and tapping the action potential of the individuals in the organization. Of course, the importance of individual initiative is recognized and given a prominent place in most contemporary and earlier visions of the new organization. Sadly, however, the solution is usually seen in changing the organization in order to reap greater benefits from human potential. The focus is on organizational context, what it does and does not do to constrain or encourage initiative, innovation, and risk, and not on individual action.[25]

The Will to Act

While it is hard to deny that organizational context has an influence on the amount of initiative taken by individuals in the organization, what is more striking is the enormous variance in the amount of initiative that individuals take in any given organization. An alternative perspective to the traditional view is to see individuals as varying in their propensity to take action, regardless of circumstances. Karl Weick notes that people often fail to act because they perceive personal limitations on themselves and constraints imposed by their situation. By not acting they fail to test these limitations and constraints. His important remarks are worth quoting in full:

> On the basis of avoided tests, people conclude that constraints exist in the environment and that limits exist in their repertoire of responses. Inaction is justified by the implantation, in fantasy, of constraints and

barriers that make action "impossible." These constraints, barriers, [and] prohibitions then become prominent "things" in the environment. They also become self-imposed restrictions on the options that managers consider and exercise when confronted with problems. Finally, these presumed constraints, when breached by someone who is more doubting, naive, or uninformed, often generate sizable advantages for the breacher.[26]

The notion that some people are more predisposed than others to act (and less likely to perceive the constraints on doing so) is an old one.[27] The experience of these people inside organizations varies. Some become CEOs. Others leave for new opportunities such as starting their own firm. The crux, however, is this: a person who has a propensity to act in the "old" organization will have a similar propensity in the "new" organization—assuming that there is even a real distinction between these forms. Similarly, a person who commonly attributes her failure to act to bureaucracy will most likely fail to act in a network organization because of conflicting goals and interests.

We could further simplify this premise by asserting (unoriginally, to be sure) that there are two kinds of people: those who act and those who react.[28] Those who act see uncertainty as a source of opportunity, seek it out, and even create it. Those who react see uncertainty as a threat, avoid it, and seek to eliminate it. People who act view the organization they are a part of, the technologies it uses, and the markets it participates in as resources for accomplishing things. People who react view the organization and its technologies and markets as constraining their ability to accomplish things.

Action and the Emergent Organization

The action perspective on organizations assumes—perhaps rather optimistically—that *most people like to act*. In acting, people dynamically create and manipulate structures, systems, and strategies. Organizational goals, where they exist, are *emergent* from individual action and, in particular, from individual action that mobilizes collective action. As Weick himself succinctly puts it: "Behavior isn't goal-directed, it's goal-interpreted"[29]—which is shorthand for saying that people generally have more of a hand in determining their own behavior than they are usually given credit for. Goals are rhetorical constructions created by actions which each person continually reinterprets. "When viewed retrospectively," Weick instructs, "[action] clarifies what the organization is doing, what business it is in, and what its projects may be."[30]

As we have said, this description is contrary to the way many managers like to talk about their work. The prevailing rhetoric in practice is that goals are set, actions are taken, variances are measured, adjustments are made, and goals are (hopefully) achieved, in which case the manager is rewarded. When they are not, the manager may be rewarded anyway. The rallying cry is, "First we have to establish our strategy!" Despite the fact that much contemporary rhetoric emphasizes the importance of individual self-determination, it still treats behavior as goal-directed and not as goal-interpreted. The underlying premise of "think before you act" is deeply embedded in our rhetoric about organizations. Through it, vision statements, mission statements, strategy, plans, and goals all come to be viewed as magical guarantees of action rather than as the rhetorical tools they really are.

An organization without these designs for action is typically perceived to be lacking in leadership, in a distinctly Western way. The leader is understood as someone who establishes vision, mission, strategy, plans, and goals *prior to* action. We want our leaders to be clairvoyant, to be better able to anticipate the future than we can. Yet, as we have tried to illustrate, a leader can also be someone who crystallizes and makes sense of *past and present* actions through the tools listed just above. This is a more enabling, facilitating, and nurturing view of leadership. Rather than expecting our leaders to be clairvoyant about the future, we should expect them to be robust actors—actors who are thoughtful historians of the past and creative participators in the present.

4

IDENTITY: THE QUEST FOR

THE PARTICULAR

"How queer everything is today! And yesterday things went on just
as usual. I wonder if I've been changed in the night? Let me think: *was*
I the same when I got up this morning? I almost think I can remember
feeling a little different. But if I'm not the same, the next question is,
'Who in the world am I?' Ah, that's the great puzzle!"
—Alice, from Lewis Carroll's *Alice in Wonderland*

So far we have focused on *how* people act in organizations. In Chapter
3's discussion of robust action for example, we painted a picture of how
effective managers combine words and deeds (and words-that-are-deeds)
in a way that at first might seem to elude rational sense—a way that is
practical, local, and always focused on particular actions and situations.
But there are still deeper questions: namely, *Why* do people act in organizations, and *Who* are these people in the first place?

We thus arrive at the final component of our action perspective, that
of *identity*. As we have suggested, organizations need to be understood
as collections of particular people who say and do particular things—
people who are not just employees, colleagues, human resources, or
even human assets, but individuals whose organizational roles and goals
must always in turn be treated in a *particularistic*, rather than universalistic, manner.

DISCOVERING PARTICULARISM

But what exactly does being particularistic entail? We begin with the
words of sociologist Carol Heimer, who says that particularism can be
seen as involving two things: "considering a person in the round rather
than [as] just a member of a category, and considering a person in the

context of his or her relationships to oneself and others."[1] To consider a person in the round requires taking account of not only some but *all* of the components that make up that person's identity. It requires careful attention to *all* the details that make each person's situation unique—details not just pertaining to occupational position (such as job, job title, skills, and seniority) but also to strengths, weaknesses, personality traits, character, and relationships. Since people act in accordance with their sense of identity, effective management only comes by taking account of these unique identities in one's daily practice. Specifically, effective managers know that their rhetoric must be crafted to mesh with the identities of others, since the way people hear things is always dependent upon who they are.

The Question of Fairness

Unfortunately, this kind of particularism is too often framed as an evasion of the fairness that comes from treating people universalistically, that is, as if people were basically all the same. Clearly, when two people are treated differently—such as in terms of office assignments or workload—charges may arise that such treatment is unfair, and that it denies people the fundamental right to be considered as equals. (To any parent or manager, and these roles have substantial overlap, such complaints are likely to be familiar.) But universalism is itself not always fair either: to treat all people the same is ultimately to be unfair to the unique individuals that they are. And it is unfair to the organization itself since the true potentials for action are likely to go unrealized.

When used correctly, the particularistic attitude not only makes for effective management, it also allows us to rethink what organizational fairness entails. For one, we find that fairness is a slippery issue: since its dimensions are many and perceptions of ourselves and others are constantly changing, there are no simple rules for what makes a situation fair or unfair. In some cases, drawing distinctions in terms of titles or gender may seem unpardonable; in others (for example, a case where women are underrepresented on an important committee) the "unfair" decision may actually be the most fair of all. Much of today's contention inside organizations about "equal opportunity" is based on arguments that certain dimensions of identity—such as sex or race—are receiving too little or too much weighting relative to other dimensions such as seniority or performance.[2]

The fairness issue is not one that can ever be solved once and for all. Instead the eternal tension between universalism and particularism is an issue managers must use their judgment in dealing with every day. Human resource systems and policies designed to relieve managers of some of this burden do so only at the cost of limiting managers' situational discretion. Through the enforcement of categories, policies, job rating systems, pay scales, and so on, managers may find it harder to exercise judgment about fairness. And today, it would seem that growing concerns about diversity—from both an individual and a regulatory perspective—are putting increased pressures on these systems and policies to either shift the balance in the direction of particularism, or redefine categories along other, or additional dimensions. Thus this eternal problem is becoming more salient and more difficult to manage.

Confronting the Universalistic Tradition

Every book about management implicitly or explicitly contains some model of human behavior or some theory about why people do what they do. A classic example of this in the management literature is Douglas McGregor's distinction between Theory X and Theory Y made thirty-five years ago.[3] From the Theory X view, which McGregor asserted was common in American industry, people are passive or even resistant to the organization's needs and "must therefore be persuaded, rewarded, punished, controlled—their activities directed."[4] Clearly, this is not a very cheery view. Yet McGregor claimed that such behavior was well documented in organizations. However, McGregor also stressed that this behavior existed not because people are naturally passive and resistant but because "management philosophy, policy, and practice" *makes* them that way. Theory X behavior, he believed, is not the cause but an *effect* of a style of managing—the management practices themselves were seen as the heart of the problem. Theory X can be summarized as: if you assume the worst in people and act in accordance with this assumption, then that is precisely what you will get.

In contrast, McGregor offered Theory Y, which he thought came closer to what people were naturally like in the absence of such negative environments. In this more upbeat view, "People are *not* by nature passive or resistant to organizational needs"; rather, "The motivation, the potential for development, the capacity for assuming responsibility, the readiness to direct behavior toward organizational goals are all present in people."[5] It is management's responsibility, he claimed, to recognize this and "to arrange organizational conditions and methods of operation so that people can achieve their own goals *best* by directing *their own* efforts toward organizational objectives."[6] Theory Y can be summarized as: if you assume the best in people and act in accordance with this assumption, then this too is what you will get.

Two things are important about McGregor's distinction between Theory X and Theory Y. The first is that it is still highly relevant today.

Managers are aware of their own assumptions about human behavior, although perhaps not expressed in such black-and-white terms, and see these assumptions in various human resource and control systems in their companies. Debates continue about which perspective is "most valid" or "most practical." And every so often, someone—such as William Ouchi in *Theory Z*, his famous book about Japanese and American management practices—comes along to propose a new spin on McGregor's original distinctions.[7]

The second important thing about McGregor's distinction is that both theories are essentially universalistic in nature. Although Theory Y perhaps contains elements of particularism ("people can achieve their own goals *best* by directing *their own* efforts toward organizational objectives"), it assumes that *all* people are as it describes, and that these people will respond similarly to a new set of "organizational conditions and methods."[8] However, as every manager knows from experience, people are different. Some are self-centered and others altruistic. Some operate in short time frames and others operate in longer ones. Some are hard working and others are lazy. Some need to be motivated, by whatever means, and others are self-starters, whatever the obstacles. As we noted in Chapter 3, people differ in their capacity to take action even when they are presented with the same circumstances.

THE NATURE OF IDENTITY

What is needed is a model of human behavior that takes into account the everyday reality of individual differences. At the same time, in order for it to be a reasonably robust model, it must apply across situations and people. It needs to move beyond the abstract poles of pure particularism and pure universalism to come up with a particularism that is practical in context.

The Pursuit of Identity

The model of human behavior that we will use is as follows: that *the primary motivation of each person is to discover and to establish one's own unique identity in the world.* What do we mean by this? To start, we do not mean to suggest that organizations are some kind of Darwinian survival of the fittest. While such may be the impression given by certain theories of individual identity, we are hardly arguing for such a position. What we mean is simply that the ongoing concern of every human being—the concern that lies behind almost every action and utterance—is the *development of a self* that can engage in meaningful relationships with other such selves in the world, whether inside or outside the immediate organization. The importance of identity is illustrated by the vertigo and even mental instability experienced by people who are in the midst of an identity crisis, a period in which they lose a sense of who they are or who they want to be.

The particularistic component of such a model lies in the fact that identity is the *uniqueness* that each person is trying to create for herself. What motivates a particular person depends on who she is seeking to be, in particular circumstances, at a particular point in time. Money, fame, power, respect, love—how important these are to a person depends on the extent to which she defines her identity in these terms and wants others to do so as well. Thus, to the oft-asked question, "Does money motivate people?," the necessarily fuzzy answer is, "Yes—but exactly how and how much depend upon the particular person."

The universalistic component of our model lies in the fact that *every* person seeks identity. It is not a concern only of young people, or of scientists, or of minorities, or of senior executives. It is the primary concern of each of us. Recognizing who a person wants to be, and realizing the implications of this for what she wants to do, is the key to creating a context in which the right kinds of action occur. Actions that are seen as contradictory or damaging to a person's identity will be very difficult to obtain, perhaps only under force and sometimes not even then. Those that are understood as contributing to a person's identity will occur easily, almost spontaneously.

Rethinking Motivation

A model of human behavior based on the concept of identity recasts the fundamental question asked by all managers: "How do you motivate people?" Again, the quick answer is, "It depends." What motivates people varies according to what they want, and what they want varies according to who they want to be. But this short answer perhaps ignores a more basic issue—which is that the question of motivation is itself somewhat ill-posed. It assumes that people do in fact need to be motivated. Yet our model suggests otherwise: people are *always already* motivated to become who they want to be—including, for example, someone who does not work very much or very hard.[9] Merely attempting to motivate such a person to work more is to ignore the power and complexity of their own identity decisions, which neither love nor money may be able to dissuade them from.

Motivation may thus not even be the best way of framing the issue in the first place. Instead, the manager's task might best be seen as simply recognizing *who* someone wants to be. For better or worse (and it always includes both), people need to be accepted—not motivated—and should be managed accordingly. This does not mean that a manager cannot try to influence the identity being sought by a person. In doing so, however, she must take into account what this identity already is and where it is going. One person may be more open to influence on certain dimensions of identity than another. Motivating someone along a dimension that is inviolate is a futile exercise, frustrating to everybody involved.

Identity as Worldly Strategy

The above discussion perhaps raises the question of whether a manager is supposed to be something of an amateur psychiatrist. While a little bit of this probably wouldn't hurt, we don't think this is the right question to ask either. *Why* a person wants to be who she wants to be may be an important question for philosophers and psychiatrists, but it is not necessarily a question a manager needs to answer. (Neither is she precluded from asking it, but the usefulness of such an endeavor has to do with how skillfully it can be done.) All a manager needs to know—and this is a lot—is *who* a person wants to be and *how* this person aims to achieve it.

Our model of human behavior is thus a sociological rather than a psychological or economic one since it is based on identity in the world of fellow human beings, rather than on inner needs and drives.[10] Identities are out there to be seen—they are constantly being established in the world through actions and words which are both observable and interpretable. As the philosopher Hannah Arendt has put it, "In acting and speaking, men show who they are, reveal actively their unique personal identities and thus make their appearance in the human world."[11] And Arendt further remarks that "this disclosure of 'who' . . . somebody is—his qualities, gifts, talents, and shortcomings, which he may display or hide—is implicit in everything somebody says and does."[12]

Yet simply because identities are revealed in words and deeds does not mean that they are easy to know and define. Personal identities are complex, notoriously slippery things—works-in-progress rather than stable, definable objects. Identities are both what connect us to and differentiate us from the world in which we live, and they constantly evolve to meet new situations and new kinds of relationships. In fact, we might use the following metaphor: that *identity is strategy for the individual person*. (Conversely, as we will explain in Chapter 5, strategy for the organization is its collective identity.) In both words and actions, a person seeks to establish both a uniqueness and a connectedness that will enable her to succeed along the dimensions she defines as important. Seen in its broadest sense, the advancing and developing of one's identity in the world is *the* primary human concern. To quote a 1923 *Harvard Business Review* article by William Whiting (more fuel for the case that interesting and relevant things have indeed been said in the past!): "To each of us today, the most important thing in all the living of our lives is the message of the meter which registers the distance we have achieved away from the hateful zero of insignificance among our fellows."[13] The process begins with the infant seeking to establish its identity separate from its mother, goes through the adolescent compelled to stake out an identity apart from the family unit, and continues throughout life as the person develops her own particular way of "being in the world."[14]

HOW IDENTITIES ARE BUILT

The pursuit of identity cannot take place in a vacuum—it is always dependent upon a social arena such as an organization. It involves actions of the self that interact with the actions and perceptions of others. According to the distinguished sociologist Harrison White, "Each person is best seen as a trace, a trace which is self-enacted and at the same time captured by observers, of what in real terms is a swirl of processes interacting to produce cognate persons and a context to be taken-as-given."[15] In yet a further descent into academic jargon, one might say that identity is *socially constructed*—that is to say, it is always produced out of some kind of social network that has a role in shaping it.[16] For Hannah Arendt, this network is seen metaphorically as a " 'web' of human relationships" in which the consequences of speech and action constantly make themselves felt.[17] A person growing up alone on an island, in other words, has no identity—no sense of a special place in the web of human activity, no sense of who she is in the eyes of fellow human beings.

Identity, Comparison, and Reputation

The pursuit of identity requires constant comparisons with others, and a continuous reevaluating of where one's actions fit in relation to one's social environment.[18] Indeed, it is because identity depends on comparisons that concerns about fairness become such a central issue in organizational life. Who one is in the eyes of others depends on who these others are, and how they are simultaneously seeking identities with respect to each other.

Strangely, the notion of who one is may thus actually be clearer to others than it is to the person herself. Arendt takes a provocative view on this point, asserting that "it is more likely that the 'who,' which appears so clearly and unmistakably to others, remains hidden from the person himself, like the *daimon* in Greek religion which accompanies each man throughout his life, always looking over his shoulder from behind and thus visible only to those he encounters."[19] The *who* someone is seeking to be always corresponds with varying degrees of imperfection to the *who* that others experience. This is one further reason why identities are such slippery things—and why a manager needs to be aware of how the identities of a person vary according to who is perceiving them. When working with a group of people, the effective manager forms a sense of each individual's self-concept of identity, as well as of the concept others have of each member, in order to manage the constant stream of action and rhetoric.

But the active management of identity begins even before two people physically meet. Before a manager gets to know a person well, she will hold an idea of that person's identity in the form of her *reputation*. A person's reputation is a pithy summary of her identity—it circulates freely in the organization and is easily determined simply by asking. It is based on a few, especially salient dimensions of her identity broadly defined. For example, a person may have a reputation for being a cost-cutter, bottom-line-oriented, good with numbers, good with people, good with customers, insensitive, ambitious, political, or untrustworthy. This reputation becomes the basis of the actions the manager takes and seeks to get from the person, as well as the rhetoric she uses in doing so.

Once established, reputations pass swiftly through the grapevine and can become objectified, especially in the eyes of people who know a person *only* through reputation. Even those who work directly with someone may filter their rhetoric and actions through the lens of her reputation in a way that confirms it for them. Thus, reputations can be hard to change, however inaccurate they may be from the perception of the person herself. This is one further reason why it is important never to assume that one's own sense of identity coincides with the identity perceived by others.

Identifications in the Social Web

Differentiations among people—along such dimensions as intelligence, appearance, personality, and so forth—provide an important mechanism by which identity is shaped, but they do not provide the only one. Equally important is the mechanism of *identification* with and within the "web of relationships" taken as a whole. To identify with a collective—

such as an organization, a profession, or a country—is to adopt a dimension of collective identity as important for the defining of personal identity. For example, companies proclaiming and acting toward a larger social purpose such as a clean environment or human rights are attractive to people who regard such purposes as an important part of who they are. These people are able to *identify with* the organization in the sense that they see their words and actions as both supportive of and supported by their company.

The Nobel prize–winning organizational theorist Herbert Simon has given us a sense of just how important this phenomenon of identification is. He asks the questions: "Why do many, perhaps most workers exert more than minimally enforceable effort? Why do employees identify with organizational goals at all?"[20] The answers, according to Simon, lie in the basic human trait of organizational identification. "Organizational identification," he argues, "becomes a major motivation for employees to work actively for organizational goals, quite apart from the mechanism of reward or the ease with which effort can be policed."[21] Two other recent writers on this issue—Peter Brill and Marshall Meyer—reason that part of the power of identification comes from the fact that "identification is not wholly conscious and does not always obey the same rational rules as conscious life."[22]

Of course, the company a person works for is only one potential source of identification. A person may identify more with her function or division for example, and this can lead to conflict with others who identify with the organization as a whole or with another function or division. A perhaps more interesting managerial situation comes when a person strongly identifies with a network *outside* her organization, such as her profession or community, for the tensions thus created may introduce a host of new identity concerns with which managers must engage. To varying degrees, managers experience such conflicts based on identification differences every day.

The rise of professions and professionalism presents a well–documented example of a form of identification that crosses organizational boundaries. While the term *profession* is a somewhat ambiguous one (one of the leading scholars on this subject, Eliot Freidson, has noted that at least as far back as 1915 there has been "a persistent lack of consensus about which traits are to be emphasized in theorizing" about the professions[23]), Magali Sarfatti Larson has defined the term in a way that captures the centrality of identity. For her, professions are "uncommon occupations [which] tend to become 'real' communities, whose members share a relatively permanent affiliation, an identity, personal commitment, specific interests, and general loyalties."[24] Common examples are lawyers, doctors, software engineers, scientists, and investment bankers. People in these professions are reputed to be more concerned with their professional objectives than with organizational objectives, and more concerned with their professional status than with their place in a company's hierarchy. As a result, their career paths are often defined in terms of movement from firm to firm rather than advancement within a single firm. Their primary loyalty belongs to the profession itself rather than to the company or firm they work for.

The inevitable tension that exists between the individual and the organization is acute for people who define themselves as professionals, and it is most acute for those who have achieved star status in their professional community. Although differences in ability between stars and others may not always live up to the differences in their reputations, such is often forgotten by both the star and the company she works for. Caught up in her own reputation and the drive to enhance it, the professional star makes demands that benefit her but that may not be in the best interests of the organization as a whole. Those on the receiving end of these demands need to weigh the costs of having a disgruntled or a departed star—with the attendant possibilities of lost clients, revenues, even other organization members in the star's orbit—against the costs of acceding to the star's demands. The benefits of keeping the star happy may be less than the costs thus imposed on the rest of the organization, especially when concerns about unfairness and favoritism lurk nervously (as they always do) just below the surface.

Multiple and Marginal Identities

As we have seen in the above examples, identities in organizations occur along many dimensions. As the eminent philosopher and economist Amartya Sen explains:

> We all have many identities and being "just me" is not the only way we see ourselves. Community, nationality, class, race, sex, union membership, . . . revolutionary solidarity and so on, all provide identities that can be, depending on the context, crucial to our view of ourselves, and thus to the way we view our welfare, goals, or behavior obligations. [25]

Each person thus stands at the intersection of many different networks of relationships, which overlap but not completely. And as we have seen, these multiple identities can be a source of conflict, especially when they are based on varying degrees of identification. When a person has membership in multiple networks, such conflicts will be inevitable as the person struggles to maintain and integrate all of her identities.

Life is made even more complicated by the fact that membership, perhaps our most important standard of identity and identification, is not always well defined. Membership comes in many different shapes and sizes, and it can include various kinds of marginal figures and "border members." Two-tier wage systems (in which newly hired employees are paid on a lower scale), the large number of consultants retained by companies (including laid-off employees who are rehired as consultants), part-time arrangements, job sharing, joint ventures, strategic alliances—all serve to complicate the attempt to come up with an easy definition of what membership in an organization really entails. Membership is something that comes in *degrees*. Exactly what part of an organization's social web one chooses to identify with, and exactly how this identification is pursued, are questions whose answers affect the kind of membership that is produced. And whenever membership is problematic, identity can be as well.

THE IDENTITY OF VICKI SATO

The dynamic and problematic nature of identity can be seen in the career of Vicki Sato, currently vice president of Research at Biogen, a leading biotechnology company headquartered in Cambridge, Massachusetts. Sato, the granddaughter of Japanese immigrants, was born in 1948 and grew up in Chicago's inner city. On graduating from high school, she attended Radcliffe College and went on to get a Ph.D. in photobiology at Harvard in 1972. She then did post-doctoral research—the customary next step in the biological sciences—at the University of California at Berkeley. While there, she decided that she was no longer interested in photobiology and that she wanted to pursue immunology instead. After a number of telephone calls and interviews, she successfully landed another post-doctoral position at Stanford in this field. About this time she also divorced her doctor husband.

Sato's Search for Identity

Sato returned to Harvard in 1977 to take an entry-level tenure track position in immunology in the Molecular Biology Department, which had promised to hire a senior person with whom Sato hoped to enter into a mentor relationship. Although this senior person was never hired, Sato developed a friendly relationship with Walter (Wally) Gilbert, a renowned molecular biologist who had just become interested in immunology and who would later win the Nobel prize in chemistry. On a whim, Sato even asked Gilbert to co-teach an introductory immunology course to which she had been assigned, even though she was "scared because he was such a legend and I didn't know that much about immunology and didn't want to look stupid."

Although the two did successfully teach together, Gilbert soon left Harvard to become CEO of Biogen, the company he had helped found with other scientists and venture capitalists. Concluding that she was a good "B + " scientist—but not of sufficient star quality to get tenure at Harvard—Sato left Harvard in 1983 after having been on the faculty for seven years. Although she "wanted to look beyond the edge and push it out" in science, Sato was "afraid that I didn't have the wherewithal to do it" and reasoned that "if I couldn't do it like that, then why bother?"

Sato decided to make a bold identity choice: to put her career as a scientist on hold and try her hand at being an entrepreneur. Technically on sabbatical from Harvard, she used her time to start a small antibody company in collaboration with one other person. All the same, she did not rule out the possibility of returning to academia with tenure at another university. While she realized that such a return might be difficult, she judged that the decision to leave was not as irreversible as she had been told.

Sato's entrepreneurial identity, however, was short-lived; it ended one year after it began when she and her partner had a falling out. Needing a job, Sato accepted her old mentor Wally Gilbert's invitation to join Biogen in February 1984, when she was already four months pregnant with her first child. (Sato had recently been remarried to Lewis Cantley, a local biochemist of decidedly A + quality.) Sato joined Biogen as director of Cell Biology and Immunology reporting to Dr. Richard Flavell, a distinguished scientist who was then in charge of Research. Immediately, she found herself immersed in cutting-edge experiments and science, some of which she confessed she "knew nothing about." It was a heady time in the life of the company as excitement about the potential of the young field of biotechnology ran high. It was also a very intense time—with so many things going on at once that Sato found herself learning a great deal about both science and management, not to mention parenting.

Living with the "M" Word

During her first years at Biogen, Sato was noticed by James Vincent who had recently been appointed CEO. (The board had asked Gilbert to resign in 1984 and Vincent—a former senior executive from Abbott Labs—was appointed in late 1985.) Working with her, Vincent found himself impressed by her "interpersonal and leadership skills and her ability to interact as a peer with the heavyweights on the Scientific Board." Initially, he gave her special projects such as studying whether Biogen should enter the medical diagnostics business. In 1988, when Flavell decided to return to academic life at Yale—proving Sato's suspicion that you *can* go home again, at least in some circumstances—Vincent took the bold move of appointing Sato vice president of Research. "We made an enormous bet on this woman," Vincent later recalled. "It was an important and significant bet on a *person,* a person who showed potential as a leader and who we felt—we hoped—would be able to develop the necessary managerial skills."

As vice president, Sato inherited a research group that had an empty product pipeline. No major scientific discoveries with commercial potential had been made since Gilbert established the basic thrust of research when he was CEO. For the next several years Sato worked hard at guiding the efforts of the scientists and bringing in scientists with important skills that were missing in the company. Within three years, a number of potentially promising products were under development.

As the head of Research, Sato demonstrated her growing skills as a manager, not only of scientists, but more generally. She now served as the only woman on Biogen's Operating Committee, and she increasingly participated in a range of business decisions involving all of the functions that affected the firm as a whole. To her initial surprise, she found that she greatly enjoyed "fitting all of the pieces of the business together." Sato, for example, proved a highly effective public spokesperson for the company, going on road shows when Biogen needed to raise equity within the investment community. Her rhetorical skills in front of large groups were based upon her great success as a teacher, an endeavor that she enjoyed very much but which had unfortunately gone largely unrewarded at a large research university like Harvard.

Yet despite her clear success as a manager—and not to mention the wealth generated through her options in a high-flying biotechnology firm—Sato was somewhat ambivalent about her role and uncertain about the identity she was seeking. Rather than describe herself as a manager—she admitted a certain aversion to using what she called the "M" word—she preferred to describe herself as "a scientist who manages other scientists." This was not to say that she found management and business uninteresting, because she certainly did not. But her deeply engrained identity as a scientist and academic prevented her from identifying with managers as a group without a certain amount of qualification.

Inside Biogen's Social Web

Sato felt that she had learned a lot about how to manage from Jim Vincent—both in terms of what to do and what not to do. She admired Vincent, for example, for his insistence on not avoiding confrontation in his efforts to make sure that all information and points of view were made available in order to make the best decision. "Jim hates conflict avoidance," Sato explained. "He is not afraid of walking through a minefield and setting things off. But as a Japanese woman I was never brought up to face conflict directly." Nevertheless, her skill in this regard had improved in her years at Biogen.

At the same time, Sato felt that Vincent had a tendency toward overcontrol, and that this created problems in a research-driven organization. As with any such company, a certain tension existed between the research function—populated by people committed to building their professional reputations in the scientific community—and the marketing, production, and business development functions, populated with more commercially oriented people, including the obligatory MBAs and ex-consultants. To say that no scientist had any interest in commercial applications or that the nonscientists had no appreciation of the science would be an obvious overstatement. But the fact remained that the two groups lived in very different worlds, relied on very different knowledge, used very different language, and understood each other very imperfectly.

The scientists often referred to the business types as "the suits." They disparaged senior managers, as one senior scientist put it, for "making decisions based on information they don't really understand because they don't have a grasp of the underlying science." The managers, in turn, often viewed the scientists as more concerned with publishing papers than with helping make Biogen a successful company. They questioned their loyalty to the organization in terms of how hard they worked and how willing they were to do "less interesting science" that was commercially more promising. Vincent in particular was concerned about whether the scientists were sufficiently focused on the right things. He was especially sensitive to scientists publishing papers quickly to enhance their professional identities when such actions might imperil the potential competitive edge of the firm. "My main concern," he explained, "is to find people of great talent who are willing to strike a balance between the mission of the firm and the mission of their own personal careers."

The scientists, for their part, felt that managers in other functions had an insufficient appreciation of what it took to do good science, *including* science that had commercial applicability. They saw their task as a creative process that would only wither under the control of oppressive budgets and deadlines. Some were concerned that this control was exactly what a new CFO was trying to implement; one scientist even commented that she was now "spending most of my time preparing reports and presentations to report on my progress against budget on a monthly basis rather than staying on top of the science in my department." As head of Research, Sato was at the center of this tension—situated between, on one hand, the need for Vincent and others to control the *business* and, on the other hand, the desires of the individual scientists to have access to all the resources they felt they needed to pursue their own *work*. (Evidence of the high value placed on scientific autonomy was the so-called 20% rule, common in biotechnology companies, which allowed scientists to spend 20% of their time on projects of their own choosing, using materials and supplies paid for by the company.) As one of the scientists explained, "Vicki's role is to protect us from the suits."

Sato was effective at managing this tension because she spoke the languages of both worlds. Through her own experience as vice president, her contact with Vincent, some training programs she had attended, and a cursory reading of Peter Drucker (his work had been distributed companywide by Vincent), Sato had learned the language of business and had gained the respect of the other members of the Operating Committee. She also read the leading journals in the scientific fields important to Biogen in order to keep up with where science was going and to retain her credibility with the research organization—she needed to be able to communicate with them in their own terms. Of course, as the scope of her responsibilities grew and as she got involved in other aspects of the business, it was increasingly difficult for her to do this. It was all the more difficult because of the exploding growth of knowledge in the biological sciences.

Sato did not see her job as dealing with two different groups that were internally undifferentiated. Ultimately, she worked with specific individuals, whether managers in other functions or managers and bench scientists inside Research. The scientists and scientist/managers ran the full gamut—from those who preferred to remain bench scientists their entire careers, to those who wanted to manage a lab or a small department, to those who wanted to run entire programs or eventually even companies. While scientists *as a group* had some characteristics that distinguished them from nonscientists *as a group*, Sato was quite aware that, in her words, there was "no general model for managing scientists."

The range of individuals Sato managed extended beyond the full-time employees at Biogen to include various border members who made significant contributions to the company. Some of the most important were members of Biogen's Scientific Board, which reviewed the company's scientific progress and evaluated the effectiveness of the Research function. Members of this board included Gilbert, who had returned to Harvard after his tenure as Biogen's CEO; Phillip Sharp, a distinguished scientist who ran the Biology Department of MIT and who had turned down the position of the school's presidency; and Jeremy Knowles, a well-known chemist at Harvard before becoming dean of the Faculty of Arts and Sciences in 1991. Managing people of this stature, intelligence, and self-confidence—individually and as a board—was clearly challenging. Sato also oversaw work being done by professors, post-docs, and graduate students in the labs of various universities that Biogen was supporting.

Sato's Dilemmas of Identity

By 1991, Sato was at something of a critical juncture in her career, with a foot and some portion of her identity firmly planted in both the scientific and business worlds. As a scientist she was an exceptional manager and as a manager she was an exceptional scientist, but Sato did not see herself as an exceptional scientist or manager: "I'm not as smart as Wally or as self-confident as Jim," she insisted. The question facing her was how long could she stretch her identities in both of these networks. Sato had been away from academia for so long and had not been a bench scientist for enough years—and therefore had ceased publishing scientific papers to any meaningful extent—that the option of returning to a major research university was now virtually gone. She conceded that one logical next step would be to become a *general* manager, such as CEO of a company, and she admitted that "the thought crosses my mind that I might *like* to be a CEO." However, she also felt that she was "less sure of that now than a while ago" because she wondered about "what mean, rotten, and ugly things I would have to do as a CEO"—and she questioned whether she wanted to "invest the kilocalories" necessary to serve in this role. But these doubts came and went.

An obvious alternative was to remain vice president of Research at Biogen or elsewhere and continue her career by establishing an identity as a preeminent research manager. As a very capable head of Research in an industry still attracting substantial amounts of venture capital, Sato was constantly getting expressions of interest from small start-up and near start-up companies. Large biotechnology companies also expressed interest from time to time. But she was not sure that she wanted to hold the same job at Biogen or elsewhere for the balance of her career. Just as "The thought that nothing would change for 35 years in academia makes me ill," the thought of not making a major move in some direction was unattractive as well. In a vivid expression of uncertainty about her identity, Sato admitted that "It is not clear who I am becoming."

LIFE IN THE SOCIETY OF INDIVIDUALS

As an individual, Vicki Sato embodies a number of themes about identity which are especially salient today. Consider a short resumé of her many facets: manager, scientist, wife, mother, Asian-American, part-time ballerina, only forty-three years old and trying to decide what to do next. To be sure, all of these elements of identity have existed in society for a long time. What is unusual about Sato is to see them all combined in one person. And although she is certainly not representative of how identities have been constructed in the past in this country, she presents a clear example of how identities may increasingly be constructed in the future.

We have stated that individual identities are at play in all societies and all organizations. Yet if there is a single development in organizations that is especially noteworthy today, it has to do with the nature of personal identity at the end of the twentieth century—and with the changes that have brought the pursuit and cultivation of identity to the fore. Of course, given that we have so far cast a skeptical eye upon claims of unprecedented change and newness, we need to be cautious here. However, we wish to reiterate that our position is not that historical change doesn't happen. Things have *always* been changing and always will be. What is really at issue is whether incorporating an awareness of a *particular* change into one's way of thinking has certain useful consequences. And in regard to identity, we certainly believe that it does.

This is not to deny the fact that modern society has always been built on a foundation of individualism, on an ethic that stresses the strengthening and improvement of one's own person. In today's world, however, the pursuit of identity occurs at a yet higher level, fueled both by a new diversity in the workplace and by an explosive growth in the number of choices open to people both inside and outside organizations. In such a context, identity ceases to be a mere background issue in organizations—as with Vicki Sato, it comes to the foreground as something that managers must constantly be aware of in everything they do.

Traditional versus Contemporary Individualism

In a sense, the entire history of modern society can be understood in terms of a growing emphasis on the importance of the individual.

From the fifteenth to the eighteenth century, the Renaissance and the Enlightenment helped give birth to the modern notion of "selfhood"— the notion of the purely autonomous individual who could succeed or fail on his or her (alas, usually his) own merits.[26] In both religious and secular forms, this ethic of individualism was crucial to the early development of capitalism,[27] and it saw itself especially glorified during the nineteenth century when new political and economic freedoms gave people (again, usually men) an unheard-of amount of autonomy in the way they conducted their lives.[28]

During the middle part of this century, of course, there was a growing concern in American society that this traditional form of individualism was being overrun by a new conformity. In the early 1950s, books such as David Riesman's *The Lonely Crowd* told a story about the rise and fall of individualism which stressed how the desire to be accepted by one's peers was creating a generation of individuals whose primary goal was simply to conform to social expectations.[29] A few years later, William Whyte's *The Organization Man* told a similar story about the disappearance of individualism among the younger generation of his time.[30] Whyte's book painted a bleak picture of a world in which young people took safe jobs at large corporations and sought simply to remain on the payroll of a single company throughout their entire working lives. Identities, Whyte feared, had come to be defined in terms of the progress the person made climbing the corporate hierarchy of a given firm, with as few lateral movements as possible. In the view of both Whyte and Riesman, the American attitude had become one of overwhelming conformity: keep quiet and don't rock the boat.

Yet as the well-known cultural critic Christopher Lasch pointed out in 1979, people like Riesman and Whyte needn't have worried: individualism is alive and well today—although it may be fundamentally of a different kind than in the past.[31] Indeed, in many ways, the "development of the self" today proceeds at a level that makes older forms of individualism pale in comparison. In earlier times, after all, individualism occurred within certain very narrow constraints: one was to look after oneself, but the range of possibilities for action was never actually as wide as it may have seemed since the various dimensions of identity were more highly correlated with each other. Being born into a certain class, or having a certain color, or being a certain sex limited the range of choices on other dimensions of identity and therefore made other choices more unlikely. Although the Vicki Satos of the world are still rare, they were nearly nonexistent at the time of Riesman and Whyte, and just as nonexistent during the nineteenth century's age of "high individualism." The individualism of the past was not so much a game of free self-expression, of actively constructing identity along many dimensions with a wide range of choices, as it was a practical matter of making ends meet. As the American legal scholar Lawrence Friedman explains this previous individualistic ethic, "People did not *choose* a particular way of life; rather, they were trained to accept a preformed, preexisting model."[32]

Yet in recent decades, Friedman stresses, it is this very issue of *choice* that is now at the very heart of the process of developing one's identity, and this is arguably new. Identity is now something that needs to be cultivated out of a range of available options that can at times seem almost limitless. In terms of lifestyle, one need only go to a local shopping mall to become aware of just how wide these options are—and in malls they are all for sale. For better or for worse, America has become a shopping mall of choices. Friedman jokes that "If [Thomas Jefferson] came back from the dead today, the range of choices would amaze and no doubt horrify him."[33] So great is the range of options and lifestyles facing the average individual that one might say that the self must literally be *invented* rather than merely developed. There is no legitimate "master plan" that tells people how to create their lives.[34]

Our modern world, asserts the British sociologist Anthony Giddens, is a place in which each person must *constantly* attend to the "unfolding of self-identity"—it is a world in which "the question, 'How shall I live?' has to be answered in day-to-day decisions."[35] In the apt phrase that titles Friedman's book, we live in a "republic of choice" where the individual can literally construct herself out of a constantly changing menu of options. None other than Peter Drucker began to sense this in 1969 when he wrote (amidst his more hyperbolic claims of transformation) that " 'What shall I do *with myself*?' is really being asked of the young by the multitude of choices around them." In his view, the range of choices in the "society of organizations" forced individuals to make difficult decisions about the ways in which they wanted to build their identities. These choices "force the individual to ask of himself: 'Who am I?' 'What do I want to be?' 'What do I want to put into life and what do I want to get out of it?' "[36]

Through constant self-defining decisions, the modern individual aims to create and to express a sense of his or her unique place in the world, often with the explicit recognition that the identity thus created is open to continuous revision. As one young researcher at the Harvard Business School said frankly of her own experiences: "I just don't think there's such a thing as a truly *permanent* identity today." In her view, the number and variety of options she faced in life meant that rigid life decisions just weren't viable. Her own view of identity—stressing flexibility, uncertainty, and experimentation—sounded remarkably close to the model of robust action we have traced so far in this book.

Of course, this brave new world of robust identity brings with it new kinds of problems and anxieties. Personal identities become highly flexible and transitory, and are less integrated into stable identifications such as organizations and institutions: the individual is free to traverse different kinds of identifications almost at will. (This is true even among the most disadvantaged sectors of society—such as in the inner cities, where the range of identity choice can be as high as it is anywhere, even if the choices are not particularly emancipatory.) In a study of this new type of individualism in America, Richard Merelman writes that the decline of traditional visions of society "has released large numbers of Americans from comprehensive group identifications and from firm cultural moorings" such that "the liberated individual, not the social group, must therefore become the basic cultural unit."[37] The result is what Merelman calls a "loosely bounded culture," a culture in which the constant development of personal identity becomes a much more salient feature than the cohesion of traditional group identities.[38]

Diversity in the "Loosely Bounded" Organization

Not surprisingly, this new "loosely bounded culture" has in turn given rise to what might be called "loosely bounded organizations."[39] As social and demographic trends have led to a proliferation of different kinds of identities within organizations, the role of the organization itself in defining identity seems to be on the wane. Strong empirical evidence suggests that the past twenty years have seen a marked decrease in employees' commitment to and identification with management and the firm as a whole.[40]

The decreased importance of organizational identification has made the idea of company loyalty something of an anachronism, at least in many circles. It is rare today, for example, for someone to spend their entire life working for a single company, and career advancement is more than likely to occur horizontally—not so much by vertical advancement within a single firm but rather by taking one's skills and talents from project to project within and *between* organizations as new opportunities present themselves. The typical career path for professionals is indeed becoming the career path for everybody. As Rosabeth Kanter describes it, "More people will be in and out of business for themselves at more points in their careers, as they enter and leave corporations, as they start and grow businesses, as they combine with peers to offer professional services for still other businesses and corporations."[41] As with Ellie Luce, our earlier model of robust action, career trajectories often are a matter of constantly seeking out new and interesting places to make a contribution.[42] The horizontal steps made in such a career are marked by growing ability and reputation, and not merely by the pursuit of "higher-level" jobs.[43]

As careers in our loosely bounded culture have become more individualized pursuits, there has been increased recognition of just how heterogeneous contemporary organizations really are. The highly publicized *Workforce 2000* report, issued in 1987 by the Hudson Institute, marshalled an impressive array of data pertaining to the changing demographic composition of organizations. Not surprisingly, "diversity" has become one of the biggest organizational buzzwords, in some corners as likely to produce groans as the equally overused and abused "empowerment." Yet while the word is perhaps overused, the fact remains that today's workforce is a startlingly heterogeneous place—the stereotype of the cookie-cutter white male executive, regardless of how applicable it ever was in its own time, in many places now fails to resonate at all. Much has been made of the fact that soon so-called minorities—racial, ethnic, sexual, and otherwise—will actually form the majority of the workplace. According to *Workforce 2000,* the net growth in the size of the workforce "will be dominated by women, blacks, and immigrants," all of whom will increase their share in it.[44] The report also presents its already-famous, although often misinterpreted, statistical projection that white males "will comprise only 15 percent of the net additions to the labor force between 1985 and 2000."[45]

While all of this is true, much of the current rhetoric about workplace diversity often fails to capture the challenges that really face managers today as a result. In obsessively reciting the statistics, we run the risk of losing sight of what the real issues are for organizations. After all, diversity in and of itself may be news, but—barring language problems and the unfortunate persistence of bigotry—it is not in itself really all that problematic. Aside from being a juicy and slightly paranoid statistic, what does it really *mean* to say that only 15% of the workforce entrants will be white, native males? What does it really *mean* to recognize—as did a long-overdue 1991 *Fortune* cover story—that a sizable (estimated at 10%), still relatively silent, portion of the workplace is gay or lesbian?

The real meaning is not that organizations are comprised of different groups of people defined in different ways. This is not to deny that this is consequential, or to say that this diversity does not lead to tensions and conflicts between groups. (It clearly does, and some of them are significant and painful for everybody involved.) But we think the real importance of diversity is that it expands the number of dimensions on which identity can be defined. For example, when we met Jack Sansolo in November 1989 while writing a case about the organizational structure of the large advertising agency (Hill, Holliday, Connors, Cosmopulos) of which he was president, Sansolo—who had already told us he had a Ph.D. in Social Psychology from Harvard—volunteered to us that he was openly gay. In doing so, he forced us and others to take account of three key aspects of his identity: gay, Ph.D., and president of an ad agency. Two years later his picture appeared on the cover of the above-mentioned 1991 issue of *Fortune* magazine. The title of the article was "Gay in Corporate America: What It's Like, and How Business Attitudes Are Changing."[46]

Since diversity expands the number of dimensions along which identity can be defined, it greatly complicates the problem of how identity is to be constructed and managed. For each person, different reference groups can serve as the basis of identification and choices will continuously be made on their relative weighting. Sato was struggling with the relative emphasis between being a scientist and being a manager. She was also struggling with balancing her roles as wife, mother, and senior business executive. Whatever the overall balance she sought, others had their own view of her. To the scientists, she was a scientist first and a manager second. To the other executives at Biogen, the reverse was true.

As diversity increases within an organization, the number of possible identities multiplies in accordance with all the possible combinations and permutations. Understanding the identities of others becomes more difficult, particularly when they are quite different from one's own. But since understanding identity is the key to organizational action, the real challenge of diversity for managers will be to keep pace with the many different dimensions of identity that diversity brings. The real challenge of diversity is not that different groups must learn to work together effectively (although they obviously must), but that managers must learn to cope with the greatly expanded *complexity* of the identities with which they will be confronted on a daily basis—including their own.

MANAGING WITH PARTICULARISM

Many organizations today claim to be confronting the "problem" (rarely is it framed as an opportunity!) of diversity. And typically, it is the human resource function that is responsible for helping managers become more sensitive to and capable of managing the consequences of this trend. Human resource professionals seek to accomplish this through various diversity programs—programs that join the total quality, customer service, empowerment, reengineering, and other such "redesign" programs already in progress. Since human resources is the people function, it seems the obvious choice to grapple with this people problem.

But is it? If our claim is true that the changing nature of identity, magnified and accelerated by increasing workforce diversity, is indeed a significantly greater managerial challenge today than it was in the past, should responsibility for it be relegated to a function that has traditionally occupied a second-class position? Of course, to even pose such a question is to fly in the face of most of the rhetoric produced by companies themselves: in virtually every organization, there is prominent talk from the CEO on down on the order of "people are our most important asset" and "the people here are very special." (Whatever the industry, we have yet to meet someone who says, "Well, our people are mediocre at best, but it doesn't matter because our market share is dominant, our strategy is brilliant, our technology is proprietary and leading-edge, and our balance sheet is rock-solid.") Yet despite the lip service paid to the importance of people—often ominously described as "human assets"—it is the rare exception where the human resource function commands the respect it would appear to deserve. What can explain this odd state of affairs?

Who Really Manages Human Assets?

Human resource departments suffer from what we might call an identity crisis, one that stems from the following nervously guarded secret: that they don't *really* manage the firm's human resources at all. Instead, as Peter Drucker pointed out almost forty years ago, a company's human resources are managed on a daily basis by people in the functions in which they reside.[47] The only human resources that a human resource department could truly hope to manage are the professionals in the department itself.

It is granted that human resource policies exist in the first place for the noble reason of trying to provide a rational and fair way of dealing with the "people question" in firms. In doing so, however, they may ultimately do managers more harm than good. One manager we talked to referred to the department in her firm as "Inhuman Nonresources"—in her experience, the function merely served to perpetuate a morass of rules, procedures, and regulations that constantly told managers why they *couldn't* do things, rather than actually helping managers with the interwoven tasks of dealing with individuals and getting things done.

To speak of these rules, procedures, and regulations in such a manner brings us back to our earlier discussion of design, and of design's proper place in management. The design tools provided for people management by most organizations are what we described at the beginning of this chapter as "universalistic." They create abstract categories that dictate how people are to be treated regardless of individual circumstance. Admittedly, these categories often have a noble intention insofar as they attempt to separate what are fair criteria for distinctions (say, performance or seniority) from what are clearly unfair criteria (such as sex or race in most circumstances).

Clearly, fairness is of utmost concern. Yet to live only by rigid universalistic categories for dealing with people is also to deny them their individuality—or, in the language we have been using, their identity. As Heimer notes, "The rules that grow up in bureaucracies tend to be rules about universalism, about how to deal with categories of people or types of relationships rather than about the need to take account of individual differences, idiosyncratic characteristics, or unusual circumstances."[48] And here precisely is the problem: until the universalistic designs of human resources are seen in the proper light, the recognition of individual differences is unlikely to proceed in the manner it inevitably must.

In the end, managers must deal with individuals in the particular. In doing so, of course, they are free to both use and hide behind the design-oriented tools provided by the organization. The former occurs for example when a manager uses a required annual performance appraisal form as a pretext for having a meaningful conversation with someone about her performance. In this case, the manager has taken a formal tool (the official performance appraisal) and has used it in solving a particular problem—namely, the need to initiate a conversation with someone. In the hiding scenario, however, the reverse regrettably happens: the manager *avoids* having a specific conversation by invoking the designs "imposed" by the organization. For example, even if it were within her power to do otherwise, a manager may cite limitations in the compensation system in order to avoid the unpleasant conversations that would result with poor performers if bonuses were tied to performance. While this tactic may seem to solve the problem in the short run, all it has really solved is the manager's wish to avoid a situation she will eventually have to confront. As we claimed at the outset of this chapter, the tension of balancing the universal and the particular never really goes away—even if the technique of hiding behind designs can temporarily make it seem as if it has.

The Challenge of Particularism

So what are managers to do? Placing greater emphasis on the validity of particularistic criteria in organizations—a task that entails taking greater account of individual identities—is the obvious solution, but it is easier to recommend than to implement. Quoting Heimer again, "The difficulty with formulating more particularistic rules is that someone has to have the imagination to dream up which variations are likely to be relevant and likely to occur often enough that they should be explicitly included in the rule."[49] If there are so many exceptions that no rules are possible, then a manager must depend only upon her own judgment. This can easily lead to charges of discrimination when a dimension of identity given special recognition for one person, such as color, is not considered for another.

Yet a close look at this very word *discriminate* allows us to get closer to meeting the challenge of moving in the direction of more particularistic criteria for managing individuals. After all, most dictionaries give two definitions of this word.[50] The first is "to have good taste or judgment." This positive definition is what managing individual identities is all about—taking people one at a time, and giving each individual case the full attention it deserves. But the other definition—unfortunately more prominent today—is "to make a distinction; to give unfair treatment, especially because of prejudice." This negative definition reflects what people fear will happen in the aggregate if particularism is allowed into organizations: to exercise discrimination with respect to one person is necessarily to discriminate against another.

We do not have any easy answers for how managers might ensure that they locate themselves more firmly in the first definition. However, we do hope to have made clear that approaches to managing diversity based upon universalistically oriented criteria are probably moving in the wrong direction—that they will tend to confound rather than clarify the issue. What is needed is a reconceptualization of fairness based on a particularistic perspective, all the way to taking individuals one at a time when necessary. The obvious implication of this need is to shift the balance from supplied design tools to applied judgment in as many managerial situations as possible. Of course, external laws and regulations designed to protect individual rights are an important constraint on just how far a company can go in this regard. Yet internally, the only constraints are the willingness of managers to accept the responsibility and the commitment of the organization to begin working toward a new conception of fairness—no small task perhaps, but one whose rewards for organizational action could be profound.

LOOKING AHEAD TO PART II

With this call for a different way of thinking about identity and fairness, it is time for us too to take up a new task. It is time to begin investigating what the insights of the last three chapters mean for the way we approach what have traditionally been seen as fundamental domains of managerial concern: strategy, structure, and performance measurement. Beginning with the concept of strategy, we will explore the various ways that the action perspective leads us to rethink our understanding of these management basics. As we go along, we will be guided by the underlying questions already established in Part I: How does language become a factor in organizations? How can managers ensure that they are taking robust action rather than being ensnared by designs? And finally, how do individual identities figure into the picture at every turn?

PART II

RETHINKING MANAGEMENT BASICS

5

STRATEGY AS A LANGUAGE GAME

"For we live not in a settled and finished world, but in one which is going on . . ."

—John Dewey, *Democracy and Education*

It is perhaps a curious habit of our everyday language that the term *strategy* is so closely associated with war. In the common parlance, strategy refers to the tactics on which wars are won or lost, and this same militaristic image tends to suffuse much of the discourse on business strategy. Indeed, *The Art of War*—the book written by the famous Chinese military strategist Sun-Tzu in the sixth century B.C.—is frequently cited by management scholars as the first textbook on strategy.[1] Of course, like generals, managers are often judged on the brilliance of their strategies. And as in war, the brilliance of a corporate strategy is typically measured in terms of the extent to which it gives the firm competitive advantage relative to its competition.[2] Yet like all analogies, this military analogy may hide some of what is most interesting about strategy in organizations. After all, strategy is not merely something that is *devised;* it is also something that *happens*—it emerges constantly in a firm as different people respond to and reinterpret their sense of the organization's identity and purpose.

WHAT IS STRATEGY ANYWAY?

To preface matters in this way is not to say that strategy isn't about creating competitive advantage—this may very well be true. But the main question for the strategist is exactly *what* leads to sustainable competitive advantage. Some believe the answer lies in building a strong market position based on offering products and services that are not easily substituted, building entry barriers, maintaining strong bargaining positions with respect to buyers and suppliers, and erecting mobility barriers that prevent competitors from encroaching on one's position.[3] Others argue that the secret to sustainable advantage is based on building market share.[4] For yet others the secret is to build a proper portfolio of cash-generating and cash-consuming businesses,[5] or to engage in only those activities in which the firm has a distinct comparative advantage,[6] or to make key commitments that lead to a bundle of unique resources and competencies,[7] or to offer products and services of unparalleled quality that uniquely satisfy customer needs,[8] or to be more innovative than anyone else,[9] or to be faster than everyone else[10]—and so the list continues.

These different perspectives suggest that there is currently no definitive answer to the question of what leads to sustainable competitive advantage in firms. And we suspect that there never will be. Like competition itself, competitive advantage is a continuously moving target. As Eileen Shapiro has wryly proposed, maybe the best that we can hope for from a corporate strategy is that a firm "make a good deal of money, a good deal of the time."[11] And if such is the case, what matters ultimately is whether a manager can translate her own theory of competitive advantage, whatever it may be, into action.

Seeing strategy from an action perspective—that is, through the prism of rhetoric, action, and identity—is what allows a manager to craft strategy most effectively. Perhaps most important, looking at strategy as a special kind of rhetoric gives us important insights into the role strategy really plays in the manager's world. Visions, mission statements, objectives, goals, and strategic plans are all examples of how rhetoric is used to impart meaning to past and present actions and to create purposeful energy for future ones.[12] The rhetoric of strategy provides a common language used by people at all levels of an organization in order to determine, justify, and give meaning to the constant stream of action that the organization comprises.

STRATEGIES, RHETORIC, AND LANGUAGE GAMES

In fact, seen from a rhetorical stance, all forms of strategy might be seen as having the character of what the philosopher Ludwig Wittgenstein called *"language games."* Dissatisfied with the traditional view that language simply "draws pictures" of an existing reality, Wittgenstein introduced the idea of a language game to explain that there isn't any one right way to view the world. By his account, all we really have are different language games that define the conventions by which we agree to talk and act. Each different language, he argued, was at heart simply a different "form of life" that expressed itself in different ways of speaking and acting.[13] Seen from this perspective, it does not really make sense to ask whether a chosen language game is a true or false representation of reality—for that, as with the quest for the true source of sustainable competitive advantage, may well be forever elusive. What matters instead is the extent to which people find the conventions and rules of their language game a *useful* way to conduct their business. And of course, different language games can prove more or less useful, depending on the situation at hand and the purposes of the players.

There are many language games—we might also call them rhetorics—that have at various times been more or less popular in the field of strategy. In the 1950s, for instance, long-range planning was the language in vogue; in the 1960s and 1970s, strategic portfolio planning and diversification became the dominant rhetoric; in the early 1980s, competitive analysis and generic strategies came to the fore and diversification lost its charm; by the mid-1980s, the emphasis had turned to sources of competitive advantage, and restructuring; and by the end of the 1980s, the new slogans were strategic thinking, core competence, global strategy, and strategic alliances.

Like most managerial rhetoric, these rhetorics of strategy were introduced as new and improved ways of formulating strategy and gaining competitive advantage. Inevitably, whenever a new perspective on strategy is introduced, it comes with a rhetoric that basically says: "This is a new idea, which represents a radical break from the past. It warrants attention because the previous concepts are outdated and no longer relevant. Leading-edge companies have embraced it and benefited from it." The implication, of course, is that if a firm wants to be leading edge, it will have to adopt this new language.

Strategic Intent and Core Competence: The New Language of Strategy

Take, for instance, the language or rhetoric that embodies two of the hottest concepts in the strategy discourse today—strategic intent and core competence. As popularizers of this new language, Gary Hamel and C. K. Prahalad brand traditional techniques of strategy formulation as worse than irrelevant and actually harmful. They contend that:

> As "strategy" has blossomed, the competitiveness of Western companies has withered. This may be coincidence, but we think not. We believe that the application of concepts such as "strategic fit" (between resources and opportunities), "generic strategies" (low cost vs. differentiation vs. focus), and the "strategy hierarchy" (goals, strategies, and tactics) have often abetted the process of competitive decline. The new

global competitors approach strategy from a perspective that is fundamentally different from that which underpins Western management
thought.[14]

Hamel and Prahalad illustrate their candidate for a new way of thinking about strategy, "strategic intent," by contrasting American and Asian
companies. Needless to say, the latter have strategic intent and the former don't. The differences between their "new" way of thinking about
strategy and the old way can be easily summarized using the authors'
own language, as we have done in Table 5-1. The descriptions in the
left-hand column of the table are those that Hamel and Prahalad attribute
to the traditional approach to strategy, those on the right the ones they
attribute to the approach they themselves advocate. The choice of language immediately makes clear which approach they consider to be superior. After all, which is better: "achieving seemingly unattainable goals"
or "matching available resources"; "inventing" new practices or "ad-
hering" to old ones?

In a subsequent article, Hamel and Prahalad introduce the concept of
"core competence," which now appears to be more likely than "strategic intent" to gain the popularity once enjoyed by strategic planning.
This still newer concept is in keeping with the authors' earlier emphasis

Table 5-1: Old and New Strategy as Described by Hamel and Prahalad[15]

Traditional View	Strategic Intent View
"Trimming ambitions to match available resources"	"Leveraging resources to achieve seemingly unattainable goals"
"A search for niches"	"A quest for new rules"
"Reducing financial risk by building a balanced portfolio of cash-generating and cash-consuming businesses"	"Reducing competitive risk by ensuring a well-balanced and sufficiently broad portfolio of advantages"
"Conforming to financial objectives"	"Allegiance to a particular strategic intent"
"Tightly restricting the means the business uses to achieve its strategy—establishing standard operating procedures, defining the served market, adhering to accepted industry practices"	"Allegiance to intermediate-term goals . . . with lower-level employees encouraged to invent how those goals will be achieved"

on leveraging internal resources: "Core competencies," they write, "are the collective learning in the organization, especially how to coordinate diverse production skills and integrate multiple streams of technologies."[16]

What strategy do Hamel and Prahalad use to create a sense of urgency about the adoption of core competence as a new language of strategy? Again, a fairly standard one—they cast the present as a time of enormous challenge and label past concepts as outdated. Asserting that "the most powerful way to prevail in global competition is still invisible in many companies," the authors argue that managers of the 1990s will "have to rethink the concept of the corporation itself."[17] And much as they did with strategic intent, they contrast the core competence approach with the traditional strategic business-unit (or SBU) approach. While recognizing that a diversified company indeed has a portfolio of businesses, Prahalad and Hamel add that it has a portfolio of *competencies* as well, the major difference being that these competencies often cross business lines. From here, it is reasonable to assume that companies that have organized themselves into relatively self-contained SBUs and that allocate capital on a business-by-business basis may be missing some serious opportunities to build core competencies. Besides, who wouldn't want to seize the opportunity to "create an organization capable of infusing products with irresistible functionality or, better yet, creating products that customers need but have not yet even imagined?"[18]

But let's back up. While much of the rhetorical appeal surrounding core competence lies in the idea's promise of offering a new path out of a bankrupt past, we might question both this portrayal of the past and the claim of newness that rises out of it. Prahalad and Hamel criticize the portfolio planning approach for paying little attention to ends and being inflexible about means. Yet to be fair, at the time portfolio planning was introduced, it *was* accompanied by a rhetoric which emphasized how these plans should influence daily actions and not just be annual events; it stressed how internal strengths (core competencies?) should be recognized when formulating particular strategies, and how flexibility of means was important in accomplishing desired ends. For Jack Welch's predecessor Reginald Jones at General Electric, strategic planning was not just a "buzz phrase or a paperwork exercise."[19] It was a *tool* that enabled him to take action toward the end of changing GE's business mix and increasing its profitability.

Though portrayed as new, the notion behind core competence is actually quite old. More than thirty years before Prahalad and Hamel proposed the idea, a number of authors—such as Philip Selznick in 1957 and Edith Penrose in 1959—had written about a firm's distinctive competencies being paramount to its competitive advantage.[20] Since then, the notion of a firm's distinctive capabilities has *always* occupied an important place in the strategy discourse, although it has been discussed under such various labels as "distinctive competencies," "corporate capabilities," "corporate strengths and weaknesses," "inimitable assets," and "invisible assets," to name just a few.[21]

The notion of internal competence—or what has come to be known as the "resource-based" view of firm strategy—has always existed (rather uneasily at times) alongside a "market-based" view of the firm. In the resource-based model, strategy is seen through the lens of the internal resources of the firm. In the market-based model, the firm itself is treated as a black box, and strategic advantage is seen to lie in the positioning of the firm in various factor and product markets. Of course, thoughtful scholars have argued that this duality doesn't necessarily require an either/or decision on the part of the strategist; Pankaj Ghemawat, for example, argues that resource- and market-based perspectives are "more illuminating if taken together than if treated as separate sources of light."[22] But such realizations notwithstanding, the strategy discourse has tended to cycle back and forth from one perspective to the other.

The End of Core Competence?

One might expect, then, that there would be a life cycle to the rhetoric of core competence just as occurred earlier with portfolio planning. At the time of this writing, there are signs that this is indeed the case. In a 1992 lead article in the *Harvard Business Review,* George Stalk, Philip Evans, and Lawrence Shulman—all vice presidents at The Boston Consulting Group, the firm that earlier pioneered the portfolio planning boom—introduced a subtle twist into the picture with their idea of "corporate capabilities."[23] While Stalk and his colleagues embrace core competence as being a complementary perspective, they feel obligated to point out its limits when not applied along with corporate capabilities. According to them, "whereas core competence emphasizes technological expertise at specific points along the value chain, capabilities are more broadly defined, encompassing the entire value chain. In this respect, capabilities are visible to the customer in a way that core competencies rarely are."[24]

And who can disagree? The dynamic at work here is one that has repeated itself throughout the history of strategic rhetoric. Legitimacy is created for an idea by cleverly showing the ways that it moves beyond the myriad shortcomings of existing ideas. And once the new idea enjoys some relative dominance in the overall language system, a host of variations appear as observers climb on the conceptual bandwagon. Over time, of course, the whole conceptual family begins to seem tired and overextended—at which point a new breakthrough concept is introduced and the cycle starts over again.

While we can only speculate about how the rhetorical winds will shift in the future, it is instructive to try. One common rhetorical shift is for virtues to become vices. Core competence may come to be criticized for paying attention to the firm itself at the expense of external competitors and product markets. The internal focus on core competencies might lead companies to attempt to preserve competencies relevant for markets that only exist in their imaginations. Investments might be made to maintain competencies far beyond any return that can be earned on them, leading to an emphasis on competence for the sake of competence rather than for meeting customers' needs.

The focus on core competencies might also be criticized for directing managerial attention away from obvious performance differences among a firm's business units. This is a valid concern: it is easy to see how investments made for the sake of an identified competence might in some cases only serve to prop up an unprofitable business. In practice, such fuzzy-headed thinking might keep managers from making the tough, trade-off decisions they are paid to make.

What will happen once these potential shortcomings of core competence are identified? For companies whose performance deteriorates because of investments in worthless competencies, the obvious antidote will be to restore focus to the business units themselves—on their performance, their competitive standing, and their potential future contribution. Those with high performance and good prospects will receive investments, as will those that show marked potential. Cash for these investments will come from businesses whose performance is good, but whose prospects are limited. Poorly performing businesses with little potential will be divested.

This great leap forward in management thinking will then replace what will have come to be branded as the naive panacea of core competence. The new rhetoric will be contrasted with the core competence approach as being more future-oriented and forward thinking. It will be pitched as especially appropriate in a world of greater uncertainty and change, in contrast to core competence which assumes that the skills of today will be relevant tomorrow. It might also sound a lot like the old portfolio planning.

What would Prahalad and Hamel have to say about this hypothetical rhetorical shift? Interestingly enough, they appear to allow for it, since they *do* implicitly recognize the importance of language for strategy. They for example write that:

> The new terms of competitive engagement cannot be understood using analytical tools devised to manage the diversified corporation of 20

years ago, when competition was primarily domestic (GE versus West-inghouse, General Motors versus Ford) and all the key players were speaking the language of the same business schools and consultancies. Old prescriptions have potentially toxic side effects.[25]

We would amend this quote slightly and observe that *all* prescriptions, old and new alike, have potentially toxic side effects if implemented poorly, too simplistically, or simply because circumstances have changed. To be sure, new strategic language can help focus attention on important issues, and it can lend existing issues a sense of urgency. This is perhaps the primary reason why managers are so willing to adopt new strategic concepts the moment they become available. Introducing new language provides a powerful way to challenge the prevailing organizational mind-set, to open up new strategic possibilities, and to take actions that can be more easily legitimized under the rubric of the new strategy. On one level, one has to applaud people like Hamel and Prahalad for having successfully introduced a language that managers have found helpful in taking action. We would even encourage managers to consider adopting a yet newer language if, in their judgment, it could be useful. At the same time, we would advise them to be careful about how any language for strategy, especially a new one, is adopted and used.

THE EFFECTIVE USE OF STRATEGIC RHETORIC

In the struggle to create effective strategic rhetoric, realizing that strategy is a language game may be half the battle. After all, while strategies may be codified in three-ring binders or certain design concepts, in the end they are about the *kinds of conversations* people have in organizations. With this in mind, the strategist's main task in shaping the game is to pay attention to four key rhetorical issues—and one important caveat.

Issue 1: Defining Powerful Core Concepts

The core concepts of any strategic language should be chosen for their ability to provide fresh and useful insights. It is this essential step that makes concepts like strategic business units and core competencies so powerful.[26] What such concepts offer is a powerful way to visualize the organization, to take stock of it, and to act on it. Interestingly enough, although their proponents may claim to have defined these core concepts precisely, their value often lies precisely in their ambiguity. In adopting them, effective managers deliberately keep their interpretations very general, open, and fairly ambiguous. From detailed case studies of how managers articulate strategies, James Brian Quinn concludes that:

> [Effective strategists] initially work out only a few integrating concepts, principles, or philosophies that can help rationalize and guide the company's overall actions. They proceed step by step from early generalities toward later specifics, clarifying the strategy as events both permit and dictate. In early stages, they consciously avoid overprecise statements that might impair the flexibility or imagination needed to exploit new information and opportunities."[27]

Fred Borch, General Electric's CEO from 1963 to 1972, is a good example of someone whose strategic rhetoric masterfully walked this line between incisiveness and ambiguity. Concerned about the decline in GE's profitability despite its phenomenal growth in the 1950s and 1960s, Borch in 1969 commissioned McKinsey & Company to analyze the problem and come up with a new strategy for GE. McKinsey proposed that GE be reorganized into strategic business units that could subsequently be managed as a portfolio.[28] Even though Borch was impressed with the McKinsey solution as a way of strategically analyzing GE's businesses, he used the SBU approach flexibly by consciously keeping the concept ambiguous at General Electric. Technically, an SBU could be a GE group, division, or department. According to McKinsey's proposal, about 80% of the SBUs could be readily agreed upon. The remaining 20% required considerable judgment—and in these cases Borch's choices were based on the specifics of the business and the specific identity of the manager running it. By allowing the particulars of each situation to determine how the SBU was defined, Borch was thus able to use the powerful SBU concept flexibly.

Issue 2: Defining Clear Guides for Action

While Borch introduced the language of visualizing units as SBUs, it was his 1972 successor Reginald Jones who defined the rules by which specific strategic actions were taken with respect to these SBUs. With McKinsey's help, Jones built a portfolio-planning model to deal with GE's problem of unbridled diversification. In this new model, SBUs were classified in terms of their location in one of nine blocks according to the scheme shown in Figure 5-1. Businesses were classified according to the attractiveness of the industry they were in and their strength in that industry. Based on this classification, the model recommended a suitable investment strategy and course of action for each business.

Figure 5-1: Portfolio Planning Model Employed by Reginald Jones at General Electric

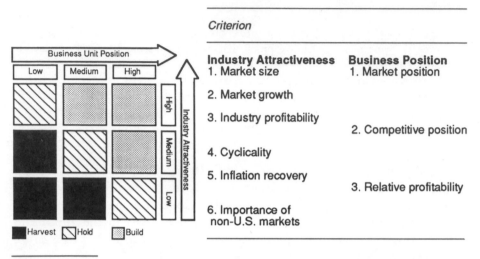

Source: "General Electric: Reg Jones and Jack Welch," Case Study 9-391-144. Boston: Harvard Business School, 1991.

According to a senior GE executive, the attractiveness of Jones's portfolio planning model was that "it not only compressed a lot of data, but contained enough subjective evaluation to appeal to the thinking of GE management."[29] While it was ambiguous enough to be flexible, the model also had the virtue of clear and specific decision rules to guide action. Once an SBU was categorized into a particular block, the model provided a clear recommendation to build, hold, or harvest the investment in the business. Jones found this model very useful in taking the strategic actions he wished to take in order to build the "new GE." In all, GE exited from seventy-three product lines during his tenure and entered into several others, most notably the 1976 acquisition of Utah International, a billion-dollar mining company with substantial holdings of metallurgical coal. GE entered the 1960s with 80% of its revenues coming from electrical equipment. By 1979, the ratio had fallen to 47%, and company earnings were up to between 6 and 7% of sales.

Issue 3: Communicating and Exemplifying the Rhetoric

Since strategy is intended to define a purpose for the entire organization and to guide collective action, finding a way to communicate the strategy and make its action implications clear is of the utmost importance. Whenever possible, managers should try to articulate simple maxims and slogans that capture the main thrust of the strategy. One superb example is Komatsu's slogan "Maru C," or "Surround Caterpillar," which served as the rallying cry for the company's successful attack against the then seemingly invincible Caterpillar.[30]

Because of the vividness conveyed by images, another powerful technique is some kind of pictorial representation of the strategy. Portfolio planning does this through the growth/share matrix, within which circles represent businesses. The core competence approach does this through a tree–like diagram picture of the company's strategic architecture, described as the "broad map of the evolving linkages between customer functionality requirements, potential technologies, and core competencies."[31] Such diagrams summarize a great deal of information in an organized way. When accompanied by a few simple rules, these pictures can be used to clearly communicate resource allocation decisions. For example, in BCG's growth/share, or "barnyard" matrix—of which more soon—the rule is milk cash cows, invest in stars and question marks, and divest dogs.

Again, Jack Welch has displayed an intuitive knack for the skillful use of rhetoric in this sense. As GE built and divested businesses in the 1980s, Welch grappled with the problem of finding a concise way of talking about GE to managers and outsiders. What he wanted was a concept that would have strategic meaning for GE and that would provide a simple description of what the company was and what it was not. With his typical flair, he drew up what came to be known as the three circle concept of GE's strategy (see Figure 5-2).[32] Welch's inventive representation visualized all of GE's businesses in terms of whether they were in or out of three overlapping circles. To be in any one of the circles, a business had not only to meet Welch's definition of what constituted "core," "high technology," and "services," but also to meet the criterion of being number one or number two in its relevant marketplace.

Communicating strategy vividly is undoubtedly important. But it is not as important as persuading people that the strategy is for real and not a passing fancy. After all, what use is a good strategy if people fail to act in accordance with it? In order for a strategy to be persuasive and be taken seriously, it often requires a highly visible and symbolic action that serves as an exemplar of the strategy in action. For instance, when Jones was CEO of GE, he used the divestiture of GE's computer business and the acquisition of Utah International as symbolic exemplars to create momentum for his strategy. Similarly, when Welch became CEO, it was his sales of Utah International and of GE's Housewares Division (which had been established at the turn of the century and was considered almost sacred) that drove home the message that when he said "number one or number two," he meant it.[33]

Figure 5-2: Jack Welch's Representation of the New GE

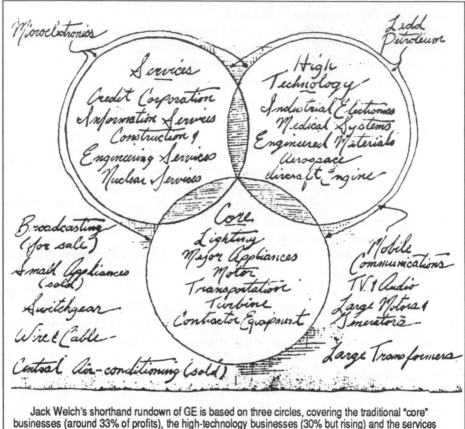

Jack Welch's shorthand rundown of GE is based on three circles, covering the traditional "core" businesses (around 33% of profits), the high-technology businesses (30% but rising) and the services (29%). Around these main groupings lie the remainder of the businesses. Some are profitable, some lose money. Among them, they account for around 13% of sales.
   These are the businesses that Welch has told to fix themselves, to become top players in their league, or they'll be sold or closed. Some, like microelectronics or Ladd Petroleum, have links to all three main businesses circles. Thay are not on the threatened list. Some, like small appliances or central air-conditioning, have already been sold or are planned to be.

Source: "General Electric—Going with the Winners," *Forbes,* March 26, 1984, p. 106.

Issue 4: Using Strategy Rhetoric for Multiple Purposes

Effective managers often adapt the strategic rhetoric they find in the world to suit their purposes and to mobilize a wide range of actions they wish to take. For instance, management theorist Richard Hamermesh found that portfolio planning, at the height of its popularity, was used to take a surprisingly wide variety of very different actions. Against the seemingly safe intuition that portfolio planning is simply portfolio planning, Hamermesh found that CEOs used the technique to accomplish *all kinds* of strategic objectives at both the corporate and business unit levels, objectives that went beyond the simple allocation of resources issue with which portfolio planning is usually associated.[34] Citing companies such as Mead Corporation, General Electric, and Memorex as examples, Hamermesh concluded that exactly how portfolio planning was used in each situation depended on the particular problem the CEO was trying to solve at the time. Sometimes it was used in the firmwide allocation of resources. At other times it was used for strategizing at the business unit level. In still others it was used to stimulate corporate management's understanding of the corporate portfolio in general.[35]

Indeed, the most effective managers will even find ingenious ways to use strategic tools that might otherwise be branded as "mere rhetoric." For example, one manager we know told us that although the consensus in her organization was that the company vision statement was hackneyed at best, she would often half-seriously invoke it to build support for specific actions that might otherwise meet resistance. Once she had identified the action as consistent with the company's avowed vision, she explained, those around her were far more likely to accept it. Of course, this inventive use of "pre-packaged" rhetoric might be labeled hypocritical, but when one thinks about it, why should a manager refrain from using tools that are there for the using? Building consensus is *always* a matter of using the rhetorical means at one's disposal. Certainly, there are situations when rhetoric used in this way is abusive and manipulative. Most of the time, however, such use of rhetoric is simply a fact of life, a powerful way of mobilizing action that often leads to improved performance.

The Caveat: Maintaining a Rhetorical Stance

To realize that strategy is a language game is one thing—but to remember it, and remember it constantly, is another. While strategists must heed these four issues, they must be equally conscious that any rhetorical framework tends to become dogmatic and ineffective once its rhetorical nature is forgotten. And it is this lesson that presents the most serious peril for the manager. Once a given way of speaking about the world has settled in, it is all too easy to forget that a *different* language game could have been chosen, and that this other game would have framed issues in a slightly different way. Gradually, the world may seem as if it is actually *composed* of the concepts one espouses. Instead of seeing the BCG growth/share, or "barnyard" matrix (see Figure 5-3) as simply one among many useful ways to represent businesses and take actions

Figure 5-3: The Strategic "Barnyard": The Boston Consulting Group's Growth Share Matrix

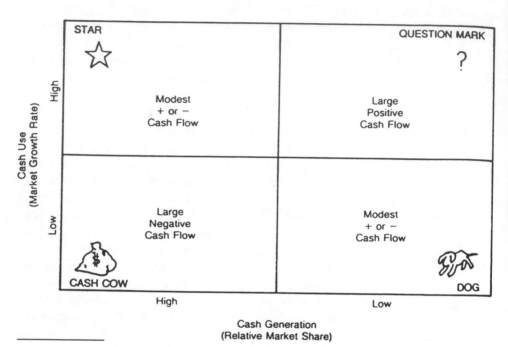

Source: Arnoldo C. Hax and Nicolas S. Majluf. *Strategic Management: An Integrative Perspective,* © 1984, p. 132. Reprinted by permission of Prentice Hall, Englewood Cliffs, New Jersey.

with respect to them, the world actually is perceived *as* a barnyard of businesses. When this happens, the truly crucial questions go unasked: "Is this *really* a dog business? Is there any way in which it can have a future?" According to some observers, it was precisely this rote application of the portfolio framework that led American businesses to exit certain industries—steel, textiles, and consumer electronics, for example—in droves, while foreign competitors eyed them differently and took actions that turned dogs into profitable businesses.[36]

A related, equally dangerous tendency in strategy "games" is for form to overtake function. Welch describes this danger well in his description of what happened to the planning system that Jones had established and used with great success. "[The planning system] was dynamite when we first put it in," Welch explained. "The thinking was fresh; the form was little—the format got no points—it was idea-oriented. Then we hired a head of planning and he hired two vice presidents and then he hired a planner and the books got thicker and the printing got more sophisticated and the covers got harder and the drawings got better. . . ."[37] The scenario Welch depicts is a fine example of what we call *creeping formalization*, a tendency managers must vigorously resist. (And of course, Welch's very invocation of the problem has everything to do with his own rhetorical strategy for mobilizing change at GE.)

While any system for producing or defining strategy must be taken seriously if it is to be of any value, system-building for its own sake can lead to disaster. The concepts must be believable, but they must not be sacrosanct. The legitimacy of the concepts should not be based upon their consistency with the past, but rather on their utility to direct present actions for accomplishing future purpose.

How does the world look when we view strategy this way? We think that taking this stance toward strategy means recognizing a constant dynamic. an ongoing process of establishing shared sets of assumptions that are treated as real until experience shows that they are not—that they are, after all, only assumptions and can easily (in theory at least) be changed. Without these shared assumptions, common purpose is difficult to establish at the rhetorical level and collective action becomes difficult. At the same time, if the assumptions are simply treated as reality, collective action can end up moving in the wrong direction. In short, what is required is a rhetorical stance that locates itself between total cynicism and naive acceptance of strategic language.

Maintaining this gentle skepticism is crucial if the strategic rhetoric a manager adopts is to be robust enough to give meaning to actions and events as they unfold. Since no manager has a crystal ball, what is most important is not predictive power, but an ability to make ongoing sense of what has happened. This is especially important because strategies rarely emerge as the grand ideas they may often seem. Usually, strategy is the product of complex sequences of action. Effective managers recognize this and accordingly exercise their judgment in prodding initiatives along, providing support and momentum when required, and using rhetoric to cast emergent actions as strategic initiatives. Robust rhetoric is used to take robust action.

STRATEGY AS ROBUST ACTION

Viewing strategy as robust action requires abandoning what might be called the grand view of strategy. Strategy should not be visualized as a cognitive activity that takes place at the upper levels of management and results in ingenious forward-looking plans for taking action that are in turn implemented at lower levels of the organization with the hope of gaining a huge competitive advantage. Strategy is instead a complex system of acting and talking, a system that occasionally manifests itself in rational designs but that more typically has to do with the entire network of conversations that exists within a firm—and with the way action is continually pursued through this network. Understood in this manner, effective strategies have the following characteristics:

1. *Effective strategies act as a bridge between the past and the future.* As corporate strategist, a manager is certainly responsible for shaping a vision of the firm's future. But she must also always think deeply about the organization's past and understand the constraints and opportunities afforded by the capabilities and language games that have been handed down. Good strategy is never ahistorical—it is always *path-dependent.* At any moment in time, the viable strategic options available to a manager are influenced by the commitments, choices, and conversations that have already occurred. This is not to say that strategic courses of action from which a manager can choose are so constrained by the past as to be deterministic.[38] Managers can certainly alter the strategic course of the firm and will oftentimes do so quite dramatically through a major acquisition or divestiture. Yet a manager must recognize that, in the words of Henry Mintzberg, the strategist "sits between a past of corporate capabilities and a future of market opportunities."[39]

Of course, managers cannot afford to spend *too* much time playing the twin roles of historian and visionary. Try as they may, they cannot escape the real and pressing demands of the present. On this count, however, they may be helped by the recognition of something that too often goes unsaid: that the oft-cited trade-off between taking actions for the short term and taking them for the long term may present a false choice to begin with—false because every short-term strategic choice, however robust, shapes the range of long-term options available. Every strategic action a manager undertakes affects the path of future strategy; like it or not, the manager is pulled into the future with every action and speech act, regardless of its scale.

2. *Effective strategies are both planned and opportunistic.* Regardless of the impressions one may receive, there is no one "best" way to formulate and implement strategy. The attractiveness of any particular approach depends largely on how it is framed. Those who extol the techniques and virtues of formal planning decry the disorder and confusion that come with informal entrepreneurialism. Those who favor the latter point to the energy it can unleash and depict formal planning as a sterile, meaningless exercise.

In practice, strategy is a messy combination of both of these perspectives—or of what Stanford's Robert Burgelman has called "induced" and "autonomous" processes.[40] Rational, top-down "strategic plans" *can* effectively set the context for individual action. But people in firms always pursue their own strategic agendas as well, and many of these autonomous initiatives can end up as an important part of firmwide strategy. Formal plans must be flexible enough to accommodate these emergent actions, which typically rely on individual intuition, timing, and circumstances.

3. *Effective strategies involve a wide variety of actions.* Contrary to the recent proposal of Pankaj Ghemawat, we argue that effective strategies do not boil down to a matter of periodically making key resource commitments.[41] Nor do they boil down—as Amar Bhide, another colleague of ours, has argued—to maintaining constant hustle in pursuing and seizing opportunities.[42] *The word "strategy" covers all kinds of things*—it is simply a word we use as part of the larger language game of management, and as such, it is not really reducible to a single essence of one kind of action or another.[43] Effective strategy simply involves combining the kinds of action listed above with a variety of other types of action. And of course, in some periods a particular form of action—and hence a particular form of strategy—may be more appropriate than in another.

In an uncertain and competitive world—and when has the world been otherwise?—managers have to use their judgment to know when to take different actions. As Elizabeth Teisberg points out, strategy involves judgments about when to commit and be willing to bet, when to delay making a commitment, when to kill something, when to hedge and ensure a bet, when to hustle, and when to try to change the rules of the game.[44] Of course, there are no easily generalizable answers for when managers should pursue which of these actions because so much depends on the particulars of the situation at hand. Quinn, for instance, notes that even if one has made a commitment to pursue a strategy of diversification through acquisition, "so much depends on the availability, sequencing, conditions of purchase, and specific management characteristics of the individual companies that [one can] only proceed flexibly and opportunistically, interactively reshaping initial visions and strategies as concrete potentials emerge."[45] And all the actions taken will have to be dressed in and mobilized through the appropriate use of rhetoric.

STRATEGY IN PRACTICE: THE STORY OF BIOGEN

The evolution of Biogen's strategy since the firm's founding in 1978 is an interesting example of the challenges of crafting an effective strategy over time. The founding vision of Dan Adams and Ray Schafer, the two venture capitalists whose impetus set the ball rolling toward Biogen's creation, was to create a trans-Atlantic firm that would pursue a broad range of commercial applications of biotechnology. When founded, the firm was basically a group of scientists scattered throughout Europe and the United States who used the initial venture funding to pursue the ongoing research projects in their own labs that appeared to hold the largest commercial potential. In practice at least, Biogen's initial strategy was thus determined largely by the identities and research interests of the scientists who agreed to join the firm, either as members of the founding team or as collaborators and members of the firm's Scientific Board.

Positioning the Firm

Encouraged by the early results of some of these projects, the founders of Biogen raised additional capital and set up laboratories and manufacturing facilities in Geneva, Switzerland, and Cambridge, Massachusetts, to pursue the further commercialization of these projects. The strategy at this stage could best be described as a diversified strategy aimed at exploring all possible avenues of biotechnology. Joe Rosa, currently the head of Biogen's department of Protein Chemistry, recalls that when he joined the firm in 1981, "Every problem was up for grabs as an area to apply this technology. It was a time to dream up great ideas. Then we developed aspartame [an artificial sweetener] using biotechnology and even though we were successful at doing it, we realized that we would never be able to match the economies of Searle." (G.D. Searle currently produces aspartame, under the tradename Nutrasweet, using conventional technology.) Rosa added: "That was one of the first times that we realized the commercial side of research."

As Biogen's original CEO, Wally Gilbert remembers always pursuing the strategic goal of building a fully integrated biotechnology firm that would develop, manufacture, and market a broad range of products. But to support the wide-ranging exploratory work that he wanted to see continue, Gilbert felt it necessary to position Biogen initially as a contract research firm, a firm that undertook research and development on projects that were licensed to be manufactured and sold by other firms. By 1983, however, Gilbert had placed his bets on gamma interferon, a cancer-fighting drug that he hoped would be the first proprietary product that Biogen would bring to market independently. To raise the capital necessary to make the transition from a contract research firm to an independent fully integrated company, Biogen went public in 1983.

Unfortunately, gamma interferon ran into unforeseen difficulties during the crucial clinical trial process. This setback—when combined with the aggressive and diversified R&D strategy adopted by Biogen during these years—led to huge losses as the firm consumed cash and generated little by way of revenues. By 1985, Biogen's "burn rate" (or negative cash flow) had reached such dangerous proportions that for a time it seemed questionable whether the firm would be able to survive. Concerned about expenditures they felt were running out of control, Biogen's board of directors recruited Jim Vincent to replace Gilbert as CEO, although Gilbert stayed on the firm's board of directors and Scientific Board.

Biogen in Transition

Had Gilbert failed? While Gilbert had certainly not been very disciplined about the manner in which he allocated the firm's resources, his broad exploratory strategy had nonetheless allowed Biogen to navigate and survive the enormous uncertainty that surrounded the field of biotechnology during this period. His intuitive approach to strategy had sown the seeds for important benefits that would be derived in the future, including royalties on patents filed on the large number of projects that he had undertaken and the European presence that would offer Biogen the option of starting clinical trials in Europe (where the regulatory restrictions were more lax during the early stages), thus speeding up product development.

But when Vincent took over, he faced a daunting challenge. Not only did he have to address certain immediate issues if the firm was to survive, Vincent also had to come up with a vision of the firm's future while building upon its past. In his actions, Vincent displayed all the flair of a great strategist and organizational builder. First, he redefined the purpose of Biogen. Unlike Gilbert whose vision was to build a diversified biotechnology firm, Vincent redefined Biogen as a "biopharmaceutical" company focused on the area of human therapeutics.

With the idea of becoming a biopharmaceutical company as a guiding vision, Vincent launched an ambitious restructuring program at Biogen. He cut costs by divesting the firm's European operations and by concentrating resources only on those projects where there was exceptional commercial promise. AIDS therapy, cancer therapeutics, and anti-inflammatory agents received top priority because they reflected Biogen's traditional expertise and also offered exciting opportunities for long-term growth. To build revenue, Vincent (along with the help of vice president of marketing Alan Tuck) negotiated a number of aggressive license contracts that substantially increased royalty revenues. In addition, Vincent actively explored new avenues for programs such as gamma interferon that had gotten stuck in clinical trials. The results: by 1988, the company had a stable recurring revenue stream that matched its expenses, $50 million in cash in the bank, and a healthy product pipeline. Having turned the company around, Vincent placed his main strategic bets on CD4, an AIDS treatment drug he had targeted over gamma interferon as Biogen's best chance for an independent product.

While Vincent's rhetoric during this turnaround period was openly critical of Biogen's undisciplined past, he did not make the mistake of rejecting the past completely. Indeed, as outlined above, he tried as far as possible to build upon and leverage the firm's previous strategic initiatives even as he made tough decisions like selling off the European operations. And by letting the Scientific Board continue to play an active role in overseeing the research being done at Biogen, he maintained an important link with the firm's past.

In all, Vincent brought a new approach to how strategy was shaped at Biogen. Building on his experience as a manager and his familiarity with a wide variety of analytic tools, Vincent introduced a more analytic and deliberate approach to strategic thinking at Biogen. Under Gilbert's leadership, Biogen had been guided primarily by intuition and experimentation. Vincent brought disciplined analysis to bear on the resource allocation process and implemented project planning, budgeting, and reviews as a way of prioritizing and controlling resources spent on the various projects. Though Vincent's approach was undoubtedly directive, he was careful not to completely squelch the autonomous and free-wheeling culture of Biogen. He continued to allow scientists to pursue their own pet projects under the "20% free time" plan. He also continued Biogen's traditional Friday evening party and "beer bust."

An Unexpected Direction

In late 1987, a young research scientist John Maraganore took advantage of the 20% plan to begin working on an interesting side project. At the start, Maraganore was trying to build the blood clot–preventing protein hiruden by combining the protein building blocks known as amino acids. The idea of building proteins this way was based on a suggestion by

Jeremy Knowles, a prominent scientist on Biogen's Scientific Board, who felt that it might be a clever way to get around patented proteins by creating their mirror images. All the same, Maraganore's reasons for choosing the project weren't strategic in any grand sense. For him, it was largely an opportunity to pursue an interest he had before joining Biogen. He chose hiruden in particular because it was a small, well-defined protein with well-known application in the cardiovascular area— in short, it was a good place to start. The project was launched on little more than an interesting idea.

As it turned out, the original idea did not work. In the process, however, Maraganore discovered a related molecule that showed impressive anticlotting activity. Excited by this discovery, Maraganore set out to build support for this new molecule, dubbed Hirugen. He knew that treating Hirugen as a potential drug candidate would represent a radical departure from Biogen's usual strategy of making drugs based on genetic engineering techniques. Strictly speaking, Hirugen was not a biotechnology product at all. A synthetic peptide, it couldn't even be manufactured in-house by Biogen. Maraganore later remembered a fellow scientist telling him at the time: " 'Even if you are successful in proving your peptide works, this is the kind of product that Biogen will just license out because it is not within the boundaries of the firm's strategy.' "

Responding to the noticeable lack of excitement among many fellow scientists, Maraganore started laying the foundations that would make it more likely for a formal development effort to be initiated. He contacted several of the leading outside experts in the area and roused their enthusiasm about his discovery. He even managed to persuade a scientist in a university to test the peptide on baboons and provide him with performance data for free. Meanwhile, he worked on implementation inside the company by winning the support of Rosa and also that of Bill Kelley, who headed Product Development and Manufacturing. All the while, Maraganore was "trying to make it as easy as possible for Vicki Sato [Biogen's vice president of Research] to support the project." As he put it, "I knew that Vicki was not an expert in this area and would ask people outside and inside Biogen whom she trusted about the merits of the project. I tried as best as I could to make sure that I had built enthusiasm among all the people she was likely to ask." By simultaneously working on formulation and implementation concerns, Maraganore was pursuing a robust strategy. He had prepared himself to take advantage of any fortuitous opportunity.

Sato, for her part, remembers having inherited an empty pipeline when she took over as the head of Biogen's research group and remembers feeling the pressing need to put something new in it. In her view,

the research group at Biogen had already begun questioning the traditional technological paradigm on which the firm's early strategy had
been based. Moreover, Sato was concerned about putting all her chips
on the increasingly chancy CD4. As Sato put it, "The ground was fertile
for something new." Hirugen offered a potential hedge, and even though
Sato was personally not wild about it, she lent Maraganore her support—"in part," she explained, "because he beat me up until I had no
choice, and in part because he had been good at building the support of
the outside opinion leaders."

Bolstered by Sato's support and by the data he had gathered, Maraganore arrived at the firm's annual planning and budgeting exercise in
November 1988 requesting a budget of $200K to procure enough Hi-
rugen to initiate clinical trials. Yet to Maraganore's dismay, Vincent
refused his request on the grounds that Hirugen had an indefensibly
weak patent position since another company had been pursuing the project for years and had already filed for numerous broad rights. Vincent
decided to use Hirugen in his own way—as an example in his continuing
attempts to articulate a policy of not committing resources to the development of any drug that did not have a strong patent position. For
Vincent, the issue was a no-brainer. He had already tried to initiate
discussions with the other company, an effot which led nowhere.
Knowing the company would aggressively defend its patent, Vincent
could tell that pursuing Hirugen was a mistake unless the patent issue
was first addressed. Yet even though he put up a wall against immediate
development, Vincent did not kill the Hirugen program. He kept the
door open and his options alive and gave Maraganore the funds to see
if he could find a way to circumvent the patent issue.

From Autonomous Effort to Official Strategy

Though discouraged to the point that he considered leaving Biogen,
Maraganore persevered. In August 1989, his perseverance paid off and
he filed a patent for Hirulog, a compound that involved a clever mod-
ification of the original Hirugen molecule. Not only did Hirulog have
a stronger patent position, it also showed more activity than Hirugen.
In the Scientific Board's quarterly review of research programs in November 1989, a number of board members—including Jeremy Knowles,
always a Maraganore champion—applauded Maraganore's genius in developing Hirulog. The board's enthusiasm, according to Maraganore,
helped catch Vincent's attention and suddenly Hirulog was no longer an
idea run afoul but a serious candidate for a new drug. Again, Vincent
was practicing robust action, exploring any and all options and getting
as much information as possible. In the annual planning meeting which

followed the Scientific Board review, Vincent approved the $200K that Maraganore requested to file an IND (an application for "investigational new drug" status) to begin clinical trials on Hirulog.

Once he received the necessary funding, Maraganore moved fast. By May 1990, Hirulog was in first-stage clinical trials—having set an industry record for the fastest time between drug discovery and clinical trials. This record speed was accomplished in no small measure because of Maraganore's ability to pull together a team of people from Marketing, Development, and Regulatory and Clinical Affairs who together formulated and executed the drug's strategy. In devising this strategy, Maraganore embraced all the precepts of robust action. "We always kept as many contingencies as possible in mind," he explained. "It's not as if I could draw a decision tree. But at each point, I was acutely aware of trying to keep as many different branches of the tree as open as possible that could serve as alternate routes to achieving my goal. In fact, I deliberately built options at each stage."

As coincidence would have it, while Hirulog showed promising results in the first stage of clinical trials, the results of the second stage of CD4's clinical trials proved disappointing. (In Vincent's words, it was a "dead turkey.") In the November 1990 annual planning exercise, Maraganore exploited this advantage to the fullest. During the two-day exercise, he pressed hard for resources that would permit a very aggressive development schedule for Hirulog. The CD4 program, which had entered the planning meeting with almost 60% of the firm's expenditures allocated to it, emerged at meeting's end only a shadow of its former strategic significance. In two days' time, Hirulog had essentially replaced it as Biogen's leading drug candidate. This dramatic shift in Biogen's drug development strategy became the overt, public strategy in January 1991, when Vincent made it the centerpiece of an important meeting with the investment community. Biogen's strategy for accomplishing its redefined mission of "building a global research-based pharmaceutical company" now hinged on a new bet—Hirulog.

By 1992, Hirulog had progressed to second-stage clinical trials and continued to move at an unprecedented rate through the testing and approval process. At the same time, Hirulog had become an exemplar for a corporate strategy now based on rational drug design. Under this newer strategic rhetoric—which Vincent had been advocating for some time—earlier research using conventional biotechnology methods of recombinant DNA and monoclonal antibody research continued, but a new emphasis was placed on research into peptides and protein chemistry. Maraganore himself was made the manager of this new strategic thrust, selected to head a thrombosis unit focused on identifying and developing opportunities for new products in the cardiovascular area.

Clearly, Hirulog's progress had been spectacular, but Vincent was still confronted with difficult strategic choices. While he was hoping that through aggressive hustle Biogen would be able to bring Hirulog to market in record time, the comprehensiveness of clinical testing meant that it would still be 1994 before the drug came to market. Meanwhile, the other leading biotechnology firms founded at about the same time as Biogen were already bringing their first products to market. To keep up, Vincent wondered if he needed to make a big move, such as a major acquisition. In addition to this short-term concern, he was also contemplating what new technological competencies Biogen had to acquire in order to stay abreast of a fast-moving scientific field and to lay the foundation for the next generation of products. He knew that the choices he made would have a crucial bearing on the evolution of Biogen's strategy and would continue to shape the firm's identity. Under Vincent's tenure, Biogen's identity as a firm—the shared sense of where the firm stood in the world—had already changed considerably from the days of Gilbert. Vincent also knew that depending on how he envisioned the firm's future place in the world, some of his managers would stay or leave.

STRATEGY IN THE PURSUIT OF COLLECTIVE IDENTITY

If Biogen's story doesn't seem typical of how strategy happens in organizations, it is perhaps because we are not accustomed to looking at strategy formation from an action perspective. The Biogen story isn't one of models, matrices, or strategic "Eureka!'s"—just a steady shifting of different actions and reactions, interpretations and reinterpretations. During slightly more than a decade, the identity of Biogen changed incrementally—sometimes in surprising directions—to yield a highly successful firm that nonetheless was probably unlike anything the company's founders would have predicted at the outset.

Crafting Identity: A Metaphor

The Biogen story may not reveal any definitively new tricks for how to corner competitive advantage. What it *does* reveal, however, is that strategy is a *process* rather than a thing—and this is no small fact to recognize. In particular, strategy as we have seen it here is a process by which a firm goes about building its identity in the world in much the same way that individuals inside the firm do. The process is neither a clean nor a quiet one: there is much talking, acting, trying on of possibilities. Seen this way, the hallmark of strategy is not the grand rational gesture, but the constant dealing with the vagaries of action and the constant need to build, and often rebuild coherent meaning in the face of uncertainty.

To employ a metaphor, the strategic process we have encapsulated above might be understood as akin to the strategic process that goes into wine making. Expert wine makers are the world's most underrecognized strategists: they deal with contingencies from start to finish, they make an enormous number of different judgments—and yet, when all is said and done, they produce a wine with distinctive identity almost year after year. How do they do it? To begin with, good wine makers think in terms of situations rather than formulas. There are unending, path-dependent decisions that wine makers must manage with good situational judgment as their main strategic weapon. In fact, Michel Lafarge, one of the most respected wine makers from France's Burgundy region, has been described as liking to change his entire strategy of fermentation in order to meet the specific conditions of each growing season: "You must ask yourself each year, 'What type of vinification will bring quality?' Each year we vinify differently and may change the length or vary the temperatures."[46] In all, producing a wine with a winning and distinctive identity demands constant attention to an enormous range of factors and a willingness to exercise one's own judgment about what action is right for each particular moment in the process. And depending on how the process evolves, one may have to be willing to make a number of spontaneous about-faces along the way.

With organizations, things are really no different, and we tend to think that most organizations would do well to take the wine maker's approach to heart. The identity of a firm is not something that can be decided once and for all; it arises as the result of a continuous stream of strategic decisions that have no real bedrock other than judgment itself. Choices are constantly made, each one adding in some way to an identity that, like individual identity, is always a work-in-progress. What businesses the firm is in, where it sells its products and services, how it interacts with other firms in its environment, what kinds of public stances it takes on certain important issues, what kind of people it employs—all these dimensions contribute to the building of collective identity inside a firm, to how individuals form a view of the firm's role in the world.[47]

Finding Identity in Diversity

Of course, building a distinctive and coherent identity for what is essentially no more than an assortment of people and resources is no easier than turning a heap of crushed grapes into a distinctive bottle of *premier cru* Burgundy. Like individuals themselves, firms can exist along so many dimensions that developing a sense of collective identity can seem a hopeless task. Yet the task is a crucial one: through an interesting quirk of organizational feedback, it is only by first projecting a coherent identity that a firm can command support of the resources necessary to maintain it. Employees, for example, partially define their own identities, and hence their actions, in terms of identification (or lack thereof) with the firm's identity. Organizational theorist Mats Alvesson notes that "by strengthening the organization's identity—its experienced distinctiveness, consistency, and stability—it can be assumed that individuals' identities and identifications will be strengthened with what they are supposed to be doing at their workplace."[48] Statements of vision, mission, values, and beliefs are all rhetorical devices designed to give employees a sense of the identity of their company. Celebrated demonstrations of this identity, such as the swift response by Johnson & Johnson to the Tylenol crisis, show just how powerful a firm's identity can be in mobilizing action on the part of its employees.[49]

At the same time, collective identity can never fully override the diversity of personal identities within an organization. As we have seen, lurking just beneath the surface of calm, rational discussions about strategic choice are powerful opinions regarding whether individual and collective identities are in conflict or confluence with one another. Especially in a world where individuals define their lives and lifestyles along numerous dimensions, building collective identity is always a delicate game of finding identity *in* differences—of providing a common language of purpose that manages to capture salient dimensions of collective meaning. The power of strategic rhetoric, and the basis of our eternal fascination with it, lies as much with how it creates a common meaning for individual and collective identity as it does with the competitive positioning of the firm.

To be sure, the very nature of some firms can make a common language of purpose difficult to achieve in the first place. The most extreme example might be seen in conglomerates. In these highly diversified firms, it is often difficult to establish any sense of collective identity across the entire organization. And the difficulty is not merely a difficulty of the employees: financial analysts and investors tend to have similar problems attaching identity to such firms, as witnessed by the low price/earnings multiples conglomerates often have in relation to industry averages.[50] Frustrated executives of these companies will frequently complain that the market fails "to really understand" their firm. But it is *meaning,* not understanding, that is the fundamental problem for these firms. The market can understand the pieces very well. It simply doesn't know what the meaning of the whole is. Recognizing Jack Welch's skills in overcoming this handicap does much to explain

General Electric's own stellar market performance of late. Although GE is a conglomerate by any standards, Welch has essentially outlawed the word and has instead used the highly rhetorical term of *integrated diversity* to characterize his company's strategy. Through Welch's attempt to highlight the integration of GE's different businesses (not always easy to do), the market has been able to attribute a sense of unified identity to the company.

Identity, of course, is a challenge for any diversified firm, even for firms merely *talking* about diversifying. Conglomerates are only an extreme case. Much like General Electric, nonconglomerates attempt to establish identity through strategies of "relatedness" or "synergy."[51] Technologies, core competencies, markets, distribution channels, products, and geographical regions are all viable candidates for defining relatedness. When done tightly and consistently, as in the case of 3M, what appears to be a very diversified firm can have a very strong identity.[52]

Yet even where identity *seems* to be under control, it can quietly be eroded through a process we call *creeping diversification,* in which linkages of relatedness are slowly overrun by the well-intentioned accumulation of different lines of business. (Figure 5-4 shows this process for a hypothetical firm, ID Enterprises, Inc.) As a company diversifies from one business to the next, a strong logic of relatedness may exist at each stage along the way. But the particular form of relatedness varies from step to step. After a certain number of such stages, there is no obvious, or even nonobvious relationship between certain businesses. As seen in the figure, between the first diversification step and the last lie a series of links among products, market segments, technologies, geographical regions, and so forth. The result resembles a peculiar-looking house on which renovations and additions have been made over many years. In time, the firm loses its identity: it becomes hard to say exactly *what* it is. As the chairman of Great Britain's GEC has been quoted as remarking, "One can say that turbines are linked to switchgear, which is linked to transformers, which are linked to control gear, which is linked to lamps. But lamps have no direct links with turbines."[53]

How can this creeping diversification be avoided? Perhaps the only thing one *can* do is realize in advance that there are bound to be times when major reorientations are necessary, and that, indeed, they come with the managerial territory. Whether by diversification, expansion, refocusing, or restructuring, it is inevitable that companies will go through periods of major reshaping in terms of the businesses they are in. The challenge for the manager is to articulate these reorientations with a clear view of the identities that will result.

Figure 5-4: Creeping Diversification at ID Enterprises, Inc.

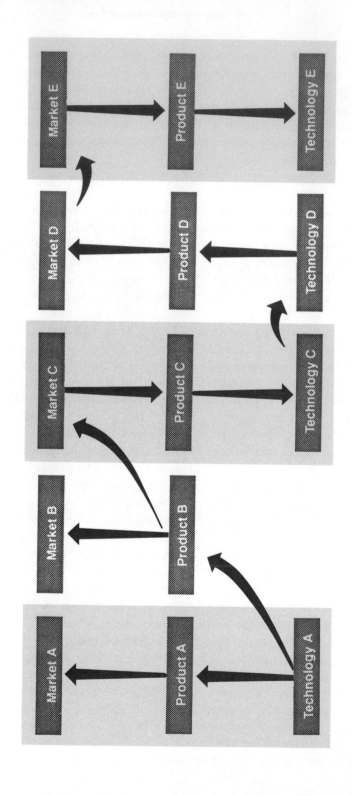

Strategy in the Social World

Building and sustaining collective identity is always a social process. It is common to hear managers describe and compare companies in the same way they do people. Conversations among peers, consultants, and academics are a marketplace where notions of collective identity are explored and refined. Industry trade journals, membership in trade associations, and transfers by managers between firms also contribute to generating information which makes these comparisons possible.[54] The mechanisms of identification and comparison are so pervasive that it is hard to find examples where strategy and identity are articulated without reference to them. For instance, Vincent frequently described Biogen's cautious growth strategy—in which the firm's use of resources was held in check until near the time of product launch—as similar to the one followed by Amgen but very different from the strategy adopted by Cetus and Genentech.

Suppliers, customers, shareholders, alliance partners, and others are also involved in a process of mutual identity formation with the firm. Like friends and relatives, they play an important role in determining exactly "who" a firm is in the world. For example, suppliers take pride in having leading-edge firms as their customers, customers emphasize that they require suppliers to practice total quality, shareholders may only invest in socially responsible companies, and alliances may only be made with companies (including competitors) that have similar cultures. The mutual identity formation at the organizational level carries down to the individual level since these relationships are ultimately based on those between people.

Perhaps what this means is that as the identities of individuals become more complex and multidimensional, it will be harder for firms to articulate a collective identity that a broad spectrum of people can identify with. And of course, we are already seeing how the proliferation of such identities leads to an interesting set of strategic choices for managers. On the one hand, there will be more opportunities to carve out narrow strategic niches that appeal to individuals with particular identities—companies such as Anita Roddick's The Body Shop, a firm that makes cosmetics that appeal to those who are against animal testing.[55] On the other hand, there will continue to be firms that will try to shape their strategies to appeal to as broad a cross-spectrum of identities as possible. Only time will tell which of these approaches will be more robust. Much will depend upon how the present conundrums of identity play themselves out. Meanwhile, managers will have to continue much as they always have—by using language to craft strategies that are as robust to evolving situations as possible.

6

ON STRUCTURE AND STRUCTURING

"The age of the hierarchy is over."
—James R. Houghton, CEO of Corning

"The managerial hierarchy is the most efficient, the hardiest, and in fact, the most natural structure ever devised for large organizations."
—Elliott Jaques, "In Praise of Hierarchy"

In contrast to something as elusive and intangible as strategy, structure seems at first a solid concept indeed. If strategy determines the collective purpose of an organization, the *structure* of the organization serves to define how people will work together to accomplish this purpose. Once strategy is determined, structure might seem to follow naturally as a design for achieving it.

If only things were so simple. Today, there are tremendous battles about what approach to structure is best for organizations, and indeed, whether structure itself is an evil to be expunged at any cost. But the battles are really only the latest manifestation of a central organizational dilemma that goes back a long time. On the one hand, organizations exist in the first place because there are gains to be obtained by the specialization of activities that comes with the so-called division of labor. On the other hand, any form of specialization raises the problem of how different activities are to be coordinated. And this creates a set of vexing trade-offs for which there are no clear solutions, even in today's celebrated Age of Information. As our colleagues Paul Lawrence and Jay Lorsch eloquently framed the problem twenty-five years ago, managers in all organizations must wrestle with the challenge of balancing these opposing forces, which they identified as those of "differentiation" and "integration."[1]

A BRIEF HISTORY OF STRUCTURE

Throughout history, most of the proposals made about structure have claimed to provide a "best" way of dealing with this problem. For much of this century, the bureaucratic hierarchy—a model of organization made famous by Max Weber—was long considered the preferred way.[2] According to Weber and many of his contemporaries (especially Frederick Taylor of the Scientific Management school), the hierarchy was simply the most rational, and hence the best, way to manage. From their perspective, the correct approach to structure was one of rational design, and their goal was the enunciation of universal, lawlike principles that would specify how to achieve optimum performance. Their concerns were timeless but were phrased in ways that seem somewhat dated today—such as the need to maintain a proper span of control or to ensure an unbroken chain of command from the top to the bottom of the organization.

During the 1960s, a new breed of scholars challenged the idea that there was a single best way to structure an organization and offered a picture of structure seen as "contingent."[3] The ideal structure was now understood to depend on a proper fit between the organization and its environment—a fit that depended on a range of contingency factors such as the firm's technology, its people, its size, its age, its strategy, and so forth. Yet even though the idea of a universal solution to the problem of organization was abandoned, the perspective adopted by contingency theorists remained one of rational design. The hierarchical structure continued to provide the main point of departure for discussions of organizational structure, with different variants of hierarchy considered fit for different circumstances.

Recent years have, of course, seen a massive attack on hierarchy itself. It is often public enemy number one on the list of culprits that are argued to be the cause of America's competitive decline. Unpopular indeed is the view expressed recently by organizational theorist Elliott Jaques that "properly structured, hierarchy can release energy and creativity, rationalize productivity, and actually improve morale."[4] For most people, this venerable organizational structure is considered bankrupt, seen as neither humane nor suitable for the demands imposed by a volatile and complex global economy. Exactly what will fill its shoes is a matter of some debate. With a variety of labels—including post-industrial, post-bureaucratic, network, federalist, learning, self-designing, and cluster organization, to name but a few—scholars, consultants, and practitioners are competing to define the contours of the new organization that will take the old one's place.[5]

Yet we should note a curious thing about contemporary rhetoric regarding organizational structure, and this is that it too remains attached to the tradition it has tried to disavow. Even if hierarchy is now a bad word, much of the focus still is on perfecting organizational design. Structure still tends to be viewed in terms of designing a particular *form* or *type* of organization—albeit now in a more turbulent and demanding environment. This emphasis on design is reflected in the comments of Henry Mintzberg who instructs that "getting everything together into a known form, if it all fits, more or less, is not a bad way to organize."[6]

Mintzberg is not really wrong on this point—it's just that "known forms," as he would probably be the first to admit, rarely get to the bottom of what structure in organizations is really about. As we will see, getting truly effective structure might better be seen as a process of *structuring,* as a kind of activity that calls upon the use of robust action. Instead of getting caught up in the contemporary rhetoric about new forms of organization and their wondrous powers, managers must take an active stance toward structure and use it as a malleable *tool* to solve problems and get things done.

STRUCTURAL RHETORICS AND REALITIES

All structural designs are really rhetorical devices. The words used to describe structures belong to one of the many categories of rhetoric we have discussed—a category that contains the labels, concepts, designs, frameworks (and even buzzwords) that managers use in everyday practice. And structure is a matter of rhetoric in a broader sense as well, since discussions about it always come down to attempts to advocate a particular way of looking at the world. In practice, then, words about structure are not so much descriptions but *ideas* about what kind of behavior is desirable in certain circumstances.

The End of Hierarchy: Yesterday and Today

The intimate relationship between structure and rhetoric is revealed in much contemporary commentary expressing disenchantment with hierarchy and calling for some kind of new organization. At the vanguard of this attack on hierarchy are a large number of management scholars and business executives, including Corning CEO James Houghton who is among the more visible figures in this brigade. Declaring that the "Age of the Hierarchy Is Over," Houghton narrated the historical evolution of Corning in a *New York Times* article, writing:

> In 1854, my great-great-grandfather founded a small glass manufacturing business, the Union Glass Company. Today it is a global corporation known as Corning Inc. Until a few years ago, like most American companies, Corning had a traditional business structure more

appropriate to the 19th century than the intensely competitive environment of the 20th. The corporate hierarchy, with tasks strictly defined by organization charts and tightly drawn job descriptions, was deeply rooted in our history.

[But,] since 1983, we have been experimenting with ways to make our management structure conform better to our business structure. As a result, Corning is now what we call a *"global network."*[7]

Houghton describes various features of Corning's "global network" in this article. The global network is "an interrelated *group of businesses* with a wide range of ownership structures." He explains that, "Although *diverse*, these businesses are *closely linked*."[8] *Alliances* and *joint ventures* are a major component of this new structure. As is a *new mindset*. The *network structure* is *egalitarian*. *Greater responsibility* is *delegated down* to line groups and *cross-functional* teams. These teams (of which there are hundreds at any one time) serve as the locus of activity, forming and disbanding according to the tasks to be completed. These teams can "spot trouble and fix it at the source *without supervision*" or top-management interference. All employees in the firm—workers and managers—have the *"power to control their own workplace lives."*[9]

Defined in the terms italicized above, Houghton's global network is a synthesis of many of the features that have been proposed by other management thinkers as the hallmarks of an emerging new organizational structure that will displace the old hierarchy and give companies, in Houghton's words, "the flexibility and strength to prosper."[10] The characteristics of this global network are based on individual autonomy and discretion, along with the concomitant need for coordination and cooperation.

So what does Houghton really achieve through his language? In actuality, he is using rhetoric about a global network structure to pursue a number of different ends: to explain actions he is taking, to exhort actions on the part of others at Corning, and to enhance his own identity as a progressive manager both able and willing to face today's competitive environment. Of course, whether Corning actually *is* as he describes it is a separate and complicated question, the answer to which depends largely on the perceptions, actions, and statements of others throughout the organization.

All the same, the objectives behind such rhetoric—namely, to create more flexible and adaptive organizations by reducing needless bureaucratic authority—are virtually the same as those from past decades. Like the closely related problem of specialization and coordination, the problem of balancing individual and collective action through structure is an eternal one. During the 1940s and 1950s, for example, a rash of articles appeared touting the virtues of decentralized structures for their contribution to "freedom," "equality," "teamwork," and the like.[11] Collectively, these articles emphasized that contemporary business pressures—such as new technologies, shorter product life cycles, greater competition, more demanding customers, and employees with higher expectations about their working environment—were making the traditional hierarchy obsolete. One 1955 article even concluded that "decentralization has become so fashionable that practically no executive today can be heard arguing for *centralized* management."[12]

It is instructive to compare Houghton's structural rhetoric with that of executives from days gone by. In 1953, A. A. Stambaugh, then chairman of the board of Standard Oil, wrote an article for *Dun's Review and Modern Industry* entitled "Decentralization: The Key to the Future." Like Houghton, Stambaugh was critical of big, centralized hierarchies and sought to build a new organization by decentralizing authority and responsibility. In the context of the large organization, he argued, decentralization meant a variety of things that sound familiar even today: a reduction in the layers of management to the minimum; an emphasis on line responsibility; decisions made as close to the problem as possible; a minimal use of staff; a working accord among all the members of the organization; and an emphasis on teamwork.[13] Barring the word *network*—a word more compelling in today's world of omnipresent telecommunications—the characteristics of Stambaugh's decentralized organization are hard to distinguish from those advocated by Houghton.

Like most of today's vilified management concepts, the hierarchical organization is an old dog that has been kicked for a long time. To make their points in a compelling way, the champions of new structural forms use the legitimate rhetorical technique of drawing contrasts with previous forms, in the process oversimplifying them or focusing on certain attributed negative aspects. And to a certain extent, whether these past structures really *were* as described is not especially important as long as people find the contrast convincing. Perhaps as long as this rhetorical technique leads people to take actions that improve their lives and the organizations in which they work, then its promise has been fulfilled.

The Use and Abuse of Structural Rhetoric

Let this not be an invitation to take all such rhetoric at face value, however. Structure is a complicated matter, and it is notoriously difficult to make blanket statements about how one organization's structure at point *a* is different from another's at point *b*. Along whatever dimensions one chooses to describe structure—from jobs and units, to reporting lines, to communication links, to task interdependencies, to status differentials, to decision rights—the structure of even a modest-sized organization is a messy and complicated affair. First of all, there is often a great deal of structural variability within it. (The research function, for instance, is often entirely different from manufacturing, which may be different from sales and marketing.) More critically, structure is always in flux. Even when formal reorganizations are not announced, a firm is constantly changing because of changes in the configuration of the whole or its parts.

As if this were not enough, there is another factor that makes structure complicated: it is as much a matter of perception as it is of objective reality. Once one gets behind officially sanctioned design concepts, rarely is there a uniform consensus among those in an organization about what the structure *is* since people all perceive it from different places and have different information about it. From the official organizational chart on down, any verbal or pictorial representation of a firm's structure must always be regarded as imperfect and incomplete at best. After all, who has ever met someone who says that the company's organizational chart is an accurate and total description of how the organization "really works" in practice?[14] The venerable distinction between a company's formal and informal organization is based on recognizing just this quirk of organizational life.

Despite the obvious complexity of an organization's structure, most people inevitably reduce it to a few words—if for no other reason than to be able to talk about it and talk about changing it. These words can be adjectives that seek to describe the structure's primary feature (as in "we are a very decentralized organization"), or nouns that describe the organization as a type (as in "we have a matrix organization"). The virtue of these characterizations is that they are fairly robust and that they connote certain configurations to people. But they are rarely used with precision, and intended meanings differ.

For instance, to return to the example we have often invoked, what does the term *decentralized* really mean when applied to a firm's structure? One common usage of this term derives from Alfred Chandler's historical account of the emergence of the "multidivisional structure" in the 1920s.[15] In his description of the structure, Chandler gives a rather clear account: the decentralized firm is one headed by a corporate office that sets long-term corporate strategy, allocates resources to self-contained divisions, and then monitors the performance of these divisions, providing help and assistance through corporate staff as necessary.

In a later empirical study, however, Richard Vancil found large differences in the extent to which the divisions of multidivisional organizations were truly self-contained, as well as large variations in the manner by which they were controlled by the corporate office.[16] Vancil's findings raise the question of exactly what is required for a structure to qualify as "decentralized" in the first place. By Chandler's terminology, decentralization refers to a structural type which can be distinguished from other structural types such as the opposed "centralized functional structure." But, in fact, nothing prevents us from extending the term to talk about situations that have nothing to do with divisions at all.[17]

Indeed, the term *decentralized* has come to be used to describe almost any organization, as long as it is one in which key decisions are made at lower levels than one might normally expect. Since the location of decisions up and down hierarchical levels can vary for any organization, this more general use is quite common.[18] Another, less common use of the term refers to the geographical dispersion of a company's assets.[19] When people, plants, and other assets are scattered throughout the country or around the world, the organization is said to be decentralized.

What are we to make of all these different uses? Although we tend to forget it, they show that to describe a structure is always to perform a rhetorical act, and that it may be impossible to clear up once and for all what a given term means. Depending on a speaker's point of view, the same structural term can be used to refer to different practices and may be cast as either good or bad. Those (like Chandler[20] and Stambaugh) who see decentralization as basically good think of it as an innovative way of allocating resources and decision making in a diversified enterprise. Those who view decentralization as bad typically define it as a variant of the old command–and–control hierarchy: for them, decentralization is a scenario where orders are passed down from the top, where managers are held to strict financial objectives, and where people are discouraged both from risk taking and from effective cooperation.[21]

Different authors thus come down on different sides on decentralization, although the term's residual emphasis on the existence of a "center" has made it rather unpopular today. Charles Handy claims that,

> Decentralization implies that the center delegates certain tasks or duties to the outlying bits, while remaining in overall control. The center does the delegating, and initiates and directs. Thus it is that we have that most consistent of organizational findings: The more an organization decentralizes its operations, the greater the flow of information to and from the center. The center may not be doing the work in a decentralized organization, but it makes sure that it knows how the work is going.[22]

Handy contrasts decentralization with what he calls federalism. "Federalism is different," he writes.

In federal countries, states are the original founding groups, coming together because there are some things which they can do better jointly (defense is the obvious example) than individually. The center's powers are given to it by the outlying groups, in a sort of reverse delegation. The center, therefore, does not direct or control so much as coordinate, advise, influence, and suggest—all words which are familiar currency in the head offices of multinationals, often forced into federalism because of the local priorities of their subsidiaries.[23]

Yet Handy has not really given us the last word—he has merely adopted a particular definition of decentralization in order to introduce a concept he calls federalism. Of course, to the extent that decentralization actually enjoys the formal meaning he attributes to it, Handy's distinction serves a useful function. Managers in companies where decentralization means what Handy describes it to mean can use the term *federalism* as part of larger efforts to change behavior by contrasting it with decentralization. But, in fact, some companies today use the term *decentralization* to mean exactly what Handy defines as federalism—and it would be hard to legislate a change in their language practices even if we were to determine that Handy's distinction was an appropriate one.

The real meaning of decentralization lies in how a community of people come to use the term in what they do.[24] There is no universally agreed upon meaning of the concept of the "decentralized organization," or for that matter of any other concept of organization structure. When it comes to structure, we would do well to heed the words of Lewis Carroll. In *Through the Looking Glass,* Humpty Dumpty insists to an incredulous Alice that "When *I* use a word . . . it means just what I choose it to mean—neither more nor less."[25] Not one to be upstaged, Alice retorts: "The question is," she asks, "whether you *can* make words mean so many different things."

Alice's insight pinpoints the issue for us: From where does the power to establish the meaning of structural terms come? Humpty Dumpty insists in reply that it is simply a matter of who gets to be "master."[26] However blunt this may be, it has a certain truth. Indeed, the structures in many organizations are so ambiguously defined that whatever meaning they have comes from the rhetorical claims of senior managers and from the legitimacy this rhetoric has in the organization. And unless behaviors and actions in the organization are coherent with these declarations, these managers are apt to have all the rhetorical legitimacy of a Humpty Dumpty.

STRATEGIES FOR STRUCTURE

In deploying structural rhetoric to create a meaningful framework for action, managers confront a number of dilemmas. As we have suggested, trade-offs are inescapable: autonomy is at odds with coordination, differentiation with integration, efficiency with innovation, a focus on markets with a focus on products, stability with adaptation, and so on. Much as managers may wish to meet *all* of these demands, they must inevitably make choices.

There are two basic rhetorical strategies for dealing with these trade-offs, each with its own implications for action. The first is simply to leave as many options open as possible when describing an organization's structure. This open strategy requires rich descriptions and the artful use of ambiguity. The second strategy is to argue that trade-offs make constant reorganizations a necessity. This more rigid, or "closed" strategy requires clarity and precision at every stage, but also requires the ability to shift gears quickly and legitimately once the disadvantages of a certain structural design become manifest.

Open Strategies for Structure

In open strategies, ambiguities are built in to the system; since the overall meaning of the structure is kept fuzzy, choices based on structural trade-offs can be invoked and taken as needed. Such open strategies are what commonly allow the various models of the new organization to be touted as effective in producing both individual freedom *and* controlled collective effort. At Millipore, a global high-tech filtration company, an executive gave us a tongue-in-cheek example of this structural approach in his description of an ideal "hybrid" structure to the company's top fifty managers at a three-day strategic planning meeting. Responding to CEO John Gilmartin's constant emphasis on structural flexibility, the executive wryly posted the following definition:

> Hybridization is an innovative, top down, bottom up, diagonally driven, vertically integrated organization, utilizing functionally focused groups with diversifying divisions supporting each other in a soft matrix format following the directions set forth by integrative devices called strategic business units.

The amusing contradictions and ambiguities of the Millipore definition may give a rather good account of how such open rhetorics actually work in practice. Indeed, the seeming contradictions of this approach have been a useful part of structural rhetoric for some time. For example, they have historically tended to be essential to the "decentralized" multidivisional firm we discussed earlier. At the time the multidivisional structure was being developed at GM, Alfred Sloan enunciated two guiding structural principles, which in their own way were just as cleverly contradictory as the Millipore executive's definition of hybridization. The first principle announced that divisions were in charge of their own destinies: "The responsibility attached to the chief executive [of the division] of each operation shall in no way be limited. Each such organization headed by its chief executive shall be complete in every necessary function and enable(d) to exercise its full initiative and logical development."[27] The second principle, however, announced that the corporate center had to take its own best interests to heart: "Certain central organization functions are absolutely essential to the logical development and proper control of the Corporation's activities."[28]

Writing about these principles forty years later, Sloan explicitly recognized the fruitful incoherence that lay beneath them: "Looking back on the text of the two basic principles," he wrote, "I am amused to see that the language is contradictory, and that its very contradiction is the crux of the matter."[29] Sloan went on to say: "The language of organization has always suffered some want of words to express the true facts and circumstances of human interaction. One usually asserts one aspect or another of it at different times, such as the absolute independence of the part, and again the need of coordination, and again the concept of the whole with a guiding center."[30] For Sloan, it was limitations in the "language of organization" that made it necessary to emphasize first one thing and then another. We would build on Sloan's insight by adding that these admitted limitations—as much conceptual as they are linguistic—can be used to a manager's advantage. After all, although a manager may believe all dimensions of human interaction to be important, in any given situation she may actually *want* to be able to emphasize one or the other to move organizational action in a certain direction.

Closed Strategies for Structure

The tendency for open rhetorical strategies to assert one structural dimension or another at different times may be experienced as a cycle, even when this is not the intention. But in the closed rhetorical strategy for managing structural trade-offs, the cycle is made explicit—the juggling of ambiguity is forgone for a procession of official, fixed designs. We can see this strategy in terms of the time-honored cycle between centralization and decentralization experienced by so many companies. Periodically, a firm introduces centralization as a way of solving the numerous problems of coordination that arise naturally in organizations. But after a time, centralization can stifle initiative, create diseconomies of scale, and inhibit innovation. So decentralization is introduced—until the old problems return and the cycle begins again.[31] (We should point out that open strategies are likely to be adopted to exploit whatever ambiguity remains at any given stage.)

Giddings & Lewis CEO William Fife suggested to us that in his experience, these design cycles prove to be about ten years long. He pointed out that "decentralization gives more autonomy but results in redundancies in divisions"—redundancies that can in turn be pared down by the "rationalization and cost reductions that centralization makes possible." At the time of our most recent conversation with him, Fife was leading Giddings & Lewis through an extensive process of centralization both in order to consolidate divisional staff into a single corporate staff and to eliminate the need for middle managers. Divisional sales functions were being consolidated into one corporate sales function (engineering, purchasing, marketing, human resources, and MIS were also centralized), and plans existed to consolidate some manufacturing facilities and reduce the number of profit centers. Fife considered these actions an important part of successfully integrating the highly decentralized Cross & Trecker Company, whose acquisition by Giddings & Lewis in October 1991 had created a level of duplication and redundancy that Fife saw as critical to contain.

The Quest for the Ultimate Design

While there is no dialectic that makes the cycles between one structure and another fully predictable, these patterns are familiar to many managers. Some accept them as an inevitable part of organizational life. Others—perhaps those more taken with the open strategy—hope for some ultimate resolution that will eliminate the need to make the inevitable trade-offs. It is this constant search for structures that provides the "best of all possible worlds" that lends so much energy to the ongoing quest for a new organizational form that might solve structural problems once and for all.

The 1970s, for example, saw the advent of the matrix organization as a promising solution for structure problems that couldn't otherwise be solved. Stan Davis and Paul Lawrence began the preface to their book *Matrix* with a fairly conventional framing of the inherent tension to be dealt with: "All forms of social organization," they wrote, "have two simultaneous needs that are often at odds with each other: freedom and order."[32] Continuing, Davis and Lawrence associated freedom with decentralization and order with centralization, and depicted existing organizational forms as representing a choice between the advantages and disadvantages of each. "The problem with the centralization–decentralization debate," they claimed, "was that the more you realized the benefits of the one, the less you got the benefits of the other."[33] Their solution—accompanied by some important caveats—was the matrix organization. For them, the matrix organization resolved the centralization/decentralization dilemma, but only at the cost of increased management and organizational complexity.[34] And because of the complexity of the matrix form, they admonished managers to go with the matrix only when circumstances pressed them to do so.

Many firms enthusiastically embraced the matrix structure during the 1970s, with varied and sometimes frustrating results. In recent years, the form has been revived as appropriate for use in geographically dispersed multinational corporations. In these situations, academics such as C. K. Prahalad and Yves Doz have argued, the matrix structure solves the problem of simultaneously satisfying the demands of local countries while maintaining a global vision.[35]

Recently, however, the matrix has fallen from favor even in these contexts. In their book *Managing Across Borders*, Christopher Bartlett of Harvard and Sumantra Ghoshal of INSEAD conclude that the matrix organization is a failure for multinational companies since "matrix companies develop a management process that is slow, acrimonious, and costly."[36] (Here is yet one more example of how yesterday's hot and leading-edge management concept is reinterpreted as the cause of today's problems, thereby paving the way for a new, hotter, and still more leading-edge concept.) Multinational corporations, these authors argue, have to find other ways to meet the three objectives of achieving global efficiency, national responsiveness, and the ability to develop and exploit knowledge on a worldwide basis.

Bartlett and Ghoshal identify three commonly used organizational models they claim are unfortunately based on the perception of "irreconcilable contradictions" among these three objectives.[37] The multinational organization, exemplified by European firms like Unilever, operates as a *decentralized federation* and emphasizes national responsiveness. The international organization, common among American firms like ITT, operates as a *coordinated federation*, and emphasizes developing and exploiting knowledge on a worldwide basis. Finally, the global organization, popular among Japanese firms such as Matsushita, operates as a *centralized hub*, and emphasizes global efficiency.

After describing these three structures, Bartlett and Ghoshal offer their own idea: the *transnational organization,* which is seen as operating as an *integrated network.* Stressing that the transnational organization overcomes the contradictions of existing solutions, they emphasize that the transnational is more than a structure—it is also a set of "organizational capabilities."[38] Making this organization work, they argue, requires management processes that are different from those found in traditional organizations: it requires new coordination mechanisms and a differentiated application of these processes from issue to issue and across businesses and organizational units. As Davis and Lawrence might have said of the matrix organization, the transnational too is "an organizational form [which] is not easy to develop and manage."[39]

The problem, of course, is that Bartlett and Ghoshal have to show that the transnational organization is *different* from a matrix organization. And this they do by insisting that coordination in the transnational is not based on a matrix implemented in terms of formal relationships, but rather on a "matrix in the minds of the manager."[40] Yet to be fair, we point out that in their day Davis and Lawrence did not view the matrix simply in terms of formal structural relationships either. In fact, they quite explicitly describe the matrix organization in terms of the following equation:

$$\frac{\text{Matrix}}{\text{Organization}} = \frac{\text{Matrix}}{\text{Structure}} + \frac{\text{Matrix}}{\text{Systems}} + \frac{\text{Matrix}}{\text{Culture}} + \frac{\text{Matrix}}{\text{Behavior}}[41]$$

Indeed, the true differences between matrix and transnational organizations may lie more in how each situation is framed than in any objective structural account. Bartlett and Ghoshal's solution is helpful insofar as it reorients our thinking about how successful action in multinationals proceeds, but it should not be forgotten that the solution is largely a rhetorical one. The rhetorical nature of Bartlett and Ghoshal's model appears strongly in the authors' caveat that "the transnational describes an idealized organization type rather than any specific company."[42] Creating an "idealized organization type" is a useful rhetorical device for directing managers' attention to the contradictory pressures that need to be addressed in any organization. And as with all rhetoric, the utility of the terms *transnational organization* and *integrated network* will ultimately depend upon the extent to which they get managers to take actions that address these tensions to the fullest extent possible.

Creative concepts such as the transnational prove that the quest for a transcendental solution to the dilemmas of structure can produce some useful results. But the use of these rhetorical models should not obscure the fact that trade-offs *always* remain: choices must be made, new problems must be dealt with, new balances must be struck. Even those concepts that employ the open strategy of "having it all" depend on a certain rhetorical robustness and ambiguity so that subsequent actions can emphasize first one thing and then another. Structures always exist *in* time, not apart from it, and they must always be adapted to deal with the issues most pressing in any particular time-bound situation.

Using Designs Effectively

Effective managers recognize the trade-offs and dilemmas within any organizational design. They skillfully use rhetoric to give a representation of the past that "explains" problems in the present. When an organization begins to suffer performance problems, these managers "discover" excess bureaucracy, a rigid hierarchy, and so forth. They present evidence in terms of examples and stories to validate this point of view. This evidence, however, is always based on a point of view presented rhetorically. It may or may not accurately describe people's felt experience of the past *when they were living it*, and it is likely to ignore or reinterpret the rhetorical explanations used in the past to validate the structure then being used. Yesterday's entrepreneurial initiatives become today's problems of unnecessary duplication, squandered control, and senseless diversification.

When the need for change becomes apparent, these managers propose a new structure that addresses these problems and offers a solution. Accompanying a structural change with an announcement about the problem to be solved immediately shows how the structure is to affect action. A new structure provides a powerful rhetorical tool by which managers can focus attention on a critical dimension and mobilize actions to address it.

Seen this way, designs such as organization charts are not so much descriptions of reality but tools for *shaping* this reality and the actions it contains.[43] Do not misinterpret us on this point: just because an organization chart is a design does not mean that its use is illegitimate or dishonest. What it does mean, however, is that it needs to be thought of as a rhetorical tool for directing action, no more, no less. In fact, implementing a new organization chart can be an extremely useful rhetorical tool, especially when it is purposefully drawn in a way that distinguishes it from the traditional "boxes and lines" approach.

Two common examples of unconventional designs are circular organization charts and inverted pyramid charts. In these and other creative designs, the general intent is to convey that the organization is not a "traditional hierarchy" and to emphasize that traditional differences in authority have been reduced or removed. The symbolic and rhetorical value of such graphic representations of a new structural form became especially apparent to us when we visited the ICCG division of Allen-Bradley, an industrial automation company.[44] Rody Salas, the vice president who headed an Ohio-based division, had announced a radical structural change by representing it in terms of a "concentric" model of the organization. (See Figure 6-1.)

Salas's representation was a powerful rhetorical device that he used to focus attention on the problems he wished to solve and the behaviors he hoped to produce. His "concentric" organization was both a description of and exhortation for the actions he considered desirable, as well as a design intended to facilitate these actions. As the industrial automation industry had changed and customers no longer wanted individual products but sought total automation solutions, Salas felt that ICCG's traditional divisional structure organized around "discrete technologies" was no longer appropriate. Often, the products and missions of ICCG's divisions overlapped or contradicted each other, making it difficult to present a coherent solution to the customer. In his view, what was needed was extensive cross-divisional collaboration and teaming, not "technological fiefdoms."

Implementing the concentric structure was both a way for Salas to clearly communicate that he wanted the boundaries between divisions to dissolve and a way to restructure the company around core strengths and customer needs. Furthermore, the circular structure allowed him to communicate that he wanted the company to move away from its traditional hierarchical organization and to embrace cross-functional teams. Of course simply drawing this picture did not create a new structure at the level of actual experience—this would only occur as the new organizational rhetoric was accepted as a legitimate part of the firm's reality.

Salas met with initial success in changing behavior through his concentric organization. However, within a few months of the new design's introduction, a number of peculiarities became apparent. While some people were reluctant to make the transition to teams, others, at the other extreme, simply became "collectors" of teams, adopting what one employee described as a motto of "whoever dies with the most teams wins." Moreover, a well-intentioned senior management had basically turned the team structure into a new form of hierarchy, with several layers of controls and performance measures to keep the lowest-level teams in line with the vision of the so-called executive sponsors in upper management. In practice, it turned out, the many ambiguities of maintaining a team-based organization had simply led to the introduction of new formal procedures for control—although nobody had yet learned to call them bureaucratic.

The ICCG story is an important lesson for those who believe that

Figure 6-1: Structure of Allen-Bradley's ICCG after Its 1990 Reorganization

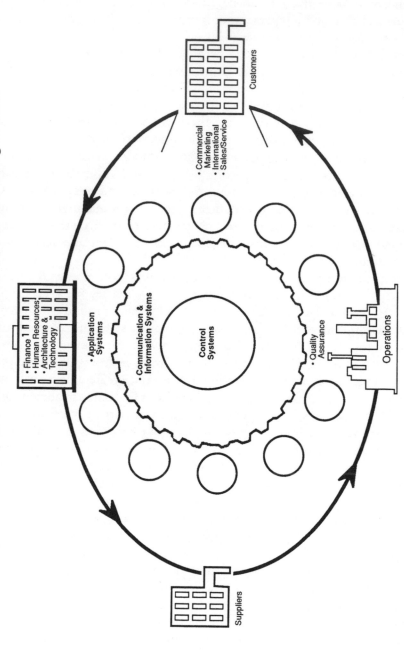

Source: James Berkley and Nitin Nohria, "Allen-Bradley's ICCG: Repositioning for the '90s," Case N9-491-066. Boston: Harvard Business School, 1991.

cross-functional teams—or "superteams" as they are sometimes called—offer the ultimate structural panacea that will break through bureaucracy's iron cage and deliver us into a new age of egalitarian management.[45] Democratic self-management is a worthy and timeless ideal, yet it rarely fails to develop its own techniques of control and stratification over time. Even in situations where teams truly do inform the general structure of an organization, there is a tendency to invent new forms of authority and control to replace those dismantled in order to form the teams in the first place. Regardless of structural rhetoric, *creeping bureaucratization* occurs in all organizations—it is the legacy of people's ongoing attempts to build their identities and achieve control in their environments.

Since people use and transform structure every day, structures constantly evolve. Like other examples we have given, Rody Salas's ICCG points out the futility of trying to identify a structural design that might conclusively solve the tensions inherent in effective organizing. Salas's new design solved certain problems and created others. He effectively used rhetoric about the concentric organization without blinding himself to its limitations. This left him free to adapt it as circumstances required.

STRUCTURE AS PROBLEM SOLVING

We repeat: all structures involve trade-offs. As an activity, organizing has eternal dilemmas and tensions that cannot be resolved by a perfect design. As we saw with ICCG, any structure generates its own set of unintended problems over time. Whether one pursues an ambiguous open strategy for structure or a precise closed one, a structure can only address a certain range of issues at a time. Eventually, either the emphases of the structural approach will have to change drastically (as usually happens with open strategies), or the structure itself will have to be replaced altogether (as usually happens with closed ones).

Structuring and Robust Action

The search for scientific principles of structural design—based upon the concept of fit or alignment with technological and environmental conditions—has blinded us to the fact that the best managers have historically used structures not to match a set of conditions, but instead to solve particular problems and to capitalize on specific opportunities. Alfred Chandler's account of the experience of General Motors, Du Pont, Standard

Oil, and Sears vividly shows how similar structures evolved as senior executives attempted to solve the particular problems they faced. "The structure that Sloan and his associates developed [at GM] came to be like the one worked out at Du Pont," he wrote. "Yet each was created quite independently of the other and for different reasons."[46]

Viewed in this way, as a mechanism for solving problems, the use of structure is an element, indeed a form, of robust action. The *appropriate* structure—not the best or the ideal structure—this is the one that solves several problems at once, that retains enough flexibility to address unforeseen developments, and that can be replaced without too much difficulty when its purpose has been served. Getting an effective structure is never a simple matter of implementing a design and leaving it to run like a machine. Instead, structuring requires constant, finely tuned action—a constant attention to the real people and situations that structures comprise. Along such lines, Giddings & Lewis's Bill Fife once described one of his favorite structural tactics as "flattening the hierarchy and then pulling it back up": when a division general manager's business was in trouble, he would temporarily suspend the existing structure by assuming the manager's job himself. From the vantage point of the manager's actual position, Fife was able to better understand where things had gone wrong and what actions needed to be taken. After a time, he would "pull the hierarchy back up" by removing himself from this position—and by either reinstating or replacing the general manager.

Perhaps not all CEOs can use structure as actively as Bill Fife does, but Fife's attitude demonstrates an important point about structure and its relation to both action and identity. People are in structures the way cells are in bodies: they do not just fill a framework; in an important sense, they *are* the framework. Yet unfortunately, our natural tendency is to think of structure in more architectural terms, as something like a building that one can simply fill and empty of people at will.

Like a body, however, the underlying structure of an organization is constantly evolving. Of course, in many companies like Giddings & Lewis, managers explicitly acknowledge this. They note with pride the pragmatic approach taken to structure as evidenced by their willingness to make structural adjustments whenever necessary. For example, at Millipore between 1986 and 1990 there were twenty major structural changes that affected the company as a whole—all generally favorably received. Yet in other companies constant structural change is regarded as evidence of senior management flailing about, of being unable to decide what to do and how to do it, of desperately lurching from one false solution to another, of declaring—like Humpty Dumpty to Alice—that the design they impose will simply mean whatever they decide it to mean.

What determines which attitude prevails? We should emphasize that we are no more arguing that constant structural change is the key to effective management than is the path of structural constancy. Indeed, in this age of the new organization, many firms have been tested to their limit by the constant declaration of new and better structural designs. The issue is whether these structures are being used pragmatically—to connect design to action and to solve important problems—and whether rhetoric is being used to make these efforts effective at all turns.

Shaping Structure

Even though it is common to think of a firm's structure as something rationally designed by very senior management, in reality it is something that is shaped daily by the actions of people throughout the organization, people who communicate and work with each other and who exchange and compete for resources. Structure is not some reified thing that people take as a rigid given and then act in accordance with. Although structure certainly constrains individual action, it is also always being shaped *by* people as they take actions to address problems and shape their identity. These ongoing actions are the very building blocks of structure and also the reason that structure is constantly changing to varying degrees.

The traditional distinctions between the formal and the informal organization are helpful. Yet from an action perspective, they may ultimately prove artificial. The distinctions are based on a misleading conception of how organizations work—that senior management's (formal) structuring efforts create the real structure, and that the (informal) structuring efforts of others are simply ways to get around whatever structural mechanisms senior management has put in place.

But viewed from the level of actual experience, structure is something that every acting member of the organization helps build. Everybody participates in the formation of an organization's structure, although some people (usually those at the top, even in the flattest of network organizations) have more influence on it than others. People at all levels in organizations are constantly confronting problems that must be solved. These problem-solving actions are the root source of organizational structures.

THE USE OF STRUCTURAL DESIGN AT APPEX CORPORATION

Appex, a cellular communications company we studied, was rated by *Business Week* in 1990 as the fastest-growing high-technology firm in the United States.[47] The company's annual revenues had grown 1,600% from 1987 to 1990, and the number of employees had increased from about 10 to more than 175 in the same period. From May 1988 to

August 1990, Shikhar Ghosh, the company's CEO, used six different structures to help him manage the problems and challenges of a new and rapidly growing company. The rapidity with which these structures replaced each other make this case an interesting illustration of how structural designs are mobilized to solve problems, including those created by previous designs themselves.

In Search of Control

Ghosh joined Appex in May 1988, leaving his job as a partner at The Boston Consulting Group where he had developed a particular interest in innovative organizational structures. On arrival at the $2 million, 25-employee company, he was faced with the challenging prospect of turning around a four-year-old company that was running out of resources and time. Like many small start-up companies founded by an entrepreneur with strong technological skills, the company was entrepreneurial, technology-driven, project-oriented, and *very* loosely structured. As Ghosh described it, "Everybody just did what they felt like." Customer service people were supposed to come to work at 8:00 a.m.; they would instead arrive at 10:00 a.m. after an early-morning basketball game. On one occasion the customer service staff even ignored the CFO of a visiting customer throughout a game, and then greeted him with sweaty handshakes. For Ghosh, such behavior was only a symptom of far more severe problems in the company—such as missed installation dates, failures in product development, and high levels of customer complaints.

Ghosh summed up the problem succinctly: "Appex needed control and structure." However, he was reluctant to move too aggressively because a large proportion of Appex's highly skilled (if somewhat unorthodox) employees were truly committed people—willing to work until 2:00 a.m. if necessary. Because the company was small and entrepreneurial, Ghosh felt that he had a good opportunity to try out some of the innovative structural designs he had encountered at BCG, structures that attempted to avoid the problems of traditional hierarchies. Yet because this was his first general management position, he was somewhat cautious about his first steps.

After consideration, Ghosh decided to implement a "circular structure" that he remembered seeing in Japanese companies.[48] Although the pictorial representation was similar to Salas's concentric organization—like Salas's model, it emphasized the easy movement of information within the organization and between the organization and its customers—there were some important situational differences. Since Salas had been concerned about rigid walls between ICCG's divisions, he defined the circles in terms of the company's various businesses in order to highlight the integration required to meet customer needs. Ghosh, on the other hand, was not concerned about barriers. To the contrary, he was concerned that not enough barriers existed, that there weren't well-identified areas of responsibility and accountability to begin with. Ghosh thus defined the circles in terms of different groups of people— senior executives at the core, functions in the next circle, customers in the final one.

The circular structure, however, met with limited success. People simply did not understand what it meant, what it was intended to accomplish, and how it was supposed to work. It had not been made compelling rhetorically. According to Ghosh: "People who joined Appex expected to see a more traditional organizational chart. They did not know with whom to talk to get things done. They did not know the power structure and who had authority to make which decisions." Nevertheless, the presentation of the circular structure at least proved a useful way of signaling to employees that more structure was necessary. It also had the unintended but desirable consequence of causing them to ask for even more structure—which probably would not have been the case had Ghosh immediately imposed a more traditional structure in the first place.

Restructuring Appex

In response to the confusion about the circular structure, Ghosh implemented a horizontal structure—essentially a functional structure turned sideway. His objective with this design was to provide more clarity about functional groupings while avoiding the problems he felt hierarchy created. This structure too was met with limited enthusiasm— particularly from the heads of the functions who called meetings to which nobody came since their authority remained uncertain.

After several months of experimentation with the circular and horizontal structures, Ghosh confessed: "My creative notions about network, nonhierarchical, team-oriented structures blew out the window." He decided that in order to establish the necessary degree of control he had to implement a traditional functional hierarchy: "I realized that I first needed control, and the way to get it was through a traditional, hierarchical structure." Nevertheless, he hoped that eventually he would be able to return to less traditional, more innovative structures: "After I achieved a minimal threshold of control, I could begin to break down the structure. But bureaucracy has some purpose."

In February 1989, Ghosh implemented the functional form he had long resisted. Hoping to preserve some of his earlier notions, he referred to the functions as "teams." Such novelties notwithstanding, implementing this more traditional structure forced Ghosh to confront some of the classic issues of structural design. How specialized should the functions be? Should sales and marketing be one team or two? How should titles be determined? (Ghosh had quickly discovered at Appex that Information Age or no, people still cared a great deal about titles.)

Yet before too long, problems began to emerge in the functional organization as well. With growth came opportunities for further specialization, and this *creeping specialization* created numerous opportunities for conflict. Power struggles erupted among people and functions as cultural and value differences between the more technologically oriented original employees and the more managerially oriented recent hires became manifest.

By March 1989, the rapidly growing Appex already had a senior vice-president level; Paul Gudonis, newly appointed to this position, worked hard to analyze the problems with the functional structure that had been implemented. He recommended to Ghosh that product teams be overlaid across the functional structure in order to improve interfunctional coordination on a product basis. Gudonis proposed that each product team be comprised of a product team manager and representatives from the functional areas. Ghosh liked the idea and implemented it.

The new cross-functional product teams improved coordination and the flow of information between functions. However, they also created problems of their own since they confused the distribution of authority. Product managers battled with functional managers over such decisions as pricing and engineering priorities. In an attempt to ensure that decisions taken in product team meetings would be implemented in the functions, product managers sought to get the highest-level functional manager possible for their team. Some senior executives began to spend nearly all of their time in product team meetings.

The large number of product teams also led to a number of resource allocation decisions that could only be resolved by the corporate management team. To keep his senior management group from being overwhelmed, Ghosh then created business teams, another interfunctional level of management intermediate between the product teams and the corporate team. Each business team, which included members of senior management, was responsible for making resource allocation decisions among a group of related products. While this approach obviously economized on the time corporate management spent on resource allocation decisions—since they now simply made overall allocations to three business teams—it further complicated an already complicated structure. Profit-and-loss responsibility became diffused and increasing amounts of time were spent debating the company's management processes as opposed to producing and delivering products and servicing customers.

The many functional and interfunctional layers of management also increased the company's cost structure as more and more people were involved in coordinating roles—this in an organization whose strategy depended on competitive pricing against much larger and better-financed competitors such as GTE, Cincinnati Bell, and McDonnell Douglas. In August 1990, Ghosh responded by implementing a divisional structure based on three divisions, two focused on each one of the company's main businesses and an Operations division which performed manufacturing for the first two.[49]

Appex's new divisional structure had a number of advantages. It improved accountability, budgeting, and planning; it focused employees on meeting financial objectives; it led to a great deal of intradivisional cooperation; and it decreased the amount of time Ghosh had to spend on day-to-day issues and resolving conflict. In short, it accomplished many of the same things that it did at General Motors and Du Pont when it was first invented and introduced.

But the divisional structure also brought its own problems, including conflicts over how resources were allocated between divisions and how shared resources were divided up and charged. Partially in response to this, division general managers began to add functions and jobs that they could control directly rather than having to share them with another division. Another problem was that intradivisional cooperation was matched by interdivisional rivalries as walls were built between divisions in the same way that had occurred at Allen-Bradley. These new rivalries inhibited the development of new products outside of existing product lines and technologies. Before long, each division began to act like an independent company by developing its own business procedures. Finally, the divisions began to play games with their financial statements in order to meet financial objectives, an activity that impeded senior management's ability to get an accurate sense of the financial status of each division and the company as a whole.

Ghosh had a number of ideas for further structural changes to deal with these problems. In particular, he felt pressured to make changes quickly because of the growth of the company's international business. (He was thinking of creating an International division.) When the company was sold to GM subsidiary Electronic Data Systems (EDS) in October 1990, Ghosh was confronted with the additional challenge of making Appex fit into a much larger organization, with all the additional constraints and opportunities that this entailed.

Assessing Ghosh's Use of Structure

Was Ghosh an effective manager of structure? In terms of such measures as growth in revenues and profits, product line extensions and additions, successful introduction of new technologies, and diversification into a large number of countries abroad, Appex is an almost unqualified success story. Part of this—a large part even—was perhaps because of the aggressive way in which Ghosh used structure to solve the pressing problems he was facing at any given point in time. From this perspective, he is to be congratulated for his willingness to make changes as soon as problems emerged. What distinguishes Appex is not so much that changes in structure were made, but the rate at which this occurred because of the accelerated time frames brought on by growth and success.

Of course, it is always impossible to know the consequences of the path not taken. There is always the possibility that results could have been even better with a less aggressive use of structure. A valid argument can be made that Ghosh could have skipped the first two innovative structures and gone immediately to the functional hierarchy, and then from there to the multidivisional structure. A less persuasive argument is that he could have immediately implemented the multidivisional form. But both of these arguments ignore Ghosh's own background and experience. Just as people in the organization were learning to work together through the structural designs he installed, Ghosh himself was learning how to use structure as a general management tool. As a consultant he had recommended such designs, but had never used them, had never lived in them. Reflecting on his experience, Ghosh commented, "What's striking to me is how quickly behavioral changes occur in reaction to structural changes." Through his rhetoric, Ghosh had made frequent structural change a legitimate and meaningful part of Appex. This is not to say that Appex employees did not occasionally register some confusion as to what the real structure of the firm was. Yet in the proper amounts, such confusion might actually provide the very spice of organizational life.

THE STRUCTURING OF IDENTITY

While structural designs may be abstract blueprints, organizational structure in practice is always about *people*. By using structural designs to solve problems, managers are never free from considering the individual identities of which their organization consists. In the Appex example, we see the trace of these identities everywhere. From the start, Ghosh's experiments with the innovative circular and horizontal structures were based on his identity as a managerial novice with a special interest in this subject. In carrying out his structural ideas, Ghosh constantly confronted the primacy of individual identities; eventually, he learned how to address individual issues *through* structural decisions. At one point, for example, he made the chief financial officer head of one of the divisions. His intention was both to help this person see how difficult it was to produce accurate plans and forecasts in the fast-moving cellular communications industry as well as to improve the forecasts of the division. Like all the best structural decisions, Ghosh's decision killed two birds with one stone.

Putting Identities First

Structure needs to be understood as a two-way street: designs must take account of individual identities at the same time that they help shape them. Unfortunately, most theories about organizational design—with all their attention to the "conditions" under which a certain design is appropriate—tend to ignore the primacy of the individuals in any given situation. To this day, most theories of organizational structure, and even theories of the so-called new organization, usually assume that the optimal structure for a situation can be designed independently of the *particular* people who will fill the boxes, rings, circles, or various other shapes that a given design specifies.

But managers effective at working with structure know better. Skillful managers know that the best structure often must be compromised in order to adapt to the particular individuals who are available. They know that a suboptimal structure that takes account of people's strengths and weaknesses is almost always better than an optimal structure that makes overly heroic assumptions about what people are capable of doing.

Effective managers know that the practice of treating individuals as movable pieces within a larger social architecture often fails—they know that, as often as not, structure must be designed around and for individuals. Clearly, this is what typically happens with the design of jobs themselves. Jobs are enlarged in order to absorb the managerial capacity of an experienced executive or in order to induce a manager to stay after being passed up for a promotion. Conversely, they are made smaller when a new incumbent is a less-experienced manager and needs time to adapt to a higher level of responsibility. Similarly, CEOs early in their tenure are typically more involved in the details of actively managing the company than they are toward the end, especially when two or three potential successors are being groomed for a horse race. A similar pattern can be observed at all levels among managers who are in the early stages of a turnaround situation or who are new in their jobs.[50] More generally, whenever a manager takes over a new job, she usually makes some structural adjustments in order to focus on particular problems, to pursue her own agenda, and to fit the job to her own management style.

Because job descriptions are constantly adjusted, even if informally, the overall structure of an organization depends on the collection of particular people performing particular roles. An organization that remains the same on paper—that is, in terms of its design—is nonetheless changing constantly as different people constantly pass through it. This active and ongoing restructuring of lived experience may not be reflected in an organization's structural design, but it is nonetheless always present: people come and go; they shift around and accumulate both control and experience.

The recognition that structure is always built out of individuals and their identities raises some vexing questions. If such changes always occur, how can we ever judge whether an organization's structure has stayed the same? Even to ask such a question is to wander onto treacherous philosophical thin ice where definitions of sameness are shaky indeed.[51] The seventeenth-century philosopher Thomas Hobbes posed the question in terms of a ship that gets slowly rebuilt out of entirely new parts, one plank at a time: Is it the same ship? Does it have the same identity? What criteria should we use to determine when a structure is different enough to warrant being called new?

Many similar philosophical puzzles can be invented to demonstrate the conundrums of organizational structure. As a variation, imagine an organizationwide instance of "musical chairs": when the music begins to play (perhaps the CEO turns it on?), each employee leaves her post and begins to wander through the organization; when it is turned off, each employee settles in the nearest job she can find. (For some readers, this hypothetical situation may bring to mind certain actual organizations.) Has the organization structure changed? Most people would say no, yet from an action perspective it certainly has. Now, consider a situation where structure is temporarily erased, only to begin filling itself in again. (Here one might imagine an anthill that, after being destroyed, begins mysteriously to rebuild its initial form.) Is the structure that arises a continuation of an old one that had merely been interrupted, or is it a new structure in its own right? As always, the answer depends on how one looks at the problem, how one frames it. Taking an action perspective is useful because it allows us to understand the dynamics constantly at work in the production and reproduction of structures, dynamics that we may often take for granted.

Building Identity through Structure

Of course, just as structural decisions must be adapted to individual identities, they also have a hand in building these identities. Contemporary rhetoric about flat organizations and the elimination of hierarchy has not eliminated the avid interest people have in titles, office size, perquisites, and other signs of organizational status—it has simply made people more subtle and inventive in their pursuit of them. Status seeking persists not because of some fundamental defect in human nature; it persists because one's place in an organizational system is a very important part of a person's identity.

Structure also provides identity by establishing the various units with which individuals identify. Functions, divisions, groups, departments, and subsidiaries are units that define membership and serve as the basis of personal identification. At Appex, identification was originally with the company as a whole before any formal structure existed. When the functional hierarchy was created, functions became an additional source of identification, to which divisions were added when the multidivisional structure was installed. (One of the problems with the circular structure was that its units were ill-defined for purposes of identification, a problem not shared by Allen-Bradley's less vague concentric structure.) As Appex's structure became more complex, the organizational identities of its employees became more complex as well.

In the final analysis, it is the reciprocal relationship between structure and identity that makes structure such a powerful management tool. To the extent that people perceive their role in a firm's structure as providing them with the opportunity to pursue their identity in the broadest sense, structure can unleash a tremendous amount of energy and creativity. Inevitably, this leads to conflict with others involved in the pursuit of their own identities, and such conflicts will occur regardless of how well or poorly the structure is defined. Structural designs may exist to solve problems, but they will never do away with conflict entirely— more often than not, they produce it as well.

Recognizing the intimate relationship between structure and identity gives us a clue into why structural change is so often resisted. Put simply, those changes that threaten a large number of individual identities will meet more resistance than those that do not. A proposed design itself may actually play little role in determining the extent to which people are threatened, for this may depend more on the rhetoric used to describe the new structure and on the particular problems it is intended to solve. After all, few things are as threatening to people as the changing of their identity by decree, which is unfortunately how structural change is often perceived in firms. It is this basic fact that makes structure an eternal source of fascination and fear, and a topic so open to well-intentioned yearnings for a new organization.

7

TOWARD ROBUST PERFORMANCE

MEASUREMENT

"Not everything is possible at all times."
—Heinrich Wölfflin, *Principles of Art History*

Taking an action perspective means being pragmatic in using the design concepts of strategy and structure. After all, while strategies and structures can be assessed along any number of abstract dimensions, their test in organizations is always how well they *work* in specific situations. In practice, managers rarely get in trouble over their strategy and structure choices as long as their choices seem to be working, as long as they are understood as contributing to a general sense of organizational performance. On the other hand, poor performance can quickly result in a manager's dismissal—however appropriate the underlying strategies and structures may appear.

But performance itself is no less riddled with nuances than the other management concepts we have discussed thus far. Of course, it is tempting to believe that performance is easily measured, that it is simply the outcome of choices about strategy and structure and the basis on which these choices are evaluated. But the situation is tricky: any attempt to measure performance feeds back into an organization and becomes a powerful *influence* on action itself. Twentieth-century science has found out that the process of measuring the physical world always has an effect on whatever is being measured. The same applies to the world of business; there is no such thing as truly objective, passive measurement.

As good managers intuitively know, and as managerial research has consistently documented, performance measurement in organizations is always plagued by uncertainty.[1] Since to measure something is to direct attention to it as important, most people in organizations cleverly direct their actions to optimize known measures to the best of their ability. The first lesson of performance measurement may be to realize that complete objectivity is a naive goal—and that the relationship between any one measurement (profits, say) and some notion of long-term performance is probably more complex than we can fathom.

PERFORMANCE PITFALLS AND INITIAL SOLUTIONS

We have been admittedly coy about getting around to defining what performance *is*. Yet if this is so, it is largely because the exact nature of performance is never entirely clear. Saying that it is what gets measured is to answer the question and to complicate it. Who decides what gets measured? Why these particular measures and not others? What makes one way of measuring more accurate than another? Of course, the most common and most widely used measures of organizational performance are financial ones, a state of affairs for which many reasons (even some good ones) exist. In our capitalist world, most organizations exist to make money. Companies and entire industries compete with each other for resources in the form of financing, people, and customers. And to varying degrees, investors, employees, and customers make choices among companies based upon their financial performance. In such a world, financial measures have the added bonus of appearing grounded and objective.

The Problem of Definition

Unfortunately, there is no universal consensus on how best to measure something even as seemingly objective as financial performance. For example, currently there is a great deal of debate about the relative virtues of using earnings as calculated by the techniques of accrual accounting versus using cash flow analysis—with the trend now favoring the latter.[2] Such debates are connected to broader, often highly rhetorical debates, such as the one over whether "shareholder value" serves as a company's ultimate economic objective. Once set in the context of these broader debates, questions of what makes the "better" measure can be phrased in almost limitless ways: Is the market which determines a company's stock price more interested in earnings or in cash flow? Which is a more accurate measure of the economic value of the firm? Which is least likely to create perverse incentives for sacrificing the long-term viability of the company in the interest of short-term objectives?

Since sound arguments can be marshalled for each position, the earnings versus cash flow debate is a complicated one that is unlikely to be completely resolved. But it illustrates an important point, which is that no measure by itself is going to suffice as an adequate snapshot of an organization's performance. To the contrary, exclusive attention to a single method of measurement will result in some things being optimized at the expense of others. And the problem only worsens when measurements are taken with greater frequency in the aim of achieving firmer "control." When the reporting period for a given measure drops (say from quarterly to weekly), so too drops the individual manager's freedom to make practical trade-offs in the name of balancing the full range of organizational variables. Especially when rewards are tied to such measures, so much time may be spent trying to hit frequent performance objectives that a manager may have little time to worry about much else.

First Steps to a Solution

What can the manager do? One obvious solution is to use a variety of financial measures (e.g., revenues, cost variances, gross margin, net income before taxes, return on investment, and return on assets) in concert with nonfinancial measures (e.g., market share, quality, customer satisfaction, employee morale, safety, and innovativeness). Although we will see that the idea itself is an old one, this solution has been growing in popularity as companies become more frenzied in their search for ways to deal with competitive challenges. While sustained long-term financial performance is still the objective, those who advocate this solution argue that such long-term success is most likely to be obtained when financial numbers alone are *not* the sole focus of performance measurement.

As an initial example, consider the measurement system implemented at Sealed Air Corporation, the specialty packaging company mentioned in Chapter 3. Following a leveraged recapitalization, Sealed Air substantially reformed its performance measurement system.[3] Prior to the recapitalization, earnings per share was the primary performance measure. Afterward, the company rank-ordered five categories of performance for which measures were developed: (1) customer satisfaction, (2) cash flow, (3) world-class manufacturing, (4) innovation, and (5) earnings per share. Placing customer satisfaction first in the priority of performance measures in company documents—such as on the little cards shown to scale in Figure 7-1—was a strong rhetorical device for signifying the company's new perspective on performance measurement. Doing so reflected senior management's belief that the key to future competitive success lay with reducing the average lead time from order of a product to its receipt, a measure that was central to customer satisfaction and hence tracked by product and by plant.

Sealed Air believed so strongly in its new approach to performance

Figure 7-1: Performance Measurement at Sealed Air Corporation

measurement that William Hickey, the company's CFO, eventually wanted to replace monthly financial statements with monthly statements of mostly nonfinancial measures. Quarterly financial statements would still be produced for regulatory purposes and for board meetings. But Hickey hoped to introduce the new nonfinancial format to the board as well once it had been adopted and understood by senior management. He and the other senior executives believed that if they achieved their objectives on cash flow and nonfinancial measures, profitability and shareholder value would naturally follow.

What are the implications of such an approach for everyday managerial practice? For one, it forces individual managers to *think*—to think hard about the trade-offs between objectives and how to achieve an appropriate balance among the different performance measures being employed. When a variety of measures are used, managers have no choice but to exercise their judgment constantly about what to focus on at any particular moment. Of course, in order for managers to think effectively about these matters, the system has to make sense. If managers fail to perceive a coherent *meaning* behind a multivariable system, it may well lead only to confusion and a lack of focus, and an inability to make any judgments at all.

So how does this meaning get created and shared in organizations? The answer is to be found in a company's use of language. At every stage of the game, the skillful use of rhetoric plays an essential role in persuading managers of the legitimacy, meaning, and relative importance of the particular performance measures which have been chosen. How the design concepts of performance measurement are used and argued for in context—and how they are given meaning in the context of a company's overall language system—is perhaps the most important issue for any performance measurement system. As with strategy concepts, a company's performance measurement system furnishes a language game. It provides conventions by which people act, helps determine how they interpret these actions, and becomes a major component of how they understand their identity within the firm.

LANGUAGES OF MEASUREMENT

As we have indicated, an important element of an action perspective on management is the explicit recognition of the strong rhetorical nature of performance measurement. True, numbers are typically used to measure performance, but they are always accompanied by words that determine *what* is being measured and the organizational *unit* for which the measure is being taken. Both the unit that is measured and the variables used in so doing require definitions, and these definitions in turn need rhetorical legitimacy. Understandably, the rhetoric varies widely from company to company. Whether the definitions are communicated formally or informally, they become an important part of a company's language system by giving managers an agreed-on way of discussing activities and of identifying what further actions need to be taken.

Performance Measurement as Storytelling

Although it is a good start, viewing the concepts of performance measurement as being rhetorical in nature is not in itself enough. Beyond this, we need to take a more general rhetorical stance toward performance and its measurement—we need to understand that the whole idea of performance is rhetorical through and through. *Taken together, the words for labeling and defining measures and units tell a story about the manager's organizational world.* This story shapes the manager's perception of that world as well as the cognitive frameworks from which her perceptions proceed. An organizational world comprised of many profit centers allowed or even encouraged to compete with each other—for example, Citibank—looks very different from a world of only a few highly coordinated centers, which was the case at IBM for many years. Each situation features rhetoric which describes a very different kind of company. And as IBM attempts to become a more agile and competitive organization, the rhetoric within the company is changing in order to tell a very different kind of story.

The common phrase that "accounting is the language of business" makes the rhetorical nature of performance measurement explicitly clear. Although accounting is in fact only a small piece of performance measurement, it represents perhaps the most well-developed and highly institutionalized rhetoric within it, a rhetoric codified in generally accepted accounting principles (grammatical rules), which are established and monitored by the Financial Accounting Standards Board (the friendly governing body of grammarians). As a recent textbook notes, accounting's odd mixture of formality and ambiguity makes learning the subject akin to learning a new language.[4] Robert Anthony and James Reece, the authors, note that differences exist among accountants in how events should be reported "just as grammarians differ as to many matters of sentence structure, punctuation, and choice of words."[5] (They also qualify this statement by warning that "just as many practices are clearly poor English, many practices are definitely poor accounting."[6]) James March, the prominent social and political scientist at Stanford University, extends this comparison of the languages of English and accounting by making the argument (no doubt to the delight of underappreciated accountants) that "an accounting report should be a form of poetry, using the language of numbers, ledgers, and ratios to extend our horizons and expand our comprehension."[7]

Explicitly viewing accounting *as* a language—a metaphor that goes beyond the simile of saying that accounting is *like* a language—makes judgment play a role in accounting just as it does in language. Within the broad confines of generally accepted accounting principles, a great deal of discretion can be exercised on such basic matters as defining revenues and costs. A range of choices exists on such issues as what defines a sale, how revenues should be split on sales that involve a number of products and services, how joint and by-product costs should be allocated, whether and how corporate overhead should be allocated, and what transfer prices should be used on internally traded goods. Empirical studies have found that a wide range of approaches are used in practice, any one of which can be rationalized through rhetoric as appropriate for a given strategy, structure, culture, purpose, and so forth.[8]

There is no one right answer to such measurement questions, although economic theory furnishes a useful, if incomplete, starting point from which to analyze the alternatives. Each choice has strengths and weaknesses. Which one is chosen depends on the actions the manager is trying to get at the time. From this point on, the manager must use rhetoric to maximize the strengths and minimize the weaknesses of the definition she has chosen.

Defining Units

Treating measurement as a linguistic or rhetorical issue applies to the definition of units as well as to the definition of measures. Of course, the two are often related, as in situations where the primary performance measure (profit, say) is used to define what kind of a unit something is. What kind of responsibility center an organizational unit should be is as vexing a management issue as defining how certain variables will be measured. While the decisions may be difficult, most of the definitions are rather self-explanatory. Profit centers are units whose performance is measured by some definition of profit, cost centers are typically measured in terms of some variance between actual and standard costs, revenue centers are measured in terms of sales volume, and investment centers are measured in terms of profits divided by the capital required to produce these profits.[9]

While each type of responsibility center creates a different set of incentives (incentives being the main focus of economic approaches to the issue), the unit names themselves have powerful connotations for the individuals who live with them. In fact, the choice of a name often defines roles and relationships in a way that may have far broader implications than the incentive structure that is thus put into place. For example, being a profit or investment center manager is almost always a higher-status role than being a cost or expense center manager. The former is seen as an entrepreneur or general manager who controls both revenues and costs, who is subject to the discipline of market forces, and who contributes to the bottom line of the company. Rhetoric describing the role of the profit center manager embellishes the rather mundane fact that all the name "profit center" really means is that the primary performance measure of the unit is profitability. Similarly, profit center managers described internally as "entrepreneurs" are accorded a grander role than those described as "product managers." Even though in both cases the same measure for profit may be used, the former clearly suggests an expansive role that encourages initiative and autonomy.

In contrast, rhetoric about cost centers often illustrates the subordinate role of the cost center manager by describing the role of such centers as the mere "servicing" of profit and investment centers. At worst, cost or expense centers are labeled as "overhead" units filled with "staff" personnel: since they are not subject to the market discipline of the bottom line, they are open to accusations of inefficiency and of interference with the entrepreneurial efforts of profit center managers. Such rhetoric—and it is common across many firms—makes very clear that cost centers are a necessary evil, whose value to the firm comes only from whatever limited contributions they make to profit center performance.

Rhetoric plays such an important role in the definition of responsibility centers that there is the occasional attempt to invent new labels altogether. In his discussion of the new information-based organization, for example, Peter Drucker states that when managers finally come to know what information they need and what to do with it, MIS departments will "become the *results centers* they should be," rather than the cost centers they currently are.[10] Although Drucker does not take the time to define exactly what a results center is, he clearly implies that to be one is superior to being a cost center.

The Performance Language System

The role of rhetoric in performance measurement goes far beyond the definition and description of measures and units. In organizations, there is a wide range of conversational practices that subtly inform the rhetoric of performance measurement. These practices usually include words such as *authority, responsibility,* and *controllability*. How these words are used becomes an important part of the general story a manager spins about performance in general. Through such rhetoric, managers propose theories about how performance and its measurement should be understood and then translate these theories into practice.

For example, the common cry that "authority should equal responsibility" can be taken to mean that managers should only be measured on variables that they can personally control.[11] By this token, corporate overhead should not be allocated to division general managers if these managers have no choice about how much of these corporate services to use.

However, an alternative view of responsibility can just as easily be put forward: that profit center managers, like true entrepreneurs, should have all costs subtracted from revenues whether these costs are controllable or not. According to this argument, the profit center manager is responsible for the bottom line regardless of whether the bottom line is the product of forces outside her domain of authority. If increases in the market prices of inputs drive costs up, the manager must simply take actions—becoming more efficient, say, or increasing prices—in order to achieve the desired profit objectives.

Accepting the rhetorical dimension of such issues makes us realize that, in the end, arguments about which practice is most accurate, fair, or optimal are actually somewhat misguided. What comes to the fore is the way that language is used to define a world view which, once accepted, simply *is* the world that contains the rules of the game by which managers will play. Rhetoric can be judged effective when this world view is accepted as legitimate in the sense of describing the conditions under which performance will be enhanced. While words such as accuracy, fairness, and optimality may be invoked in describing this world view, their role is largely a persuasive one and should not be confused with the search for truths on which the right answers can be based.

The rhetorical nature of performance measurement extends to all types of measures. Quality, customer satisfaction, innovation, human resource development—these measures depend on the effective use of language just as much as more traditional measures do. If anything, the role of rhetoric is probably even greater with these less-traditional measures since universal definitions from widespread practices do not exist.

The only possible exception to this proliferation of different vocabularies is in quality, where the Malcolm Baldrige Award has played an important role in creating a good deal of common language. David Garvin, an expert on quality who teaches at the Harvard Business School, notes that the award "has created a common vocabulary and philosophy bridging companies and industries."[12] The development of a common vocabulary has helped companies learn from each other's experiences through benchmarking and other activities. (This learning was in fact one of the initial objectives of the award.)

While the sharing of a common language system across companies has clearly been important in the case of quality, what is perhaps most crucial is that a powerful language system exist *within* the organization. Motorola, the winner of a 1988 Baldrige Award, is a particularly good example in this regard. In the early 1980s, Motorola established its now-fabled "Six Sigma Quality" program (note the catchy effectiveness of the name) with the goal of achieving 99.99966% defect-free products by 1992 in order to meet the threat of Japanese competition. Robert Galvin, CEO at the time the program was started, signaled its importance by making quality the first item on the agenda at board meetings.[13] Soon, the concept of quality expanded to include all kinds of activities—from organizational leadership to internal and external communications, even to janitorial services. As the notion of quality was linked to other performance issues such as employee involvement and customer satisfaction, it became a fundamental part of the company's language system, taught throughout the global company in extensive training programs.

Remarking that "we talk the Six Sigma language around the world," current CEO George Fisher now sees the company as built on a "common linguistic foundation."[14]

Before Six Sigma, Motorola focused mostly on performance measured in financial terms. But this changed as quality became an increasingly important part of the company's language system. The new language introduced by Six Sigma changed Motorola's definition of performance in general. While Motorola's experience is perhaps a special one, the underlying dynamics are hardly unique. Every company has its own language system by which performance is defined, and every manager uses rhetoric to build its meaning and coherence. How *effective* the rhetoric and how *useful* the language system—these are the issues that separate companies like Motorola from the rest.

FROM MEASUREMENTS TO ACTION

The way a company defines performance in its design concepts and overall language system provides the context in which action takes place. To paraphrase a saying: be careful what you measure for you are likely to get it. When a measure is taken and attention is directed to it through meetings, discussions, and formal performance appraisals, actions have a way of aligning themselves along the dimension that is measured.

How Measurement Shapes Action

Consider how the performance measurement system at Cypress Semiconductor shapes behavior. T. J. Rodgers, the CEO, believes in always meeting quarterly revenue and profit targets, despite the high degree of uncertainty characteristic of the semiconductor industry. In order to do this, Rodgers has installed a measurement system that enables him to know within fifteen minutes such measures as revenues per employee (and how these compare with competitors'), delinquent orders, average outgoing quality in each production line, and yields, costs, and cycle times at every manufacturing operation. Maintained in a weekly reviewed database that also contains the short-term goals of Cypress managers, such information has been described as allowing the company to react "instantaneously to unforeseen competitive developments."[15] In any given week, a total of 6,000 goals becomes due.

Some Cypress goals, such as delivery dates to key customers, are monitored by so-called killer software, which shuts down a manager's computer systems if they fail to be met. The failure is brought to Rodgers's attention and the problems that led to it must be solved before the software is allowed to work again.[16] Such a detailed, short-term-oriented measurement system no doubt focuses Cypress employees on objectives and makes them take actions to achieve them. Whether these advantages outweigh the obvious disadvantages of an unremitting attention to short-term objectives is hard to say, but clearly Rodgers feels that they do.

Like decisions about structure, measurement decisions need to be made in the context of practical objectives. In fact, structure and performance measurement are actually two sides of the same coin. While one defines relationships and the other variables, both are essentially a way of clustering activity in certain ways, or of getting action to align itself along certain dimensions and not others. Like structure, performance measurement is best treated as a hands-on, practical activity that is permitted to evolve constantly to meet managers' particular situations.

The advertising firm of Hill, Holliday, Connors, Cosmopulos is an interesting example of how measurement can be used to accomplish specific objectives.[17] Like many agencies, Hill, Holliday had established profit centers based on its internal businesses of general advertising, market research, direct marketing, public relations, and so forth. Each profit center provided services to the agency's accounts. When the market changed, however, and the advertising industry in general became more sluggish, it became clear that it was time for a change. Customers had become more cost-conscious, the delivery of the various services had become harder to integrate, and talent had gotten harder to attract. In response, the company reorganized and created profit centers based on account groups, which contained all types of services. In addition to placing the major interdependencies within each profit center, the change also anticipated that profit centers might actually compete with each other for new accounts. Of course, the primary measure—profit—remained the same, but the structural unit for which it was measured had been altered in order to respond to the particular challenges facing the company during a period of changing and decreasing customer demands. Indeed, when the firm's conditions improved, it reverted to its original structure and measurement system.

Multiple Measures for Multiple Actions

The example of Hill, Holliday would be hardly noteworthy were it not for the fact that it demonstrates something that is often overlooked: choices about performance measurement should always come down to sober reflections about what units and measures will work best to address *specific* challenges. Depending on the circumstances, revenues may be more important than profits, growth may be more important than gross margins, quality may be more important than earnings, customer satisfaction may be more important than employee morale—or the reverse of any of these may be true. This is not to say that such pairings necessarily involve major trade-offs; while trade-offs will of course always exist, their significance depends largely on how well such issues are treated rhetorically inside the company. But it is to say that the variable emphasized through measurement is the one more likely to be optimized, and thus that there is a pressing need to keep a stock of different measures on hand that can be deployed in different situations.

Clearly, this view of performance measurement is at some odds with the view that advocates establishment of a small set of (usually financial) measures to be kept fixed for a long period of time. And we admit, fixed measurement systems have a certain reassuring appeal. They afford the possibility of making easy comparisons between a company's past and present performance. And in the terms we used earlier, this stability is often believed to make it easier for people to have a stable idea of what performance *means*.

While stable measurement systems have their benefits, there are nonetheless three major shortcomings to such an approach. The first is that keeping performance measurement fixed limits the extent to which it can be used as a tool for shaping action. While a given measure may encourage certain kinds of actions, rigid systems make it more difficult to see how measures are connected to discrete circumstances. Second, since measures provide the rules of the game by which managers play, over time managers learn how to bend and get around the rules. When this happens, measurement can be a game in a quite negative sense. Third, since measures typically represent *outcomes* of processes, they do not always provide the best information about what actually *occurs* behind the scenes of these processes—or how these processes are related to one another in the big picture.

Recognition of these problems, and in particular the third one, has led to a flurry of writing about the need to move to a new paradigm of performance measurement. More specifically, the call has typically been to supplement the traditional small set of outcome measures with nonfinancial measures of the processes that lie behind them. Contributing to the general exhortations about the need for post-modern management practices, one of the authors of this book (Eccles) has even called for a revolution in how companies measure performance, with the exhortation that "within the next five years, every company will have to redesign how it measures business performance."[18] With the bravado of assumed originality, his 1991 manifesto for the *Harvard Business Review* urged that nonfinancial measures such as quality, customer satisfaction, innovativeness, and human resource development be put on the same level as the traditional financial ones. Other academics, consultants, and managers have recently made a similar argument.[19] And a number of companies, such as IBM and Du Pont, are already at work experimenting with this "new" approach.

But the idea of putting financial and nonfinancial measures on an equal footing is certainly not new. In *Relevance Lost*—a critical historical review of accounting's waning importance in business organizations— H. Thomas Johnson and Robert Kaplan remind us that "until the 1920s, managers invariably relied on information about the underlying processes, transactions, and events that produce financial numbers."[20] They argue that "a call for more extensive use of nonfinancial indicators is a call for a return to the operations-based measures that were the origin of management accounting systems."[21]

Johnson and Kaplan's study does not investigate how fully the range of nonfinancial measures used decades ago extended beyond measures of operations processes to include some of the more unorthodox measures being implemented today. Yet the impetus to include such measures has clearly been present. Under Ralph Cordiner, General Electric embarked on precisely this task through a "Measurements Project" that began in 1951 and included Peter Drucker as a consultant.[22] The task force recommended eight different classes of measures: profitability, market position, productivity, product leadership, personnel development, employee attitudes, public responsibility, and balance between short- and long-range goals. Ten years later in 1962, a McKinsey consultant wrote an article that criticized the information systems in most companies for failing to provide the broad kinds of measures recommended—but, alas, never fully implemented—by the General Electric task force.[23]

In fact, whenever the issue has been raised, the basic arguments about supplementing financial with nonfinancial measures have been roughly the same. Here is a brief summary of them:

1. *The use of nonfinancial measures prevents managers from being absorbed in a narrow, short-term view of performance.* Especially in situations where financial measures are taken over short time intervals and are linked to rewards, the introduction of nonfinancial measures broadens the manager's range of attention and brings a longer-term orientation. Within this argument, a further distinction is often drawn between internal nonfinancial measures (such as quality) and external nonfinancial measures (such as customer satisfaction and benchmarking). In particular, external data provide a good reality check on a company's own perceptions of performance.

2. *Nonfinancial measures are necessary in order to capture the variables that are the most meaningful and useful in managerial experience.* Financial measures are far removed from the manager's daily reality and are thus not particularly actionable. As studies have shown—and as managers know from experience—accounting-based measures may provide targets, but they rarely provide the information to make the decisions necessary for achieving them.[24] In fact, managers often devise manual or PC-based "shadow systems" in order to get the measures they really use to make decisions, measures that might better be collected formally. In any case, it is clear that the collection of nonfinancial measures of things such as production, delivery, and market position gives a more meaningful picture of organizational performance than do financial figures used alone.

3. *Nonfinancial measures can serve as* leading indicators *of financial results.* Since nonfinancial measures often reflect the processes that yield financial results, they can be used to indicate future financial performance, and thus be made legitimate even to people for whom the bottom line is everything. (Figure 7-2 schematically represents the relationship between such a leading indicator and financial results.) Obviously, many

Figure 7-2: The Search for Leading Indicators

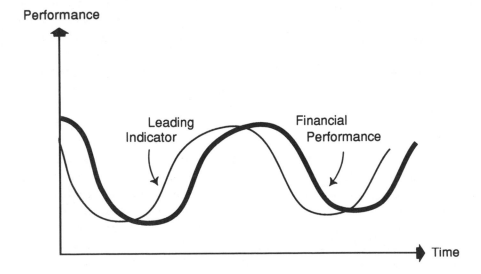

managers and investors alike are interested in knowing if a certain input variable (sales inquiries, for example) can be explicitly correlated with future financial results. When an identified leading indicator goes up or down, a manager can take actions to minimize or maximize the anticipated impact.

Making Measurement Robust

These justifications for a more extensive set of performance measures than purely financial ones are grounded in two fundamental truths about performance measurement. The first is that no single performance measure provides a perfect context for action. As people focus on getting a measure to "come out right" (e.g., profits should be high and variances should be zero), both desirable and undesirable behavior will emerge. An array of different performance measures—both financial and non-financial—expands the dimensions along which action can be guided and gives managers a broader sense of the different actions that may be demanded.

The second truth is that no one measure perfectly captures all aspects of performance, even allowing for time lags. In a provocative paper, Wharton School professor Marshall Meyer points out what this chapter has tried to explain from the start: "that commonly used performance measures can and often do diverge, and sometimes dramatically so." Meyer rightly calls this quirk "the nemesis of measuring organizational performance."[25] If return on investment, quality, customer satisfaction, employee morale, and so forth were all perfectly correlated with one another, only one measure would be necessary. Simply looking at this measure, a manager would know the company's performance on all other measures. But since performance measures have complicated and often unknowable relationships with each other, multiple measures are always necessary.

When used properly, multiple measures are a central ingredient of robust managerial action. Taking robust action means that first one thing and then another needs to be emphasized as conditions change and as the consequences of action unfold. Having multiple measures, including nonfinancial ones, gives the manager a larger rhetorical vocabulary to mobilize action. It legitimizes discussion about actions that affect a range of outcomes in a way that simply focusing on the bottom line does not. For a certain period, attention can be directed to measures of quality in order to improve that dimension. Subsequent attention can be shifted to measures of customer satisfaction, as a way of aligning action along that dimension.

Of course, if the various measures are not being taken, it is all the more difficult to talk about them, especially when financial results are encouraging. One of the great traps of focusing on financial measures alone is that it gives people the ammunition to argue that their actions are undiscussable as long as they are meeting their numbers. But for performance to have any real meaning, dialogue about its nature must always remain open—and having a broad range of shifting performance measures is one way to make sure that the relevant conversations are occurring.

The approach we are advocating is not without its own pitfalls. Perhaps the most serious is what we call *creeping numeration*, which refers to the temptation to turn every measure deemed relevant into a crucial part of an official measurement system. Once the decision is made to expand the class of measures from a single financial category to three or four categories, and four or five measures are developed for each category, a company can quickly have twenty or more key performance measures.

The obvious problem here is one we articulated in the epigraph to this chapter—that not everything is possible at once. With so many measures, attention and meaning are spread too thin for the average mortal to deal with them effectively. Most managers simply cannot pay attention to twenty measures at once—let alone optimize them—despite company rhetoric that implores them to do so. What measures make sense depends largely on one's situation; the full range of possibilities will never be implementable at any one specific time. Telling people that each of these measures is equally important only pushes the problem of devising a meaningful performance measurement system down to the level of each frustrated individual.

Of course, managers are understandably concerned that relaxing their emphasis on any one key performance measure will result in that measure being totally ignored. But there are some workable strategies for managing with a large number of performance measures. One is for the manager explicitly to establish relative priorities among them, as we saw at Sealed Air. A manager may even define a business model of what she regards the cause and effect relationships among the measured variables to be. (An armchair example of such a model, taken from the implicit model we have seen in many companies, is given in Figure 7-3.)

While most managers use their experience to make judgments about how measures are related, they usually do so two or three variables at a time and rarely combine all into a general model. Such models are hard to build and not necessarily useful unless they can be revised to keep up with changes in the world. Yet there are benefits to be gained from trying. Explaining a business model is a rhetorically powerful way to describe how the world works. Even if the world is not exactly as

Figure 7-3: "Spinning a Story About Performance": An Example of a Business Model

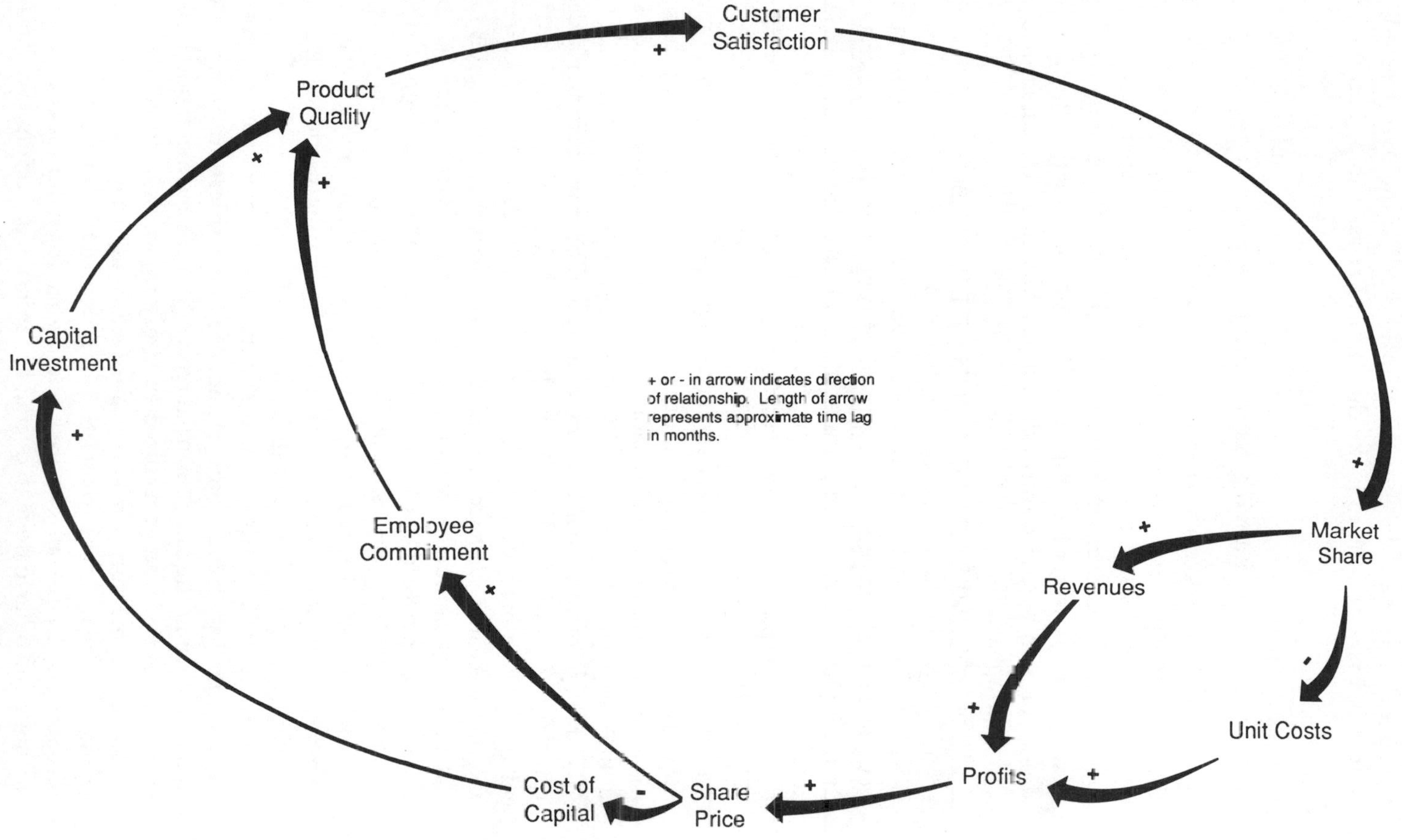

+ or - in arrow indicates direction of relationship. Length of arrow represents approximate time lag in months.

Customer Satisfaction

Market Share

Unit Costs

Revenues

Profits

Share Price

Cost of Capital

Employee Commitment

Product Quality

Capital Investment

the model describes, the model can make itself come true if people accept it and take actions to make the implied relationships become real.

Leaving Room for Judgment

Whether a business model is made explicit or not, a performance measurement strategy grounded in multiple measures and robust action must be flexible and changeable. A truly robust performance measurement system must include a significant role for the exercise of judgment about how frequently to report a measure, how uniform measurement reports should be, and when measures should be added and deleted, emphasized and de-emphasized.

At present, most companies simply report financial measures on a monthly basis in varying degrees of detail—a cycle based on the monthly ritual of closing the books. But when performance measurement goes beyond financial numbers, the period of reporting should be reconfigured. Some measures change more often and are more frequently available, such as yield rates on a production line. Information technology has made it possible to get vast quantities of data almost instantaneously.[26] How much of these data should be reported as performance measures and how often they should be reported depend on how quickly they change and how important they are for decision making. In some cases, performance measures should be reported weekly, daily, or even hourly.

Other measures, such as market share and overall customer satisfaction, change more slowly. Quarterly or even annual measures may be adequate. As a practical matter, measures that are difficult and expensive to collect because they are not readily available from a company's internal processes cannot be reported as frequently. Rather than having a template for performance measurement that is the same from period to period, reports can and should vary according to what measures are included. Again, this is not simply a matter of amount of detail, as is common in financial reports, but also of what the particular measures are that are reported for any given period.

Variations in reporting format should also be tolerated when a company's strategy entails some meaningful diversification. The existing practice of using the same financial report for each business, questionable in itself, need not be generalized to apply to a newly broadened set of performance measures. What measures are important, how often they should be taken, what their relative importance is, and what the implied business model is—all can vary somewhat from business to business without much harm done to overall coherence. As a result, each business may come to have its own dialect of performance measurement complete with slightly different words, definitions, grammars, and rhetorical strategies. A few aggregate financial measures may end up being all that is needed to give a requisite sense of commonality and fairness across the different businesses.

Finally, it should be anticipated that methodologies for taking measures will change over time, as will the measures themselves. Just as words in a language become archaic and cease to be used as new words appear, performance measures will evolve over time. When such change should be sought and when it should be resisted are again matters of management judgment. The virtue of keeping the same measures for a period of time is that it enables historical comparability and perhaps rough empirical validation of presumed business models. The vice is that new measures can always be found and may be quite important, and unless some existing ones are eliminated, creeping numeration will be the result. The discipline needed to discontinue irrelevant performance measures should not be underestimated.

PERFORMANCE MEASUREMENT AT CROMPTON GREAVES

Crompton Greaves, an Indian conglomerate, is a good illustration of a robust approach to performance measurement using a number of types of measures.[27] CEO K. K. Nohria, known as KKN within the company, had implemented a measurement system that played an important role in his successful attempt to resuscitate one of India's largest companies, a company in serious financial difficulty when he became president and managing director in 1985. The Crompton Greaves example shows vividly how issues of rhetoric, action, and identity are all intricately interwoven in a company's performance measurement system.

KKN's Performance System

Crompton Greaves's system was made up of three classes of measurement: operations management, improvement management, and strategic management. KKN's choice of terms is telling: operations management referred to financial outcomes, improvement management to processes that produced these outcomes, and strategic management to external and longer-term outcomes that were a consequence of the first two. While there were no priorities among the three classes, a simple but clear business model was nonetheless implied, which included a variety of financial and nonfinancial measures from both internal and external sources.

Measures in the operations management category included five standard financial indicators of performance: profit before interest and tax, revenues, cash flow, manpower cost, and capital expenditures. In the improvement management category were measures of management processes felt to lead to improved outcomes, including measures of productivity, quality, cost savings, and employee involvement. Finally, the strategic management category focused on measures of performance relative to key competitors such as market share, customer preferences, and so on.

After the performance of each divisional manager on these measures was collected each quarter, all divisions were rank ordered according to their performance on each indicator. The resulting data were made public, which served to heighten awareness of their importance. It also contributed to the self-identity and reputation of managers since explicit comparisons were made and communicated.

The measures obtained from this basic system were useful both to KKN and to the managers of the divisions themselves. For KKN, the measures were a way to evaluate the company's numerous divisions on a variety of dimensions. Which measures he paid the most attention to depended on the characteristics, strategy, and problems of the individual business. The large number of measures—combined with KKN's willingness to shift emphases across divisions and over time—provided effective ambiguity. Depending on his concerns at the time and his agenda with a particular division, KKN could simply focus on the measures that most enabled him to engage in the kind of dialogue he desired. Conversations between KKN and his managers were about performance in its broadest sense, and not dissections or debates about why a single measure had or had not been achieved.

Because the measures were far from perfectly correlated, it was rarely the case that a division was doing well or poorly on all of them. The lack of correlation and the fact that managers could only optimize on a subset of these measures at any given time meant that variance along each measure was high. This wide distribution of measures made laggards really stand out publicly, which of course increased the pressure on managers to improve. Even in the divisions that were performing well in general, there was room for improvement along some performance dimensions, a fact that KKN would frequently emphasize.

In creating a performance measurement system based on a number of measures, KKN had muted the distinction between measurement units based primarily on profits and primarily on cost variances. He eliminated the labels of profit and cost centers and introduced the neutral term *performance centers,* which applied to every unit in the company. ("Profit and cost centers," he explained, "are accountants' terms, not managers' terms.") Through this rhetorical device, he sought to make clear that managers of all types of units—product divisions, marketing regions, and even corporate functions—were responsible for unit performance broadly defined and for the performance of the firm as a whole. By calling all units performance centers, he eliminated much of the invidious comparisons, distinctions, and finger pointing between cost and profit centers, since all units were now essentially members of the same class. He had made clearer the interdependence between them and reinforced their joint responsibility for outcomes.

Meeting Objectives at Crompton Greaves

In order to ensure that managers were committed to achieving their targets, KKN typically allowed them to set their own objectives: "I let managers set their own targets and only revise them downward," he often said. Accompanying this rhetoric of individual responsibility and his own reasonableness, KKN used a number of mechanisms to prevent targets from not being sufficiently ambitious.

First, managers had to make commitments in front of their peers. Just as performance was publicly evaluated, so too were commitments to perform publicly made. Since the public forum gave them the opportunity to distinguish themselves as individuals, managers usually volunteered targets that were rather heroic. On some occasions, KKN would give managers a chance to lower these targets, sometimes even making this offer several times. Whether they did or not, the exercise further reinforced that the managers were responsible for achieving the targets—the targets were *theirs*, not KKN's. The commitment managers felt for their targets was expressed by Ranjan Dasgupta, vice president of Control Systems:

> If I cannot deliver on my own operational commitments, then only I am held responsible. Since I am not told what to do, my inability to meet my commitments reflects a failure in either my judgment or my actions, and neither can be condoned. Even if failures result from environmental contingencies, there may be compassion for me, but I am still not off the hook. I am expected to forecast and hence held to be responsible for the impact of contingencies.

A second mechanism for putting upward pressure on objectives was that KKN set long-term benchmarks against international standards toward which he constantly urged managers to progress. For instance, claiming that the international quality standard was zero defects (a clever rhetorical move, we might add), KKN suggested the reasonable target of each division halving its number of defects each year in order to reach international standards "eventually." Since some divisions at Crompton Greaves had defects up to 10%, this seemingly modest proposal was in fact a real and constant pressure to improve performance.

KKN's System in Action

KKN used performance measurement in a number of different ways to facilitate taking robust action. Most fundamentally, the new measurement system had created a new language in the company through the names and definitions of units and measures. Combined with the actions KKN took in using it, this new language system helped create a sense of commitment and responsibility on the part of his managers—a commitment driven by their common desire to establish identity rather than by KKN's imposition of external standards.

The new language of performance measurement at Crompton Greaves broadened the horizon of managers. Many innovative ideas were generated out of this new approach to measurement—ideas such as a zero stock day, a program to call on customers, and various value-engineering programs. Every idea was explicitly tied to improving performance along one of the measures in the system.

Performance measures also contributed to robust action in resource allocation and promotion decisions. Even though the performance system was not directly tied to compensation or capital expenditures, managers were acutely aware of their performance in terms of their so-called hit ratio. The ratio reflected the number of times they achieved targets or succeeded in the creation of a new business that was number one, two, or three in its market. Like the performance measurement system itself, the hit ratio contained some ambiguity since it was not a formal numerical measure. Within broad limits KKN could define it in whatever way he wanted to in order to justify decisions made about capital or personnel. Thus, while he liked to say that he had made the performance evaluation system so transparent that the numbers alone determined who should be promoted—thereby eliminating concerns of politics or favoritism—in reality the hit ratio left him with substantial discretion.

The performance measurement system was robust because KKN changed it incrementally all the time. New measures were constantly being added and ones that were no longer relevant were dropped. International standards were revised as they improved. By keeping the system from going into a steady state, KKN kept it from becoming an end in itself. He always tried to prevent managers from gaming the system by constantly changing its features. These constant changes were a clear signal that the system was simply a tool for improving performance and could be adapted as circumstances changed. In the end, it was company performance—and not performance measurement *per se*—that was KKN's ultimate concern.

MEASURING UP: PERFORMANCE AND THE INDIVIDUAL

While company performance is always the proper goal, we have yet to consider fully how the individual manager figures in the process. If one thing is clear from the example of Crompton Greaves, it is that performance measurement is very important to individuals, because measures are an important component of their identity. But how can robust action apply to the measurement of individuals in the same way it does to performance in general?

Rewarding Individuals

When considering the role of individuals in performance measurement, the first issue that comes up is that of rewards. Whether, how much, and in what way to link individual rewards to performance measures presents managers with some of their greatest dilemmas.[28] At one extreme, rewards—typically financial ones—are clearly and explicitly linked to performance measures in a pay-for-performance scheme. In order for people to see a true link between performance and pay, such a system should allow bonuses of up to 50% of base salary or more, while preventing such bonuses from being seen as entitlements. Of course, this is easier said than done: systems of this nature require significant dispersions in performance ratings, a state of affairs often difficult to achieve in practice.

Even when meaningful dispersions in ratings can be achieved, a problem with this approach is that the more highly formalized the pay-for-performance system, the more likely it is to be treated like a code to be cracked. Individual managers (and who can blame them?) find innovative ways to defeat the system. Like card counters at a blackjack table, they learn how to calculate what their bonus will be for a given level of performance, and adjust their actions accordingly.

To be fair, the clarity of such formalized reward systems is a virtue; it allows the managers who implement them the security of appearing objective and impartial, and it lets individuals know exactly how they will be rewarded for their service. Yet once an overformulation of individual performance measures sets in, the objectivity of numbers, measures, and formulas can start to become a little too real. Of course, any performance system—and especially one that explicitly links pay with performance—has to accept its own concepts and measurements as true. But this can quickly devolve into a hyper-rationality about numbers that leads people to treat them as a totally accurate and complete representation of the situation at hand. When this happens, great emphasis is placed on ensuring that actual measures match projected ones and that every action or decision serves to improve a measure.

Pushed to an extreme, hyper-rationality about measurement is what creates the context for gaming. People begin to focus solely on getting the right numbers to show up in their measurement reports, even if this entails actions the person knows are likely to hurt performance more broadly conceived. These actions can range from padded or conservative budget forecasts (accompanied by rhetoric about how difficult it will be to achieve them), through moving revenues and costs between accounting periods, to outright fraud.[29] If these actions become sufficiently ingrained, the performance measures *lose* their legitimacy as representations of reality and come to be treated as arbitrary confections.

A more subtle problem with a pay-by-numbers approach lies in the actions that it *doesn't* create. All too frequently, enforced performance measures stifle innovation. By being overly clear about what *is* being measured, a manager is very clear about what is *not* being measured—and thus what can be safely ignored.

Of course, there is always the option of managing individuals without recourse to any measures. While this approach may be used by some entrepreneurs and by managers in certain industries, in a pure form it is hard to find in practice. It is, however, common to find situations where the measures used to manage the business are not used to determine rewards. In these cases, compensation is based on a salary administration system which emphasizes such things as job grade, hierarchical level, and seniority. To the extent that bonuses are paid, they are based on profit sharing and are allocated in a way to make them the same for all people in a particular job category.

Critics of this approach argue that it doesn't provide sufficient incentives for people to strive for truly superior performance. They also charge that people won't take the numbers seriously and that the measures will lose their meaning as guides to action; people will find other purposes to guide their decision making, purposes such as empire building or the pursuit of leisure time. Strangely enough, the result may be exactly the same as what happens when measures are taken *too* seriously. The measures become divorced from the lived reality of the organization, and are seen as arbitrary indicators of irrelevant variables. The game with no rules at all ends up being indistinguishable from the game overrun by them.

Robust Measurement for Individuals

Here, we must confess to the use of a rather transparent rhetorical ploy by describing two extreme scenarios concerning measurement and individuals. But we want to posit that robust action may provide us with an effective, if elusive, middle ground. In general, taking the path of robust action has meant applying to performance measurement the kind of rhetorical stance we are elsewhere advocating. Measures are treated as real, but within limits. They are regarded as rhetorically constructed proxies for the reality they represent, not as a reality themselves. A healthy skepticism exists about the accuracy and completeness of any one measure or combination of measures, and the methodology and composition of the key measures are constantly updated. In this scenario, judgment is exercised about how much emphasis to put on a measure or group of measures in a given situation, and about when changes in the overall system should be made.

But perhaps the most important arena in which such judgment needs to be exercised is that of individual identities. Measures have to be linked to rewards, but in a way that involves substantial managerial judgment about *who* is getting measured and how the measures and rewards are interpreted personally. In practice, what this means is that people in what might appear to be identical jobs—such as divisional general managers within the same company—might actually need to be regarded quite differently with regard to performance measurement. It also means that reward systems based on formulas must give way to a system in which rewards and measures are linked to particular individuals in a way that will prove effective at mobilizing action.

Of course, the ambiguity introduced by robust action can lead to charges of subjectivity and unfairness. The fact that these feelings may be based on exaggerated perceptions of the recognition other people are receiving is irrelevant: this is simply part of the messy reality with which the manager must cope. In the real world, a manager has no choice but to be as objective as she can in her judgments, while realizing that pure objectivity never really exists. In the manager's pursuit of robust systems of performance measurement, the basic challenge is thus always the same: to weave together measures, rewards, and rhetoric to create fair and legitimate stories about organizational performance and the individual's role within it.

PART III

LESSONS FOR THE PRESENT

8

MAKING THE KNOWLEDGE

SYSTEM WORK

"Knowledge must come through action; you can have no test which is not fanciful, save by trial."

—Sophocles, *Trachiniae*

Clearly, today's managers depend on a wide array of knowledge—including several different *kinds* of knowledge—in order to get things done in organizations. It is perhaps in recognition of this that the word *knowledge* has gained such rhetorical currency in management. According to the familiar story, the dynamically changing environment of the exciting new information-based service economy places a premium on knowledge since "the body of knowledge is growing at an accelerating pace."[1] And this contemporary knowledge explosion, it is said, requires explicit attention to developing the knowledge stocks of managers, professionals, and workers so that they can cope and compete successfully.

MANAGERIAL KNOWLEDGE RECONSIDERED

But as we have seen, there is another side to the coin that is too often forgotten: that the need to generate and use knowledge in its many forms is nothing new. Managers have *always* been concerned with making sure they have the necessary skills to do their jobs. It comes as no surprise that in 1946, Robert Calkins noted that "business has in large part ceased to be the simple art of making and trading that it once was," and that "decade by decade it is becoming more technical, more intricate, more highly organized . . . and more deliberately managed."[2] We might ask if there was *ever* a time when organizations—and not just business organizations—were unconcerned with the collection and application of knowledge about management.[3]

The Roots of Knowledge

In their attempts to mobilize action, managers rely upon their knowledge at every turn. Exactly where this knowledge comes from is a complex matter: if asked, most managers would tell an interesting story about the sources that have contributed to the ways they think and act. Indeed, management knowledge comes from everywhere: it comes from a manager's own experience, from the experiences of others, from books and articles on a variety of topics, from videotapes and live speeches by managers and management scholars, from formal education in business school MBA and executive programs, from training programs, and, increasingly, from consulting firms. Each manager's unique knowledge about the world ultimately gets filtered into her rhetoric and actions; it is incorporated into everything she says and does in the organization.

Yet an important lesson of the action perspective has been that action does not merely follow knowledge—it also produces it. From the expected and unexpected consequences of words and deeds, a manager formulates more or less explicit ideas about what works and what doesn't. These models or theories then inform her future actions—which in turn revise her base of knowledge. For many years, Chris Argyris, a professor at Harvard Business School and a long-time champion of this kind of "action science," has studied how managers and others make sense of their world.[4] He notes that people "design action to achieve intended consequences, and monitor themselves to learn if their actions are effective. They make sense of their environment by constructing meanings to which they attend, and these constructions in turn guide action."[5]

The knowledge thus gained by the manager also contributes to the learning of others. Those who witness a manager's actions draw their own lessons, which are then added to their own stocks of knowledge. More formalized learning occurs when the actions of managers are studied by academics, consultants, and journalists who disseminate this knowledge to the world both socially and officially. And these observers of managerial action are not always passive voyeurs: frequently, they play an active and important role in the situations they study—in the parlance, such interlopers are known as outside "change agents."[6] But regardless of how these interactions occur, the important point is that those most involved in producing knowledge for managers are absolutely dependent upon them for the data and even many of the insights on which this knowledge is based. Managers, it must be remembered, are both the producers and the consumers of the knowledge they use to do their job.

Is this knowledge *true?* Is it an absolute, objective reflection of the way the world is? Obviously, the answer is no—but this does not detract from its status as knowledge. Knowledge about management always exists in a rhetorical form—in various concepts and language systems that will never serve to explain every managerial situation. It is intended to be applicable for many managers across a range of situations, but it is never perfect or complete. As we have seen, it comes from the experiences of particular managers solving particular problems and taking advantage of particular opportunities. Data from a number of particular situations are compiled to identify patterns that are the basis for more general theories or models. But because these general theories are always applied in particular circumstances as well, they are constantly adapted in practice. It is managers themselves who are responsible for making general theories meaningful with respect to the specific issues they are addressing.

Knowledge and action, theory and practice, follow one another in a cycle of contemplation and application. Which comes first is often difficult to say and is in the end unimportant.[7] What *is* important is that a manager learns from her own experience and that of others, and that she uses this knowledge toward the end of effective action.

What Good Is Formal Research?

Traditionally, of course, the task of producing knowledge has been seen as the province of academics. We call this "formal research" since it is explicitly about producing codified knowledge about the world in which managers act. Usually, the validity of formal research is judged by criteria that attempt to define good "scientific" research, such as statistical significance, replicability, and predictive power.[8]

The knowledge produced by such formal research may or may not prove useful to managers. To be fair, the process itself makes a certain amount of learning almost inevitable. Since formal research often involves interactions with managers who are engaged in projects of their own, managers are bound to take away certain immediate rewards from this kind of interaction, however minor they may be.

But the question remains: Just how useful to managers are the fruits of formal research by business school professors? The unfortunate answer is that it seems to be hardly useful at all. An article in *Business Week*—in which it was estimated that $240 million per year is spent on research by the top twenty business schools—posed the question in its title: "Is Research in the Ivory Tower 'Fuzzy, Irrelevant, Pretentious?' "

The swift answer was a resounding "Yes!"[9] To make matters worse, such a claim cannot be written off as the hyperbole of an excitable journalist; it was supported by a comprehensive study of business school education conducted by two business school professors themselves. Lyman Porter and Lawrence McKibbin found that "many key managers and executives pay little or no attention to such research and its findings."[10] Grimly, they concluded that "if impact is measured in terms of whether managers are directly influenced in their day-to-day actions by the latest research articles and scholarly books, then one would have to conclude that such effects are virtually nil."[11] Biogen's CEO James Vincent, also a member of the Board of Overseers at the Wharton School, had a more charitable assessment, albeit one with the same criticism: "Obviously business school faculty have a skill set which is relevant, but they tend to overdo techniques and formulas at the expense of people and leadership issues."

While the marginal relevance of formal business school research is certainly not surprising to managers and shouldn't be to business school professors, it is food for thought. After all, the situation contrasts sharply with the research done by academics in other professions such as the sciences, engineering, and health care. For example, professionals in the health care industry—and here we can include the doctors and scientists employed by hospitals, pharmaceutical companies, biotechnology companies, and various agencies—avidly follow research in their fields, and in some cases conduct it themselves as well. In some professions, staying on the cutting edge of knowledge is considered essential for survival. For example, Biogen's vice president of Research, Vicki Sato, spent a great deal of time reading scientific journals such as *Cell, Science,* and *Nature.* For her, this was not a trivial pursuit: it was absolutely necessary in order to make the kind of intelligent resource allocation decisions that would reflect the current state of biological knowledge.

It is clear that formal research about management *per se* serves no such crucial role in organizations. We might attribute some of the irrelevance of business school research to two influential reports published in 1959, based on studies sponsored by the Ford Foundation and the Carnegie Corporation.[12] Among the many similar recommendations the two reports made for improving the quality of business schools were calls for more serious research in basic social science and quantitative disciplines such as psychology, sociology, economics, and mathematics. Frank Pierson, an author of the Carnegie study, summed up the prevailing attitude about management knowledge when he argued that "not until the data are embodied in principles or generalizations which can be said to 'explain the facts' can research attain general significance."[13] The alternative of focusing on the writing and teaching of case studies was labeled as inadequate, since case studies were considered unlikely to "contribute substantially to constructing a larger body of discipline-tested knowledge of business behavior."[14]

The recommendations of the Ford and Carnegie reports were implemented with a vengeance. Today, business schools are largely comprised of faculty who hold Ph.D.'s in social science or quantitative disciplines, or who hold similar degrees in hybrid fields such as organizational behavior, marketing, and business policy. Reflecting on the Ford and Carnegie studies, a 1990 report on management education notes that, indeed, "during the past three decades the social and management sciences have come to dominate the curricula and research agendas of most business schools, as well as the daily activities of faculty members and students."[15] Increasingly, the research conducted in business schools has involved mathematical models, laboratory simulations, or large sample surveys in order to control for all of the variables except for the few that are being examined. What is the ultimate purpose of all this research? Mainly, it would seem to be developing or testing the theories of those who conduct it.

The ironic result is that while the academic stature of business school professors has improved over the last forty years, the improved stature has come at the expense of relevance to managers. Even before the Ford and Carnegie studies, a 1948 survey of executives concerning management education found that many of them were "of the opinion that the universities teach too many theories and too few practices."[16] Since then, the successful campaign to make business school research more "scientific" in a classical academic sense has simply exacerbated this problem.

Managers as Researchers

Today, managers and academics use and generate knowledge in almost entirely different ways. Most formal research conducted by business school professors is directed toward discovering general principles of design through the rational control of narrowly defined variables. Managers, however, do not have the luxury of ignoring all but a few variables, although they do have to decide which ones are most important in a given situation. Although managers do formulate certain inferences about causal relationships, these relationships are conditional and situational, guided more by pragmatism than rationality. And unlike researchers—who have the opportunity to gather data from a large number of cases—managers must formulate models of the world based on a very small collection of data from their own experience and the experiences of others.

As should be clear, a manager cannot defer action until enough such data points have been gathered to test for statistical significance. And even when a manager is aware of studies that *have* established statistically significant relationships, it does not mean that such awareness is necessarily a useful guide to action in her particular situation. The variables controlled for in formal research are rarely under the immediate control of a manager; indeed, if they were, there would be little to manage in the first place. As a result, her situation will almost always differ greatly from the academic's statistically artificial situation created to produce significant correlations.

Effective managers are productively anarchistic in their search for knowledge: they constantly manipulate first one variable and then another, often without any purely rational justification for why they proceed the way they do. (In fact, the philosopher Paul Feyerabend has powerfully argued that "anarchism" is the best way for *anyone* to generate knowledge, and that most true scientific discoveries have actually been made in precisely this way.[17]) If a certain manipulation proves effective, the variable is left alone until the manager has reason to think it should be changed. If manipulations do not accomplish the desired objectives, then the manager keeps experimenting until they do—or until the issue becomes irrelevant. Over time, these experiences coalesce into more or less explicit models that a manager has about how things work in her world. Accompanied by rhetoric aimed at legitimating them, these models in turn become part of a company's language system.

But while the models and language systems thus created can be useful guides to action, they can also be very problematic when used unreflectively. Simply because actions based on a particular view of the world have been effective in the past does not mean that the same actions will be effective in the present. Things change, and sometimes these changes make new ways of thinking and talking necessary. As Eileen Shapiro has noted in her book *How Corporate Truths Become Competitive Traps:* "In my experience . . . when the 'truths' held within organizations are incorrect, they lead to a pattern of poor decisions that cannot be corrected until the 'truths' themselves are corrected."[18] Failure to recognize when a new model is necessary is one of the most common causes of performance declines in companies. As a result, one of the most important reasons for hiring managers from other companies—not to mention for retaining the services of consulting firms or for participating in academic research studies—is to get exposure to different models that might work better than present ones. Knowing when one's knowledge is no longer useful is the beginning of wisdom.

WHAT KIND OF KNOWLEDGE IS USEFUL TO MANAGERS?

While experience is probably the most important source of managerial knowledge, effective managers take knowledge where they can find it. They are constantly looking for simple but robust concepts, models, frameworks, diagrams, words, and stories that can be applied to their situations.[19] These tools are adopted not because they are necessarily *true,* but because they are useful rhetorical tools in the creation of action. For example, is The Boston Consulting Group's growth/share matrix explored in Chapter 6 really a true statement about the world? Similarly, do organizational legends—such as the one about the engineer at 3M who persevered without support to develop the Post-it™—need to be absolutely true in order to serve as a kind, albeit a special kind, of knowledge? Managers are looking for knowledge that can be readily translated *into* action, which is not true of most formal research. Most of the ideas that have truly affected practice were not ones first published in academic journals, and are the very ones often regarded by academics as not based on true research.

Making Knowledge Robust

The pursuit of robust action requires robust knowledge that can be stretched, adjusted, and interpreted as necessary. What managers want is particular, concrete examples of what others have done—examples that reveal the complexity of the real world in all its messiness. This holds especially true for those taking a general management perspective where uncertainty and ambiguity are high. For example, Biogen CEO Jim Vincent says that in reading the general management literature, he is "particularly interested in the experiences of other companies and industries in order to see the patterns of what happens and why." He adds that he is also quite interested in reading about the role of "organizational behavior and leadership" in making these things happen. And in regard to more well-defined functional issues such as finance and marketing, Vincent claims to be on the lookout for "specific techniques for doing things, such as benchmarking."

Like Vincent, most managers consume and circulate vast quantities of information that they glean from the media and the popular press; many of them even order books and articles in bulk.[20] Traditionally, academics do not consider these information-hungry managers to be engaged in anything like real research. The practice has even been slighted by a *Fortune* article which discussed "the growing popularity of books about business and business leaders" in order to conclude that "they may never be the most thoughtful books on a subject" since they "favor anecdote over rigorous research and analysis."[21]

Yet the *Fortune* evaluation is based on a mistaken sense of what kind of knowledge is useful for managers and what kind of criteria managers use to assess its relevance. The rich and often evocative detail in these popular accounts enables a manager to decide the extent to which the example applies to her own situation. Sometimes even one example can be enough to convince a manager to take a particular course of action if it is sufficiently compelling, even though in a strictly scientific sense it has no validity at all. And if the manager makes this single example compelling enough to others, it may lead them to take the same course of action. Of course, the credibility of the company or manager that is the source of the story greatly influences how compelling it is seen to be. While the knowledge thus disseminated may not be scientifically rigorous, it is very robust since it can be put into practice in any number of ways.

One of the reasons case studies and other forms of rich description are so effective at helping managers generate actionable knowledge is that they too are very robust in terms of their lessons. In a discussion of a case study, differences in character and experience among the participants mean that only rarely will a complete consensus emerge. For managers in sufficiently different circumstances, it is even quite possible that opposite but equally valid lessons will be drawn. Similarly, different instructors often use cases to illustrate different, and even contrasting, lessons about good management practices. In fact, the most skillful instructors will often *vary* the meaning, depending on the particular audience to whom the case is being taught.

Case studies are also robust because their meanings change over time. Yesterday's good management practices are today's example of what has gone wrong with contemporary management—even of what has caused a decline in industrial competitiveness.

An interesting example of this flip-flop of managerial knowledge can be found in the tight financial control system described in the 1964 Empire Glass Company case study still taught at the Harvard Business School.[22] The case, set in 1963, describes the budgeting process and measurement system for a single division in a diversified company. Going back to the teaching notes from twenty years ago, one finds a convincing, if somewhat counterintuitive, rationale for measuring plants as profit centers, based on the argument that doing so improves quality and customer service. Seen from today's perspective, however, what is most striking about the case is the strict emphasis on financial measurement and control. In fact, no data at all are given about measures of quality and customer service, despite their avowed importance in the case and in the teaching notes. And even though past teaching notes contain no discussion about actually measuring these things, the issue is likely to come up in a contemporary discussion of the case.

In fact, not only does our renewed interest in nonfinancial performance measures lead today's readers to see things missing at Empire Glass, but we may even decide that the company's practices are downright harmful. Of course, old teaching notes point out the virtue of a tight financial control system in a division of a diversified company whose stock price depends on a steady increase in quarterly earnings. Now, however, with the bloom off the rose of conglomerates and the massive divestments and restructuring which many have since experienced, Empire's obsession with financial control can be seen as an indication of a failure to make the best use of company assets.

What Is Excellence Anyway?

Similarly, consider the lessons about management Tom Peters and Bob Waterman drew from their study of excellent companies in *In Search of Excellence*.[23] A number of writers, including Richard Pascale, have since noted the decline of many of these excellent companies. Analyzing the forty-three companies five years after Peters and Waterman published their book, Pascale describes fourteen as still excellent, ten as solid but as suffering from a loss of leadership, eleven as in a weakened position, and six as actually troubled.[24] Nearly half of the excellent companies had serious performance declines only five years later. (One might add that among Pascale's still excellent companies were DEC and IBM, both of which have since experienced enormous fiscal losses and have reduced their payrolls by tens of thousands of people.)

Another writer, Michelle Clayman, confirmed these findings in a study which examined the performance of twenty-nine of the excellent companies relative to the S&P 500. Citing *In Search of Excellence*'s "heartwarming" descriptions of creative managers who "actually visited factories and offices to see what was happening," she admitted that "the excellent companies have qualities we would all love to see in our own companies."[25] Yet she also discovered that their financial health, measured by the same variables Peters and Waterman had used in selecting them, "began to decline virtually across the board starting right from the date on which they were selected as 'excellent'."[26] Clayman decided to try an experiment: she went out "in search of disaster" to identify companies that would have yielded the worst combination of the same six financial characteristics used by Peters and Waterman. The perplexing result: a portfolio of decidedly unexcellent companies outperformed the S&P 500 by 12.4% per year, as compared to 1.1% per year for a portfolio of excellent ones.[27]

What are we to make of this? Were the excellent companies whose performance had declined not truly excellent after all? Were the management practices that supposedly made these companies excellent not sustained in the ones whose performance deteriorated? For example, did Avon and Revlon, two of the excellent companies who became troubled ones, fail to stick to their knitting—or did they simply stop being close to their customers?[28] Did those companies that were still excellent five years later *change* their management practices in response to new circumstances, while those whose performance declined failed to keep up? Are today's excellent companies tomorrow's mediocre ones and vice versa?

Answering such questions is difficult because it requires firmly demonstrating cause and effect relationships through the use of traditional academic research techniques. Yet by the nature of their jobs, managers cannot wait for these statistically significant relationships to be demonstrated in a convincing way. And even if they were to be demonstrated, they would probably have little application to what managers do. Managers are interested in *new* ideas and examples of *best* practices. They are interested in ideas that are established by the reputation of a particular country (e.g., Japan), company (e.g., General Electric), manager (e.g., Jack Welch), consulting firm (e.g., McKinsey), educational institution (e.g., Stanford), or professor/consultant (e.g., Peter Drucker) that is the source of a particular concept, model, framework, diagram, word, or story.

In applying these excellent ideas to her own practice, the manager always creates her own meanings—shared ones if she is successful at using them to mobilize action. And with these new meanings come a new vocabulary, which must be incorporated into the existing language system of the company. A recent *INC* magazine article about a reading program that involves all 210 employees at Texas contract manufacturer Web Converting, Inc. shows just how noticeable this process can be. In the article, vice president of sales Daniel Ott remarks about his company's adoption of such terms as *learning organization* and *localness* from Peter Senge's *The Fifth Discipline:* "That book in particular has created a vocabulary around here."[29] Ott's remark vividly illustrates how meaning crystallizes around a new word or phrase once it has been introduced into a company.

The exact meaning of certain terms will thus vary from company to company, often even within a company. In one situation, "empowerment" and "participation" may be treated as synonyms, whereas a clear distinction may be made between them in another. In some companies the vision and mission statement are one and the same; in others they are distinct. Companies spend a great deal of time through training programs, consulting projects, and management meetings deciding on the meanings of words. Universal meanings—so necessary in order for academics to pursue their formal research—simply do not exist, either in organizations or among them.[30]

Managing the Language Cycle

Although managers are concerned with getting the right amount of clarity (sometimes a lot and sometimes a little) about the meaning of a word or phrase intended to represent a new concept, the fact that this word or phrase may resonate differently elsewhere need not be a major concern. A manager wants to use the concept to mobilize action. The president of a billion-dollar division of a large company made this point very clearly while discussing the concept of core competence with us. When asked whether it mattered if the term had different definitions in other companies, he replied that it didn't as long as employees in his organization weren't personally aware of them. He feared that if they were, they might become confused, making it difficult for him to use the concept in the way he wanted to.

His concern illustrates a basic dilemma about concepts used in management practice. On the one hand, broad dissemination of a concept or a term gives it credibility and helps establish its meaning. On the other hand, as the concept spreads, it begins to mean different things to different people. Orit Gadiesh, the managing director of Bain's Boston office, explains that "a word will take on different meanings in different companies" because of the fact that "managers are using it to discuss different problems." Over time, this can lead to confusion and the degeneration of the concept into a buzzword or fad, which diminishes its credibility and utility, especially when there are many meanings of the same word within the same company. The eventual result may be the need to replace the now discredited word with a new one—which sets the entire process in motion over again.

Clearly, the introduction of new words often brings a number of advantages. Like old clothes, words that have been around for a while lose their excitement as the situations that made them relevant fade. Even when the issues to which the words are attached remain salient and their meaning precise, the introduction of new words often proves invigorating. When people with a variety of work experiences are hired into a company, for example, they bring not only their skills but also their word meanings from former employers—by reframing the way people see things, these new words may open up whole new spaces for action. Introducing new words also indicates that the manager and the company are using leading-edge management practices.

Taken to excess, however, the pursuit of new management ideas can create problems as well as solve them. People quickly come to see through the rhetorical strategy of using new words for essentially old concepts. They become cynical or simply confused, and may wonder why anyone ever bothered to make a change in the first place. While there will always be valid reasons for introducing new words, managers need to think hard about the problems it can create. Gadiesh summarizes the dilemma in terms of the lack of a better alternative: "People see through most things most of the time," she admits, "but there is really no better way of communicating change than by using a new vocabulary. Ultimately, a new concept will stand or fall on its own merit."

THE SOCIAL PRODUCTION OF KNOWLEDGE

The large number of business school academics, consultants, journalists, and managers who disseminate new words and concepts may create rhetorical dilemmas for managers—but it must be remembered that their ultimate purpose is to serve them. As we have seen, managers are at the center of a vast institutional apparatus—an entire social system devoted to the production of knowledge about management. In theory, managers could exist without all these sundry people, but the reverse is not true. Without managers and companies, these other professions wouldn't have people to teach, to study, to consult to, or to write about.

Appreciating the Intermingling Roles

While the dealings among them certainly aren't perfect, people in these roles actually mix with each other a great deal; sometimes the roles even overlap. Virtually every company we are involved with in some capacity (research, case writing, or consulting) is engaged with one or more consulting firms, has graduates of business schools on staff, and in many cases is involved with faculty from business schools. Business school professors and consultants work with managers on consulting assignments, research projects, and product development. Managers get MBAs, attend executive education programs at business schools, and receive management training from independent training firms who have contracts with their employer. Over the course of a career, a person may experience the social production of management knowledge from many different perspectives, sometimes even simultaneously.

Managers are thus embedded in a dense network of relationships—

many of them quite active and long term—with a variety of people who are all concerned with the development of managerial knowledge and who constantly depend on them for data and insight. In turn, managers benefit from the opportunity to discuss issues with people who bring a different perspective and training, and who can compare the experiences of one manager to those of others. This ongoing interaction is invaluable to managers since it gives them the opportunity to reflect on the relation between theory and practice.

A natural division of labor exists in this knowledge-production system, one that the manager should exploit as effectively as possible. It is the manager herself who has the most direct experience with the problem of using rhetoric to get action by managing individual identities. But she also has the least time for reflection and is least able to step back to assess what is similar and different between her situation and others.

What Academia Can Offer

Academics are in an opposite situation from managers. They are less immersed in the phenomena, but also have the time and training to reflect upon these phenomena in order to derive concepts that will prove useful in practice. The issue is simply whether they are interested in doing so. On average, academics are better trained and more up to date about managerial theory than managers or consultants. However, they need to be challenged to bring these theories to bear on the practical concerns of managers to the fullest extent possible.

The fact that most managers find academic research irrelevant does not mean that they aren't curious about the knowledge academics have. Quite the contrary. As teachers and consultants, academics convey ideas and examples that often prove extremely useful. Optimally, they adapt and apply their theoretical knowledge to practical problems and communicate it through nonacademic rhetoric. We certainly do not advocate that academics cease doing research intended to contribute to theory; nor are we suggesting that there isn't value in their communicating with each other in their own language—something every profession does, including management. What we are suggesting is that academics work harder at fusing these two, often highly differentiated, parts of their professional lives: research and teaching/consulting.

Clearly, a better integration of practice-focused research into academia will entail cooperation with managers. Managers need to understand that they are more than the mere source of academic data, that they play a valuable role in providing and critiquing the ideas that academics develop. In writing this book, for example, we benefited enormously from conversations with managers that went far beyond the collection of data. There was much discussion of ideas, much proposing of new paths of inquiry, and—not infrequently—times when we were sent back to the drawing board. In the end, the production of knowledge about management is very much a collaborative social process.

Of course, there are some important obstacles that need to be overcome before academics will place more emphasis on communicating with managers and allow problems from management practice to shape their research agendas. Prime among them is the fact that most academic institutions don't reward these activities very highly.[31] As a result, such research and writing are rarely conducted by nontenured professors. To the limited extent that academics conduct problem-focused research or apply theoretical knowledge to practical problems, it is largely done by tenured faculty. Problem-focused research needs to be made more legitimate in academic environments, clear standards for evaluating it need to be developed (collaboratively among academics, managers, and consultants), and people who do it well need to be rewarded.

While this may seem an obvious solution, in practice it will be very difficult because of strong academic traditions and the criteria universities use for granting tenure. In many business schools it will be difficult to convince deans and faculty that managerially oriented research and writing is as important as academically oriented research and writing. It will be even more difficult to convince the provosts and presidents of the universities with business schools, since few of these people have come from business school faculty.

What Consultants Can Offer

Consultants occupy a middle position between academics and managers in terms of their role in the production of management knowledge. Although they are more directly connected to practice than pure academics, they are not as directly involved as the managers they advise, except insofar as they have management responsibilities within their own firm.

Consultants also tend to be more familiar with formal theory than managers, but less so than academics. Although they certainly spend more time working with managers than most academics, and thus have a better sense of the urgent problems that managers face, the economic pressures for billable time make it difficult for them to distill their data and write up what they have learned from it. Sometimes they are even reluctant to do so because of the fear of losing a proprietary knowledge advantage. They are also under some constraints from clients who understandably do not want certain information made public.

Yet despite these limitations, consulting firms, particularly the larger ones, *do* engage in valuable research. In fact, some of the best problem-focused research is done in these firms since they have a natural economic incentive to produce knowledge that will contribute to their work with clients. Most firms have people trained in the methods of formal research, often including ex-professors—it's just that the research is usually of a different nature than in academia.

The problem-focused research done by consulting firms typically involves clients in a number of different ways—from on-site interviews to so-called multiclient research programs (in which participating companies typically supply partial funding and send representatives to periodic meetings in order to share learning). The knowledge generated by this research is distributed through many of the same channels used by academics—books, articles in business and trade magazines, educational programs, conferences, videotapes, and so on. While consultants rarely publish in the most serious academic journals, they have an equivalent distribution channel in the form of firm-sponsored newsletters, reports, and even magazines.

The web of relationships in which consultants partake is quite complex. Perhaps because of this, it is also one that contains perceived conflicts over intellectual property rights, access to research sites, and sources of revenue. Yet we feel these conflicts are exaggerated on both sides—after all, academics *should* spend most of their time teaching and doing research, not consulting—and, what is worse, they preclude the possibilities for more productive working relationships. One such possibility is an arrangement by which academics could work with consulting firms to distill a firm's accumulated knowledge and make it more generally available. Consulting firms are a great source of semiprocessed ore in the form of data and client experiences, ore that needs further refining in order to become gold. While time and travel schedules usually prevent such refinement, academics have the ability to help consulting firms develop their data in much the same way that consultants are able to refine and analyze data for their clients.

Getting the Most from the System

In the end, what can managers draw from our depiction of the social web of management? Our central message is that they should look for creative ways to take advantage of *all* the different skills and perspectives of those around them. Managers need to be conscious of and take explicit responsibility for their central role in the social production of management knowledge. In particular, they need to work with academics, consultants, and other managers to develop concepts and rhetoric that are appropriate for their situations. As we have said often, it is unlikely that buying ideas "off the shelf" will prove effective since these ideas are designed for the general case, which describes no particular case. Ideas need to be adapted and customized to a manager's particular circumstances by being integrated with her experience and the existing language system of the company.

In some cases, this may mean that some of the basic terminology will need to be changed in order for the rhetoric to be as effective as possible. No doubt some academics and consulting firms will be uncomfortable with this suggestion, as to do so can sometimes cause tension and conflict. People and firms build their professional reputations and identities by being associated with certain ideas that have *particular names*. They are very concerned about having "their" ideas taken by somebody without appropriate attribution and economic compensation. The importance individuals and firms attach to being identified with these names is revealed in copyrights and service marks. For example, The Boston Consulting Group has service-marked the term *time-based competition*. Other consulting firms have done the same: for example, CSC/Index for *business reengineering*, and Booz, Allen & Hamilton for *strategy-driven systems*.

These efforts to protect claims on intellectual property are understandable and will not disappear. In practice, however, defending them may be difficult: very little in this world is truly new and proprietary, and even when it is, knowledge is diffused in many of the same innovative ways that physical products are reengineered to get around patents. An ironic consequence of the attention to the preservation of identity claims on certain concepts is that a term can start to mean many different things as different knock-off concepts proliferate. Another problem— and one we have identified as central—is that the term becomes perceived by others in the company as simply another brand-name management fad purchased from some fortunate consulting firm or academic.

Since meaning is always shaped according to particular circumstances, a manager might as well do it explicitly. Core ideas obtained from a consulting firm, academic, or another company should be developed with the active collaboration of the manager—both in content *and* in rhetoric—so that the ideas will be most effective at producing meaning and action. The result may well be a greater variety of rhetoric used across different firms for the same ideas, and those who provide this rhetoric may find themselves adding value more from their role in the creation of action than from having their name attached to a certain word or phrase. This is particularly important for those consulting firms for whom "implementation" is the currently popular buzzword for describing how they add value. If implementation is about taking action, then these firms should be more concerned that the right actions occur than with insisting that their language be adopted by clients.

Obviously, the point is not differentiation of language for its own sake, but the creation of language that will enable the manager to take effective, robust action. For academics and consultants to pay more than lip service to the process of implementation—always the managerial test of these ideas—they must accept managers as full partners in the development of knowledge. This means that managers will have an active and sometimes overriding voice in determining the rhetoric appropriate in their particular case. As always, the language used to represent the ideas should be considered inseparable from the ideas themselves.

9

PUTTING CHANGE IN PERSPECTIVE

"The thing that hath been, it is that which shall be; and that which is done is that which shall be done; and there is no new thing under the sun."

—Ecclesiastes 1: 9

"All is flux, nothing stays still."

—Heraclitus, Fifth Century B.C.

We began this book by posing the question of whether massive, transformative changes were occurring in the business world and society at large. While we suggested that obsession over this issue was naive and prevented managers from seeing what effective management was really about, the question itself still lingers. After all, the management knowledge system we have portrayed is, for the most part, still dedicated to propagating the idea that certain historical discontinuities demand revolutionary changes inside organizations. Before concluding, we need to consider the implications our perspective has for the way we look at these notions of change.

Where has the action perspective left us? For one, it has suggested that recent hysteria over revolutions and transformations may be missing the point. Instead, looking at management through the lens of rhetoric, action, and identity has allowed us to see that both organizations and the world change incrementally, day by day.[1] Admittedly, this is a different way to think about change than the one to which most of us are accustomed. Yet in the long run, it is nonetheless the most useful approach that managers can take.

THE RHETORIC OF CHANGE REVISITED

Change is the way of our world. Much of traditional Western thinking—and here we speak not only of past decades but of past centuries—

has been based on the deeply held belief that change is progress and progress is good.[2] To change is to be responsive, adaptive, and competitive—even excellent. Organizations have traditionally insisted on the need for change and enumerated its many benefits. Actions of competitors, needs of customers, desires of employees, improvements in technologies—all these factors serve to make change a daily reality in organizations. Wherever we have looked, arguments for maintaining the status quo have been hard to find and even harder to defend.

So why then all this talk about a new age that will finally allow us to break through traditional organizational inertia? Perhaps the current hysteria for organizational change comes from our tendency to adopt a so-called punctuated equilibrium perspective on change, a view that the world consists of periods of relative calm interrupted by periods of upheaval.[3] Daily, we are bombarded by the idea that we are living through a unique age of momentous and discontinuous change—a societal transition from one equilibrium state to the next, a transition that makes the need for sweeping organizational change more powerful than ever.[4]

Is it wrong to look at the world this way? No, not entirely. So many authors have identified and documented various forms of discontinuity that it is clear that something very interesting *is* happening in the world right now. Yet accepting this view at face value ends up occluding what managers most need to know about change. After all, interesting discontinuities are *always* happening in the world. For managers at least, reality is about understanding these multitudinous changes at a concrete, practical level—how they work, who is behind them, and the particular games and strategies that they make possible or even necessary.

Change in the Age of Information

Consider for example the impact of information technology (IT), one of the most frequently cited forces leading to transformative changes in the nature of organizations and work. Peter Drucker's new organization is information-based.[5] Shoshana Zuboff speaks of the emergence of the "informated organization."[6] For Charles Handy, it is the emergence of an information economy—the combination of modern information technology and an economic environment favoring knowledge work— that has created the conditions for discontinuous change and an age of unreason.[7] Every one of these authors cites continuing advances in information technology as opening up entirely new organizational possibilities, which will in turn help shape the organization of the future.

Information technology introduces a host of new mechanisms into organizations, this is true. But consider the issue from another angle, an historical one. If the constant concern of organizations has always been the efficient coordination of knowledge and labor, then the new technology simply represents the latest phase of innovations that firms have absorbed in order to deal with an *eternal* problem. This is not to deny that computers and telecommunications offer some fundamentally new strategies for dealing with coordination; indeed, they *do* allow certain firms to pursue innovative new structures and strategies. At the same time, the changes brought by IT are not always as punctuated and revolutionary as they are made out to be.

We do not wish to be thought of as taking the Ecclesiastes-like position that there is nothing new under the sun. To the contrary, precisely what is interesting about something like information technology is that changes, discontinuities, and opportunities have been occurring all the time, even if at certain times these discontinuities have been experienced more saliently than others. The telegraph, the telephone, the typewriter, the calculator, the computer, and the facsimile machine have all had far-reaching consequences when integrated into the functioning of organizations. But as recent historians have rightfully argued, focusing on any one event or series of events as a watershed of change is to ignore the ongoing forces that determine what change looks like and how it happens.[8]

In the final analysis, what is all too often ignored is the role of human agency in bringing about change—and thus just how unstable a process change is. The insights of Zuboff's work on information technology come from her insistence that it is in actual human situations—both major and minor—that the consequences of technological change play themselves out. Zuboff's studies of the introduction of IT into the workplace highlight not the cleanness of different organizational phases but instead the complexity of organizational transitions, of those periods where everything seems to be up in the air and the future is difficult to predict. What is interesting for Zuboff is not the new technology *per se,* but the innovative and even contradictory ends to which it can be put by specific people in specific contexts—and the existing uncertainty about what path certain of these developments will take.[9]

Change is always grounded in the particular—in particular things, particular people, particular struggles. Typically, organizational change does not come from flick-of-the-switch transformation or from calm and steady evolution. Instead, as with information technology, it emerges from ongoing attempts by individuals to pursue their own identities in processes that, on the surface, may actually seem arbitrary and disordered. The choices individuals make and the continuing inventiveness with which they marshal resources to take actions—*these* are the real motors of change.

CHANGE AS MICROPOLITICS

What we are suggesting is that managers get down to the nitty-gritty of how change happens. Understanding change's basis in human agency means adopting a *political* perspective on organizations, in both the positive and negative sense of the word. In the positive sense, politics is about getting collective action from a group of people who may have quite different identities and interests. It is about being willing to use conflict and disorder creatively. The negative sense, of course, derives from the fact that attempts to reconcile these interests result in power struggles and organizational games that can sometimes take on a thoroughly unproductive life of their own.[10]

How Coalitions Make Change Happen

At all times, organizations consist of competing political coalitions of people engaged in legitimate and illegitimate conflicts to define the agenda of the firm and to shape its course of action.[11] What makes change difficult is not that people resist it, but that they have different opinions about what actions or changes are necessary. When people resist change, it is not because they are opposed to change *per se,* or even that they only want to have a *voice* in the change, as so many organizational consultants would have us believe. Rather, it is often because they are opposed to the particular change or action being proposed. People are not dupes: most of us tabulate fairly quickly how even the most abstract of changes may affect us personally.

While people may resist specific changes that they find threatening or disagreeable, most people are basically not opposed to change itself. We disagree with authors like Charles Handy who contend that, left to their own devices, most people opt for the status quo.[12] To the contrary, we believe that most people naturally and actively pursue change on a daily basis. The real issue is not that action is hard to get—it's that coalitions of all sorts are constantly competing with each other to define what *kind* of action is to be taken. Sociologists Eric Leifer and Harrison White have referred to this "wheeling and dealing" as the true source of organizational change; it is, they tell us, "part of the daily reality" of organizations.[13]

It is thus to the political nature of organizations that managers should first look when they confront the issue of change. To manage politics well consists in using rhetoric and action to reconcile—always messily, always imperfectly—competing collective and individual interests. Those who take an action perspective are willing to accept the chaos and imperfection; those who prefer to see change as a well-planned transition from one state to the next are quite uncomfortable with organizational politics and often hide behind it as an excuse for their failure to take effective action.

The Rhetoric of Political Coalitions

Constant organizational rhetoric about stagnation and the need for change exists not because the world really *is* a stagnant place, but because political coalitions *use* this rhetoric in order to further their agendas. A particular coalition will often frame their vision in terms of a dire need to overcome one or another kind of organizational inertia. (This is not unlike how politics works on a national scale.) Another coalition that might disagree with this vision is then labeled as "resisting change." Currently, it is fashionable for senior managers to make this indictment of much-maligned middle managers. For example, when Al Giacco was CEO of Hercules he referred to this layer of management as "permafrost."[14]

Naturally, middle managers don't *see* themselves as a rear-guard coalition that exists for the purpose of resisting change. From their perspective, they work hard to take the actions they genuinely believe will contribute to the effectiveness of the firm. They may even see senior management as an obstacle in its own right, or at least as unreasonable and irresponsible about how organizational change might best proceed. Part of the problem, however, is that middle managers usually aren't a well-formed coalition in the first place—there are too many of them and their interests are too poorly aligned. In truth, it is usually senior management that legislates who is part of the solution and who is part of the problem.

But the fact that senior management has the dominant voice should not blind us to the reality that power coalitions form and shift daily—and that these blocs have the power to create and institutionalize change. Little things are constantly happening: confusion erupts, power struggles emerge, individuals and coalitions jockey for positions. An attempt to create change in a more directed and grandiose sense must always start with the awareness that change is grounded in and shaped by the micropolitics of the organization. It cannot happen by decree.

GETTING CHANGE IN ORGANIZATIONS

How then to get change? The disorderly and political nature of the change process means that most of a manager's efforts to bring about change are about mobilizing action in a highly dynamic situation. Change isn't a mystical or mysterious substance—it's about action, pure and simple. James March has rightly noted that our tendency to glorify organizational change prevents us from seeing it for what it is: "Theories of change in organizations are primarily different ways of describing theories of action in organizations," he writes, "[and] not different theories."[15]

How to Get Change—And How Not to

Unfortunately, most existing theories of how to get change in organizations are not very helpful. Nearly all of them start from the false premise that change is difficult to accomplish because people resist it out of fear, uncertainty, and slothfulness. As a result, their emphasis is mistakenly placed on finding fresh ways to convince people to be receptive toward change.

A traditional change program in organizations might incorporate the following elements: an emphasis on motivating employees, an attempt to formulate a clear vision of the desired end state, careful attention to the mechanics and logistics of the effort, extensive communications, an exhortation for broad participation, the involvement of training and other forms of staff support, detailed action plans, and mechanisms to measure the undertaking's extent and consequences. In practice, these well-meaning efforts often are lumped into an official change program with a particular theme. (Almost any theme can be turned into a program: quality, empowerment, pay-for-performance, culture, customer service, and becoming a world-class competitor are just a few.)

Despite their prominence in today's business media, the worth of these so-called activity-centered programs is often dubious. Management consultants Robert Schaffer and Harvey Thomson maintain that "the momentum for [such programs] continues to accelerate even though there is virtually no evidence to justify the flood of investment" in them.[16] According to Schaffer and Thomson, these programs often fail to deliver—yet they persist because of "the fact that hundreds of membership associations, professional societies, and consulting firms all promote activity-centered processes [which] lends them an aura of popularity and legitimacy."[17]

In *The Critical Path to Corporate Renewal*, Michael Beer, Russell Eisenstat, and Bert Spector use the label "programmatic change" to describe the idea behind such programs[18]—and they too are chary of the results these programs produce. Their research led them to conclude that many of the major change initiatives described so enthusiastically by CEOs and senior human resource executives "not only failed to make a significant change in the corporate culture, but also instilled cynicism, making future efforts even more difficult."[19] Beer and his co-authors posit their own reasons why such programs are nevertheless so popular: (1) "programs represent actions that can be put into place quickly"; (2) "managers like to emulate well-known success stories"; and (3) "programs are tangible and therefore easy to measure."[20]

Why are these well-engineered attempts to get change failing? We contend (to return to what we said earlier about action in general) that clean, rational plans for action, and especially for collective action, simply fail to take account of how the world really works. In too many programs, change is approached analytically, divided into concrete segments of rhetoric and action that have far too little to do with one another. First, of course, comes the rhetoric: an awe-inspiring array of consultant studies and surveys, speeches, focus group discussions, interviews, plans, memoranda, newsletters, diagrams, milestone charts, graphs, tables, and thick manuals in three-ring binders. The idea of the rhetoric is to explicitly secure the buy-in of the whole organization. Action, it is supposed, will come later.

We are not opposed to clear and participatory rhetoric when situations so demand. But the rhetoric needs to be seen not as *motivating* action but as *mobilizing* it toward an end that may only become clear once the process is underway. Exhortative rhetoric often does need to be used to heat things up—but the actions produced should, in turn, become the basis for generating further rhetoric and giving meaning to it. Rhetoric and action must follow after and generate each other in a rapid sequence that will often take the form of fruitful chaos.

MAKING AND MANAGING CHANGE: AN EXAMPLE FROM MOTOROLA

An excellent example of a change process conducted in the spirit we have outlined is an initiative started by Bob Galvin in 1983 when he was CEO of Motorola.[21] The situation is taught as a series of case studies at the Harvard Business School—not because it is a textbook notion of the change process, but because it is so different from the conventional wisdom about how this process occurs.[22]

Setting Change in Motion

Galvin set Motorola's change initiative in motion through a speech he gave on April 24, 1983, at the biennial meeting of the company's top 153 officers. Although the company's performance was good and immediate prospects were bright, Galvin thought things were not as rosy as they seemed: there were too many levels of hierarchy, too many bureaucratic turf battles, a lengthening product development cycle, a focus on technology instead of customers, and an emphasis on short-term results over long-term competitive strategy. In short, he saw in Motorola the usual list of ills plaguing American companies. A surprise even to Motorola's top-management team and human resource executives, Galvin's speech called for managers to take a fresh look at their organizations in order to create smaller, more focused units, eliminate layers of management, and get management closer to the product and market.

The reaction to his speech was one of confusion: What was he talking about? No one was sure what the proximate cause was, although some opined that a recent trip to Japan and the fact that he had read *In Search of Excellence* on the trip may have stimulated his thinking—thinking perhaps abetted by the fact that the book didn't pay as much attention to Motorola as it did to other, ostensibly more excellent companies.

Whatever the reasons, Galvin had decided that the time had come to take the plunge. In taking the plunge, however, he had given no specific prescriptions for how change at Motorola would proceed. He had made only a prophetic announcement: "When we come together in two years," he announced, "we will report and share the changes made and the lessons learned."[23] While his message was urgent and pointed, it was also admittedly ambiguous. He left people wondering why he talked so much about Motorola's structure, whether he regarded growth and increased sales as a problem, and if he was simply proposing a new executive training program for the company.

While the dust was still settling, Galvin clarified matters somewhat. To begin, he wrote a memo about the need for a "change in managing." He elaborated on the need for a more responsive organization, but again intentionally did not specify particular actions or the expected results of these actions. What he clearly hoped for was that others would determine these actions for themselves. Yet even though Galvin's managers were used to his management style, they wanted more clarity and needed more persuasion that action was necessary. During the rest of 1983, Motorola initiated a survey of the top 1,000 managers, an outside consultant was hired,[24] and several drafts were prepared of a "guidelines paper" that would define both the means and ends of the change process at Motorola.[25] The consultant and human resource executives wrote the first draft and Galvin wrote all subsequent drafts. The paper remained unfinished at the end of the year.

Amidst some consternation that it would become "simply another acronym in the 'alphabet soup' of programs at Motorola," early 1984 saw Galvin's initiative named the Organizational Effectiveness Process, or OEP.[26] Members of the Policy Committee (the company's top twelve executives) were asked to identify a few key areas or breakthrough projects where they could begin to apply OEP. Galvin met personally with each member to convey the importance of this process. The guidelines paper was revised until it was sixteen pages long. Yet despite the continual revisions of the guidelines, the actual output in terms of documentation, definitions, and directions was minimal—Galvin still refused to specify what actions should be taken. And while the head of human resources constantly pushed for greater clarity, he too was wary of institutionalizing OEP too soon lest people enact it procedurally rather than spiritually. Finally, the guidelines paper listed not a forty-eight-step action plan, but forty-eight *questions*.

From Confusion to Action

OEP was ambiguous and somewhat confusing. Soon, however, something interesting occurred: action began to occur throughout the organization—varied, creative, and spontaneous. Some managers took OEP as an opportunity to try new and innovative experiments. Others accelerated things they were already doing. And some did nothing more than relabel their current actions as examples of OEP. The content of the actions varied from structural changes to the design of new management control systems to efforts to reduce the time and cost of product development. Some of the particularly successful actions were hailed as breakthrough OEP projects and broadly communicated throughout the company. As these actions took place, they contributed to the rhetorical clarity of OEP and became the basis of other actions.

While pressures to institutionalize OEP had existed from the beginning, it was not until the program was well underway, in 1985, that institutionalization actually began to occur. In order to disseminate the fruits of the program throughout Motorola, a wide variety of design tools were implemented across the company. Mechanisms of institutionalization included OEP Plan Books submitted with the annual financial and quality plans, a "7S" model for implementing OEP, workshops, integration of OEP into existing training programs, incorporation of OEP evaluation measures into the Motorola Executive Incentive Plan, and the development of an "Action Framework" (presented at the 1985 Motorola Officers' Meeting), which identified the four OEP focuses as strategy, structure, process, and performance. Formal designs for OEP thus came not at the beginning but almost two years down the road.

Understanding "Wheeling and Annealing"

The Motorola example is a richly evocative story, but can we get behind the facts to come up with a conceptual understanding of what occurred? As is usually true with attempts to describe such active and chaotic processes, a metaphor may work best here. When organizational change proceeds like it did at Motorola, it can be compared to *annealing*—a chemical process by which new crystal formations are obtained by heating up and cooling down a system. Eric Leifer and Harrison White have proposed annealing as a model for how change gets steered in "messy" large-scale organizations.[27] Here is how, in their words, annealing works:

> In crystal formation . . . a system of particles at high temperature can be cooled very slowly, allowing equilibrium configurations to form at each temperature change. At the temperature zone where crystals begin to form, the cooling process can be repeatedly reversed until a satisfactory initial configuration is obtained (which shapes the progressive refinements). Reversal is the key to the annealing process, as it allows one to avoid "bad" local optimums.[28]

In order to get change at Motorola, Galvin didn't start out with a precise goal in mind; instead, he followed the principles of annealing—he simply heated things up and then waited to see the unpredictable ways in which change would "settle out," once things began to cool. Throughout the process, he refrained from laying out any explicit plan for change; he let plans emerge from the "wheeling and dealing" among managers who scurried to take advantage of the opportunities his original speech had helped open up.[29] Indeed, in a variety of ways—for example, the surveys and the ambiguous guidelines paper—Galvin created political arenas to stimulate managerial wheeling and dealing, recognizing that that would ultimately serve the process of change. Galvin was willing to make the system "worse off in an effort to right itself."[30] He also showed his willingness to start an occasional fire so that existing patterns of interlocking coalitions could dissolve and form anew.

THE AMBIGUITIES OF CHANGE

As we saw with Motorola, the annealing approach to change consists of periodically shaking things up to open cracks in the power structure, cracks through which new individuals and new initiatives can surface. One of the key challenges in this process, of course, is knowing *when* to heat things up and when to let them cool down. The metaphor suggests that managers heat things up when they perceive that organizational action has entered a pattern they consider suboptimal. But how is the manager to evaluate the results that ensue?

The Challenges of Evaluating Change

Knowing exactly when and how to initiate change is perhaps a skill that can only be learned with experience.[31] Similarly, *evaluating* organizational change is always a matter of judgment as well. Consider the problems in evaluating the change process at Motorola. In the third quarter of 1985, reactions to OEP were mixed. Some felt that it had enabled the company to accomplish a great deal and had led to some dramatic successes that wouldn't have happened otherwise. People also praised OEP for lending itself to customization. Others were more critical. They felt that the program was too ambiguous and as a result it had not been implemented as quickly as it might have been. Concerns were also expressed that it had not been disseminated broadly enough. The vice president of human resources worried that "OEP might have been 'one of the better kept secrets at Motorola.' "[32]

The difficulties of evaluating the extent and consequences of change suggest that maybe the best thing to do is simply to focus on measures of organizational performance—to evaluate change in terms of its outcomes. If the bottom line of change is to affect the company's bottom line, then perhaps that is all that is important. Rather than worry about how much change is occurring or has occurred, maybe we should look only to financial performance measures.[33]

We don't agree. To see why, let's take a look at the complicated picture provided by Motorola's numbers. Table 9-1 shows revenues, net income, and average share price for Motorola in the years 1980–1990. We see sales increasing from 1983 to 1986, with the biggest improvement from 1983 to 1984 when OEP was just being developed. Net income also increased impressively between 1983 and 1984. Financial performance suffered during 1985, at the same time the company began to institutionalize OEP. During this same period, Motorola's stock price declined, yet it rebounded in 1990 to almost double its 1985 price. In fact, between 1985 and 1990, revenue and profit growth steadily increased as well.

Unfortunately, these numbers don't tell us much about the success of OEP. Are we to draw from them that the confusion surrounding OEP's introduction led to short-term performance declines in the mid-1980s? Or, conversely, are we to infer that OEP's long-term benefits began to show up later in the decade? Did the increase in stock price

Table 9-1: Motorola's Financial Performance

Year	Revenues ($ millions)	Net Income ($ millions)	Stock Price ($)
1980	3,098.760	186.081	19.29
1981	3,335.865	174.990	22.89
1982	3,785.845	177.961	22.43
1983	4,328.000	244.000	41.48
1984	5,534.000	387.000	37.10
1985	5,443.000	72.000	34.35
1986	5,888.000	194.000	40.60
1987	6,707.000	308.000	54.19
1988	8,250.000	445.000	44.64
1989	9,620.000	498.000	52.12
1990	10,885.000	499.000	65.88

reflect a true change in company value and performance or just the vagaries of Wall Street?

The numbers are especially meaningless since it is impossible to know the relative effects of other things going on at Motorola on financial performance measures. Other programs were being pursued such as Participative Management and Six Sigma Quality (which began before OEP and outlasted it), new products were developed and sold, changes were made in strategy and structure, Galvin retired and was replaced by George Fisher, new technologies emerged, and changes in the market environment occurred. All of these factors contributed to Motorola's performance during the 1980s. Some of them probably were affected by OEP and affected it in turn. Clearly, it is impossible from the data we have to make any definitive statements about the contribution of OEP to financial performance.

Facing Up to Uncertainties

Indeed, perceptions about the effectiveness of a change process can vary widely—perhaps they even should. No one involved in a change process is an objective and unbiased observer. Each manager experiences change in a unique way. As its major architect it is not surprising that Galvin was positive about the impact of OEP. Skeptics probably remained skeptical.

Even those outside the change process—such as academics and consultants—are not objective. Such individuals bring their own theories, models, beliefs, and biases to their observations. While they can give an informed opinion, and perhaps stimulate some reevaluations by those involved in the process itself, there is no reason to treat external evaluations as reality.

There is no bedrock to evaluation. Every evaluation of a change process is a rhetorical act that becomes an important part of the process itself. And given the political nature of the process, there are bound to be struggles about whose version of reality is the right one. In organizations, different people will point to different events and situations as "evidence" that change is either happening or not happening. Perhaps people will have started to work longer hours. Perhaps the time cycle for product development will have fallen noticeably. One thing is for sure, however: rhetorical struggles will and should occur as people renegotiate a consensus of their social and organizational realities. In fact, these struggles—with all the productive chaos and disorder that may temporarily swirl around them—are often our best indication that meaningful change is in the works.

10

Coda: Rediscovering

Managerial Practice

"Managers have to learn to know language, to understand what words are and what they mean. Perhaps most important, they have to acquire respect for language as [our] most precious gift and heritage. The manager must understand the meaning of the old definition of rhetoric as 'the art which draws men's hearts to the love of true knowledge.' "
—Peter F. Drucker, *The Practice of Management* (1954)

Four decades ago, Peter Drucker eloquently expressed the fundamental thesis of this book: that to see management in its proper light, managers need first to take language seriously. That this elder statesman of modern management made this point so many years ago does not surprise us. To the contrary, given our call to get back to managerial basics, we are heartened to find that something we think so important has been said before—even if said by someone with whom we have earlier taken issue for his willingness to herald a managerial New Age. Hopefully, what this book has shown is that proclamations of change and newness only begin to scratch the surface, and that a careful inquiry into language is necessary to arrive at any deeper understanding of how management is practiced.

While language has been the cornerstone of this book, our more general purpose has been to offer a coherent overview of management based on three particular words—rhetoric, action, and identity—used in particular ways. This point of view, which we have labeled the action perspective, is a synthesis of ideas, research, and experience, and, we are pleased to note, it is already practiced by effective managers.

Unfortunately, since an important component of our action perspective has been that managers must adapt words and concepts to their own circumstances, we cannot offer a pithy concluding statement regarding "what you should do next." Of course, we hope that while reading this book, you have gained insights relevant to your situation, which you will apply when the opportunities arise. In summary, therefore, we take this opportunity to ask some questions organized in terms of the concepts we have used—questions designed to enable you to reflect on the ways you exercise your identity as a manager.

SHAPING IDENTITY

Who are you in the organization you work for? We have defined identity as the unique place a person seeks to establish in the world. We have also argued that the dimensions along which this identity-seeking occurs are a matter of personal choice. Money, status, power, professional accomplishment, and altruism are but a few examples of the dimensions along which identity can be built. How much a person wants of these and other things depends on what one wants to be known for and as, to one's self and to others. Identity, we have argued, comes from both actions and words; it is about both being and becoming.

So who do you want to be in your organization? What are you trying to accomplish? What contribution do you want to make to the firm's strategy? After all, strategy is not something that is "out there." You are a *part* of it because in seeking to establish your own identity you affect the strategy of your company. In turn, the strategy of the firm influences your personal strategy for who you are and who you hope to become.

Assuming you know what identity you want to create, how do you go about achieving it? How do you *implement* your personal strategy? What are the points of reinforcement and conflict between your strategy and that of the firm? What do you do on a daily basis that works to shape your identity?

For example, how do you use rhetoric to communicate to others the person you want to be? As we have seen, language is a direct and explicit way to establish identity. What you say about yourself, what you say about others, and how you compare yourself to others are important aspects of the person you are. What you say about others says much about yourself—and your words are often heard this way whether you intend it or not.

Your actions are another important element in the construction of identity. Who you want to be influences the actions you take, and the actions you take in turn inform your sense of identity. Because the consequences of actions are not predictable or entirely controllable, you may thus find your managerial identity taking some unexpected turns.

Indeed, identity is never entirely under your control. The people you work with form their own opinions of you through their interpretations of your words and deeds. What you say is not always the same as what others hear, your intentions are not always the same as what other people think they are, and what actually happens may be different from what you intend to happen. For the people who know you, who you are in the world may or may not correspond closely with who you see yourself to be.

How you see yourself—who you want to be—always exists uneasily with how others see you. This tension is difficult to manage since your self-image is undoubtedly clearer to you than the image others have of you. But you must remember that for all practical purposes, the view others have of you is the real you for them. Knowing how others see you is thus essential for being effective at taking action.

To be sure, uncovering this aspect of your identity can be a tricky endeavor. It depends on the rhetorical skills of other people and their willingness to express their views of you. It also depends on your willingness to ask, "How do you see me?"—and not many people are comfortable doing this. To the extent that others have some idea of how you see yourself—and they usually do—they will be understandably reluctant to challenge your views. Hearing you are not as bold, as ingenious, or as capable as you may think you are is not a pleasant experience.

But finding out how others see you depends on your ability to listen nondefensively to your colleagues' impressions. In order to better understand the identity people are responding to (versus the one you *think* you are projecting), your skill as a *listener* is of paramount importance. Being who you want to be depends on a realistic knowledge of what others think of you, and this knowledge is especially useful in addressing and mediating the differences that arise in organizational life.

Your managerial identity, then, depends on a complicated interaction of your own intentions and other people's interpretations. It is never completely fixed or defined, but varies according to the individual and over time. Every day, both intentionally and unintentionally, you work at constructing your identity. How aware are you of this continual process?

TAKING ACTION

As we have noted, your managerial identity is formed through actions and words. The *kinds* of actions you take and, more generally, how effective you are at taking them are perhaps the most crucial determinants of your success. Since as a manager you are constantly making decisions, we ask: How capable are you at taking action?

It is unlikely that your immediate response to this question is "not very." Most people see themselves as at least reasonably capable of taking action and are skilled at formulating rationales for why some things work out and other do not. Most people are well intentioned and do their very best to get things done. But we are concerned here with *robust action*—action that accomplishes short-term objectives while preserving long-term flexibility. So how capable are you at taking robust action?

Robust action does not occur in a vacuum. While you are acting, so are others. These people have initiatives and objectives of their own, based on the identities they wish to establish. They are trying to influence the strategy of the firm, use structure to solve problems of their own, and measure performance in a way that enhances their identities. To practice robust action successfully, you need to be constantly *aware* of the actions of others and the intentions behind them. You need to find ways to capitalize on efforts that support your own initiatives and counter those that do not. Blunt as it may sound, taking action and blocking action are equally important—although it is nearly always more difficult to do the former than the latter.

Of course, a simplistic "win/lose" framing ignores the fact that robust action is about getting beyond such starkly opposed outcomes. In the ambiguities of organizational life, winners and losers are not as well defined as in certain other domains. What appears to be a loss can often be turned to your advantage, just as what appears to be a victory can end up working against you. Effective robust action plays off the actions and reactions of others in a way that allows individual and collective objectives to be achieved as often as possible. Even when this is done with great skill, however, there will always be trade-offs to manage.

As Part II of this book sought to show, strategy, structure, and performance measurement are all about managing trade-offs in the pursuit of robust action. In the case of strategy, we saw that one's success at this depends on how well rhetoric is used to mobilize future actions and interpret past ones. Similarly, in the case of structure, we saw how rhetoric must be used to specify a course of action with sufficient clarity that it influences the actions of others, while being ambiguous enough so that others can decide for themselves which actions make the most sense to them. Finally, in the case of performance measurement, we saw how flexible rhetoric makes it easier to redirect actions and measures according to one's changing circumstances.

The ambiguity and flexibility dictated by robust action means that you must rely on your own judgment about whether you are doing enough of the right things given your circumstances and objectives. This self-assessment requires the same kind of discipline and honesty that we urged you to bring to questions about your identity.

You need, for instance, to reflect soberly on the actions you have taken in the past. Which ones were more effective than others? Performance measures and management theory may of course help in this inquiry, but they are always incomplete and must be supplemented by your own judgment. As we have consistently argued, there is no single path to effective robust action. Becoming adept at it simply requires learning from your successes and unlearning those strategies that have ceased to be effective.

USING RHETORIC

Rhetoric is not only an important element of managerial identity, it is itself a particular form of action. Although managers may be reluctant to admit that they are not particularly effective at taking action—after all, this is what good management is all about—they are less reluctant to admit that they could be more effective rhetoricians. Many people feel that they could do a better job of public speaking, of dealing with difficult interpersonal issues, and of improving their writing and communication skills. The common cliché that actions speak louder than words may fail to capture the truth of the matter: that words have an enormous potential either to make organizational action happen or to inhibit it.

The basic message of this book has been that without the right words, used in the right way, it is unlikely that the right actions will occur. Words *do* matter—they matter very much. Without words we have no way of expressing strategic concepts, structural forms, or designs for performance measurement systems. In the end, there is no separating action and rhetoric. Concepts and designs provide the rhetorical frame in which action takes place and, in turn, emerge from action themselves. Clearly, language is too important to managers to be taken for granted or, even worse, abused.

Thus the question, "How skillfully do you use rhetoric?" is intricately bound up with the question about how capable you are at taking robust action. Your ability to take action depends on how effectively you use rhetoric, as a speaker *and* as a listener. Your effectiveness as a speaker and writer determines how well you are able to get others to do things. Your effectiveness as a listener determines how well you understand others and do things for them.

In the course of this book, we have used the term "rhetoric" in a number of different ways to refer to the different roles that language plays in management. The first, of course, corresponds to the most common definition of the term: using language for persuasion. As we argued, managers spend a great deal of time in one-on-one conversations, small group discussions, and presentations to large audiences in order to frame situations in certain ways and influence others to take certain actions. How aware are you of shaping your message to the audience it is addressed to? Because certain forms of rhetoric are so common (exhortations about the need for change, return to basic values, and capitalizing on opportunity, for example), it is easy to fall into a rhetorical rut. Unless you have achieved a high level of proficiency in rhetoric (not something most of us can claim, the authors included), you may need to make conscious and explicit choices about your rhetorical repertoire—and you should be creative in thinking of ways to improve it.

Another kind of rhetoric used by managers is what we have broadly referred to as design concepts—the rational systems, structures, and frameworks of organizational life. While these designs don't usually *seem* rhetorical, we have tried to show how such concepts do much more than neutrally represent a situation, that they always use language to frame it in a particular way. We have also argued that it is your responsibility to adapt design concepts to your particular circumstances. So we ask: Are the concepts you are using meaningful and mobilizing to the people you work with, or are they mere slogans? Finding out whether others regard your rhetoric as effective is as difficult as finding out how others see your identity, but feedback is essential to make sure that your words are not falling on deaf ears.

The final way we have used the term rhetoric is with reference to the language systems that exist in and among organizations. Every organization has its own pattern of talking, one that includes all of the various design concepts used in particular ways. The question here is, "What effects do my actions, including the words I introduce, have on the language system in my company?"

Making this assessment has two elements. The first entails assessing how you use words, especially new ones, that have been introduced by someone else. "Core competence" introduced by the CEO, "reengineering" introduced by MIS, and "empowerment" introduced by human resources are examples of new rhetorical tools made available to you in this way. If they have broad organizational legitimacy and clearly have something to offer, you should feel free to use such terms for your own ends. The second element, however, entails assessing the effectiveness of words *you* are responsible for introducing to the organization.

Given the large number of buzzwords rapidly cycling through companies today, you must use discretion in introducing yet another one, especially one that purports to represent a "new" management concept. As always, the question to ask yourself is whether introducing such terms will enhance or inhibit the use of language for mobilizing action.

SOME PARTING WORDS

In summarizing the three basic concepts on which this book is built—identity, action, and rhetoric—we have asked a number of questions about how you manage these elements of the management process. Our goal in doing so was to provide a personally grounded recapitulation of the key ideas that have gone into our own thinking. The utility of these questions will be determined by the extent to which they have allowed you to reflect on your own managerial practice and to begin thinking about how you might proceed from here.

We are *not* advocating that you develop an action plan, a decision tree of actions and outcomes. The organizational world is too ambiguous, uncertain, and complicated for such an approach to have much utility. What we *do* advocate is that you take an *action perspective* which recognizes that the purpose of management is fostering action and then making that action meaningful to people both collectively and individually. As we have argued, this requires not only the skillful use of rhetoric, but, more generally, taking a rhetorical stance vis-à-vis the practice of management. Part of this rhetorical stance is a healthy dose of skepticism about the quick-fix solutions flooding today's managerial literature. While some of them may be helpful, they will not in themselves ensure you or your company a long and prosperous life. It is *you* and your colleagues who are responsible for this every day. By accepting this responsibility, you can move beyond contemporary hyperbole and rediscover the essence of what management is all about: the effective use of language to get things done.

NOTES

PREFACE

1. Robert G. Eccles and Nitin Nohria, "The Post-Structuralist Organization" (Boston: Harvard Business School Working Paper, 1991). Eager to join the new organization bandwagon, we wrote:

> In the past decade, a great deal has been written by academics, managers, and journalists about the need for a new management paradigm in response to dramatic changes in the business environment and the characteristics of organizations. This new management paradigm is being shaped by firms that are experimenting with new approaches to structure, systems, strategy, resource allocation, and human resource policies. . . . But because these experiments are still in their early stages in most companies . . . it is too early to expect a definitive statement of this emerging paradigm.

We should add that the term *post-structuralist* was by no means our own. Instead, we had merely appropriated it from recent theoretical work in the humanities, where this term has come to be used in a fashion that is perhaps more in line with the present book than with the above paper.

2. Jeremy Main, "Manufacturing the Right Way," *Fortune* (May 21, 1990): 54–64.

CHAPTER 1: GETTING BEYOND MANAGEMENT HYPE

1. Charles Handy, *The Age of Unreason* (Boston: Harvard Business School Press, 1990).

2. Kenichi Ohmae observes: "On a political map, the boundaries between countries are as clear as ever. But on a competitive map, a map showing the real flows of financial and industrial activity, those boundaries have largely disappeared" (Kenichi Ohmae, "Managing in a Borderless World," *Harvard Business Review*, 67 [May–June 1989]: 153).

3. The term *post-industrialism* is one that has been around for quite some time. As discussed in Chapter 2, it has been used at least since the time of World War II to identify a "new" social and technological regime marked by a decreased importance of traditional forms of large-scale industrial production. The

term became widely popular only later, however, after the publication of Daniel Bell's well-known book, *The Coming of Post-Industrial Society* (New York: Basic Books, 1973).

4. William B. Johnston and Arnold H. Packer, *Workforce 2000: Work and Workers for the 21st Century* (Indianapolis, Ind.: Hudson Institute, 1987).

5. Michael C. Jensen, "The Eclipse of the Public Corporation," *Harvard Business Review*, 67 (September–October 1989): 61–74.

6. Tom Peters, "Get Innovative or Get Dead (Part One)," *California Management Review*, 33, no. 1 (1990): 9–26; and Peters, "Get Innovative or Get Dead (Part Two)," *California Management Review*, 33, no. 2 (1990): 9–23.

7. See Mary Parker Follett, *Dynamic Administration: The Collected Papers of Mary Parker Follett*, eds. Henry C. Metcalf and L. Urwick (London: Sir Isaac Pitman and Sons, 1941). Suffused with a range of knowledge that spanned psychology, philosophy, law, economics, and the sociology of industrial organization, Follett's work remains a remarkably fresh statement of creative interdisciplinary thinking about management. In particular, her ideas about management (and life itself) as a continuous *process* serve as important forerunners of the ideas that will be developed throughout this book.

8. Follett, "The Meaning of Responsibility in Business Management," in *Dynamic Administration*, 147.

9. Ibid., 148.

10. Ibid., 158.

11. Ibid., 154.

12. American sociologist Daniel Bell has captured this celebration of the new particularly well in his writings about art and culture. In his view, modern society shows "a dominant impulse toward the new and original, a self-conscious search for future forms and sensations, so that the idea of change and novelty overshadows the dimensions of actual change." He continues: "Indeed, society has done more than passively accept innovation; it has provided a market which eagerly gobbles up the new, because it believes it to be superior in value to all older forms. Thus, our culture has an unprecedented mission: it is an official, ceaseless search for a new sensibility" (Daniel Bell, *The Cultural Contradictions of Capitalism* [London: Heinemann, 1976], 33–34). We hope it does not prove controversial to argue that whether a practice is new or traditional is unimportant as long as it is effective.

13. See Frank H. Freeman, "Books That Mean Business: The Management Best Sellers," *Academy of Management Review*, 10 (1984): 347: "Dieting, sex, whimsy, food, money, and gossip are no longer first in the hearts of bibliophiles . . . *Publishers Weekly* exclaimed, 'Without contest, business was the hottest bestselling subject in 1983.' . . . [Yet] this publishing event may not be so much a unique event as it is just another sign that we are now in the *business decade*. Corporate America is back in good standing, along with the reemergence of pride and hope in the business citizenry." The distinctly early-1980s optimism that Freeman recounts, however, would soon—with the October crashes and the return of recession—turn sour.

14. The share of worldwide motor vehicle production occurring in the United States fell from 28% in 1970 to 22% in 1989. Similarly, U.S. market share in

the semiconductor industry fell from 57% in 1982 to 37% in 1989. Japanese industry, not surprisingly, shows the reverse trend. For example, between 1970 and 1989 the Japanese share of the motor vehicle market (counting only vehicles produced *in* Japan) went from 18% to nearly 27%. In semiconductors, the Japanese share went from 33% in 1982 to 50% in 1989. (Automotive data are taken from *World Motor Vehicle Data,* 1991; data on semiconductors are taken from Richard Brandt, "The Bad Boy of Silicon Valley," *Business Week* [December 9, 1991]: 64–70.)

15. An infatuation with Japanese management has been an American fixture for over a decade. In particular, many books were published during the recession of the early 1980s, arguing that American companies needed to start taking lessons from the Japanese. See for example William G. Ouchi, *Theory Z: How American Business Can Meet the Japanese Challenge* (Reading, Mass.: Addison-Wesley, 1981); and Richard Pascale and Anthony Athos, *The Art of Japanese Management: Applications for American Executives* (New York: Simon & Schuster, 1981).

Given signs that the Japanese economy of the 1990s is entering its own period of difficulty (with Tokyo's Nikkei Stock Average down almost 50% from its 1989 peak as of March 1992), one has to wonder how resilient the model of Japanese management will ultimately prove. One also has to wonder what our prescriptions of good management would be like today if Germany, which has also witnessed a period of enviable economic progress, had instead become the focus of our attention through the publication of a hypothetical *Theory G* in the early 1980s. With the arrival of Europe 1992, and if Germany creates an even greater economic powerhouse by successfully integrating East Germany, we may yet see something like this come to pass. (Nikkei data from Robert Neff, "Can Tokyo Keep the Nikkei from Going Through the Floor?," *Business Week* [March 2, 1992]: 34.)

16. See Peggy Langstaff, "Success Stories: Business Books That Lead to the Top," *Publishers Weekly* (August 9, 1991): 15–23.

17. "Is Anybody Listening?," *Fortune* (September 1950): 176.

18. Aristotle, *On Rhetoric,* tr. and ed., George Kennedy (New York: Oxford University Press: 1991), 22.

19. In recent decades there has been a resurgence of interest in the concept of rhetoric which has resulted in several works that might be seen as forerunners of our discussion here. For example, in economics, see Donald N. McCloskey, *The Rhetoric of Economics* (Milwaukee: University of Wisconsin Press, 1985); in literature, see Wayne Booth, *The Rhetoric of Fiction* (Chicago: University of Chicago Press, 1961) and "The Revival of Rhetoric" in Martin Steinmann, ed., *New Rhetorics* (New York: Charles Scribner's Sons, 1967); and in science, see Alan G. Gross, *The Rhetoric of Science* (Cambridge, Mass.: Harvard University Press, 1990). An important, less-disciplinary treatment of rhetoric is in Chaim Perelman and L. Olbrechts-Tyteca, *The New Rhetoric: A Treatise on Argumentation,* John Wilkinson and Purcell Weaver, trs. (Notre Dame, Ind.: University of Notre Dame Press, 1958, 1971).

20. Now over two millennia old, the debate over rhetoric has been a remarkably constant one. Indeed, Plato's fascinating dialogues (written in the fourth

century B.C.) use a highly rhetorical style to argue that rhetoric is (mainly) a bad thing, thus laying the foundation for most contemporary attitudes about language. See in particular the "Gorgias" and "Phaedrus" dialogues, in Edith Hamilton and Huntington Cairns, eds., *Plato: The Collected Dialogues* (Princeton, N.J.: Princeton University Press, 1961). For an overview of the debate that seeks to restore rhetoric's good name, see Chapter 20, "Rhetoric," in Stanley Fish, *Doing What Comes Naturally: Change, Rhetoric, and the Practice of Theory in Literary and Legal Studies* (Durham, N.C.: Duke University Press, 1989).

A discussion of language's "framing" role in management can be found in Jay A. Conger, "Inspiring Others: The Language of Leadership," *Academy of Management Executive*, 5 (1991): 31–45. The idea that our everyday use of language dictates the way we see (and act in) the world has been of paramount importance to philosophers throughout the twentieth century, although it is perhaps only in recent years that the implications for management science have begun to be appreciated fully. Among numerous philosophical discussions of the role played by language in determining our understanding of the world, see J. L. Austin's *How to Do Things with Words* (Cambridge, Mass.: Harvard University Press, 1962); Richard Rorty's *Philosophy and the Mirror of Nature* (Princeton, N.J.: Princeton University Press, 1979); Ludwig Wittgenstein's classic *Philosophical Investigations,* tr., G. E. M. Anscombe (Oxford: Basil Blackwell, 1974); or, in a slightly more analytical vein that stresses the importance of "conceptual schemes," Hilary Putnam, *The Many Faces of Realism* (LaSalle, Ill.: Open Court, 1987). An interesting attempt to apply Wittgenstein's notion of language games to managerial behavior can be found in Louis R. Pondy, "Leadership Is a Language Game," in Morgan W. McCall, Jr., and Michael M. Lombardo, eds., *Leadership: Where Else Can We Go?* (Durham, N.C.: Duke University Press, 1978).

21. Chester I. Barnard, *The Functions of the Executive* (Cambridge, Mass.: Harvard University Press, 1938, 1968), 194.

22. In addition to Follett and Barnard, we might cite such theorists as Karl Weick, David Silverman, and Chris Argyris as examples of others who employ some variety of action perspective in their writings on organizations. See Karl Weick, *The Social Psychology of Organizing*, 2d ed. (New York: Random House, 1979); David Silverman, *The Theory of Organizations: A Sociological Framework* (New York: Basic Books, 1971); Chris Argyris and Donald Schön, *Organizational Learning: A Theory of Action Perspective* (Reading, Mass.: Addison-Wesley, 1978); and Chris Argyris, Robert Putnam, and Diana McLain Smith, *Action Science* (San Francisco: Jossey-Bass, 1985). Peter Drucker has been another important advocate of an action perspective, although—as discussed in Chapter 2—his varied writings have at times emphasized newness and design in ways we have protested against. Yet see Peter F. Drucker, *The Practice of Management* (New York: Harper & Row, 1954), for a comprehensive discussion of management that certainly merits mention here (and to which we will return in this book's conclusion).

CHAPTER 2: RHETORIC: THE WORK OF WORDS

1. Brian Dumaine, "The Bureaucracy Busters," *Fortune* (June 17, 1991): 36.

2. Like most popular terms in contemporary management theory, the precise genesis of the term *adaptive organization* is difficult to trace. Alvin Toffler, the author of *Future Shock*, wrote a report for AT&T in 1972 entitled *The Adaptive Corporation*, although the term may well predate his use of it. See Alvin Toffler, *The Adaptive Corporation* (London: Pan Books, 1985).

3. William H. Whyte, Jr., *The Organization Man* (New York: Simon & Schuster, 1956).

4. Regarding this early use of the term *post-industrialism*, see for example Paul Meadows, "Post-Industrialism," *Technology Review*, 49 (December 1946): 101–103 ff. Meadows's article outlined the development of a "post-industrial" society a good twenty-five years before Daniel Bell's announcements in the early 1970s. He wrote in terms that sound strikingly contemporary:

> [Post-industrialism] suggests a new system of industrial technics, evolved out of the old, and already present in many forms; it refers to reaction tendencies generated by industrialism itself. . . . It expresses a dissatisfaction with the forms of industrial life as we have known them; it is tired of big business, big industry, big cities, big labor, and big government. . . . Post-industrialism is a decentralized way of life: its key word is decentralization. . . . Production revolves around more flexible machine arrangements, and remote control of industrial operations becomes possible and necessary. Automatic manufacturing becomes of increasing importance and a new type of industrial worker emerges . . .

5. That the concerns of the 1950s were not that unlike the concerns of more recent times can be demonstrated simply through glancing at the management literature of the past. See for example George R. Price, "How to Speed Up Invention," *Fortune* (November 1956): 150; and Armand Feigenbaum, "Total Quality Control," *Harvard Business Review*, 34 (November–December 1956): 93.

In particular, Feigenbaum's article on quality control provides the opportunity to examine a specific situation in which the current rhetoric deceives us into stereotyping and misunderstanding what really has gone on in management. To look at most recent books and articles, one would think quality to be an invention of the last decade. In truth, however, much of what is today said in the name of "total quality" has been said, in various ways, for quite some time. Feigenbaum's *Harvard Business Review* article anticipated much of the current emphasis on quality and customer satisfaction, and couches these concerns in a language of competitiveness almost identical to what is tossed around as new thinking today. The author proclaimed then what is now chanted as a new mantra:

> To design, process and sell products competitively in the 1956 marketplace, American businessmen must take full account of crucial trends: Customers— both industrial and consumer—have been increasing their quality requirements very sharply in recent years. This tendency is likely to be greatly amplified by

the intense competition that seems inevitable in the near future. These trends spell out the twin quality objective that 1956 competitive conditions present to American business management: (a) considerable improvement in the quality of many products and many quality practices, and at the same time, (b) substantial reductions in the over-all costs of maintaining quality.

Was the American management establishment not listening, or do we have a short memory?

6. Perrin Stryker, "The Subtleties of Delegation," *Fortune* (March 1955): 94–97, 160–164.

7. Ibid., 95.

8. Ibid.

9. Ibid. There are of course some differences to be noted in the use of the terms *decentralization* and *empowerment,* but their effect upon organizational practice runs the risk of being overstated. In particular, the 1950s rhetoric of decentralization usually retains connotations of hierarchy and the division of labor. The newer rhetoric of empowerment, on the other hand, tends to minimize all notions of structure and coordination, stressing instead the sense of fuzzy "boundarylessness" that has become fashionable today. Whereas it might be said that empowerment extends deeper into an organization, this would be to ignore two things: first, that many defenses of decentralization (such as Ralph Cordiner's below) have clearly been meant to apply to practices outside the domain of the high-ranking executive or manager; and second, that—rhetoric to the contrary—issues of coordination and control cannot be made to disappear. The confusion surrounding the precise meaning of decentralization today will be further treated in Chapter 6.

10. These lectures, substantially as delivered, were published as: Ralph J. Cordiner, *New Frontiers for Professional Managers* (New York: McGraw-Hill, 1956).

11. Peter F. Drucker, "The Coming of the New Organization," *Harvard Business Review,* 66 (January–February 1988): 53.

12. Cordiner, *New Frontiers for Professional Managers,* 87.

13. Ibid., 21.

14. Ibid., 47. We concede that some interesting arguments have been made for seeing today's new "rage for smallness" as indicative of a transition to an entirely new form of capitalism, one often known by such labels as "flexible accumulation," "Post-Fordism," or even "late capitalism." Even so, it is important to acknowledge that management values did not simply switch from big bureaucracy to nimble "smallness" overnight; rather, the values of bigness and smallness tend to interpenetrate each other in every age, even if they ultimately are expressed in different ways. For more on this see for example David Harvey, *The Condition of Post-Modernity* (Cambridge, Mass.: Basil Blackwell, 1989) and Michael Piore and Charles Sabel, *The Second Industrial Divide* (New York: Basic Books, 1984).

15. Ibid., 49–50.

16. Jack Welch, "Management for the Nineties," speech delivered April 27, 1988, in Waukesha, Wisconsin (General Electric: GE Executive Speech Reprint, 1988).

17. As Welch remarked in an interview: "Don't forget, we built much of this company in the 1950s around . . . POIM: plan, organize, integrate, measure. We're trying to make a massive cultural break [from that]." See Noel Tichy and Ram Charan, "Speed, Simplicity, Self-Confidence: An Interview with Jack Welch," *Harvard Business Review,* 67 (September–October 1989): 112.

18. Indeed, the rhetoric of change and of the need for a new model of organization and management was as salient in the 1960s as it was in the 1950s. As early as 1960, Robert L. Katz declared in a *Harvard Business Review* article that "the conventional way of thinking about how an organization should be organized and administered is obsolete" (Robert L. Katz, "Toward a More Effective Enterprise," *Harvard Business Review,* 38 [September–October 1960]: 80). And in an article called "The Firm of the Future," H. Igor Ansoff similarly outlined this new vision:

> The forces which will shape the future firm are already at work. In fact some of them have been at work for a number of years. . . . All available evidence suggests that acceleration of product changes is going to continue. New technologies will continue to spawn new products and to invade older technologies and the life cycles of products will become shorter. . . . Demand is shifting to new market areas. . . . By the 1980s, a majority of U.S. firms will be trading in truly international markets; many firms will become multinational. . . . The future firm will remain a profit seeker, but its search for profit will be strongly affected by an awareness of social consequences. Extrapolating the external forces which are at work today, we thus see that the keynote of the next two decades is change: growth of new products and services, expansion and restructuring of markets, and a redefinition of the firm's relationship with society. The fact that the prospects are for radical changes should not be surprising to students of the business scene. *Change has been the dominant note throughout the entire history of American business.* (H. Igor Ansoff, "The Firm of the Future," *Harvard Business Review,* 43 [September–October 1965]: 162, emphasis ours)

Finally, we might consider the imagery of the "free-form corporation" as proposed by Max Ways in another *Fortune* article of July 1966:

> As it stands today on the threshold of the final third of its first century, modern management seems pregnant with another metamorphosis . . . Whatever of truth there once was in the myth of the modern organization as a tyrannical machine has been diminishing for fifty years. The myth never took account of the modern organization's essential involvement in change. As this involvement has deepened, reality and myth have drifted even further apart. In the sixties, a typical company makes scores, perhaps hundreds or thousands, of products which it knows it will soon have to abandon or drastically modify; it must select others from millions of possibilities. Most of the actual and possible products are affected by rapidly changing technologies of production and distribution.
>
> In this situation, a company cannot be rigidly designed, like a machine, around a fixed goal. A smaller proportion of decisions can be routinized or precoded for future use. The highest activity of management becomes a continuous process of decision about the nature of the business. Management's degree

of excellence is still judged in part by its efficiency of operation, but more by its ability to make decisions changing its product mix, its markets, its techniques of financing and selling. Initiative, flexibility, creativity, and *adaptability* (emphasis ours) are the qualities now required—and these are far more "human" than the old mechanical desideratum, "efficiency." (Max Ways, "Tomorrow's Management: A More Adventurous Life in a Free-Form Corporation," *Fortune* [July 1, 1966]: 85).

19. Drucker, "The Coming of the New Organization," 53.

20. Peter F. Drucker, "Long Range Planning: Challenge to Management Science," *Management Science,* 5 (1959): 238–239.

21. Themes of unprecedented change and discontinuity run throughout Drucker's work. Compare for example Peter F. Drucker, *Landmarks of Tomorrow* (New York: Harper, 1959), ix–x: "At some unmarked point during the last twenty years, we imperceptibly moved out of the Modern Age and into a new, as yet nameless era"; Drucker, *The Age of Discontinuity: Guidelines to Our Changing Society* (New York: Harper & Row, 1968), 9–10: "The last half-century has been an Age of Continuity. . . . Now, however, we face Age of Discontinuity in world economy and technology"; and Drucker, *Managing in Turbulent Times* (New York, Harper & Row, 1980), 9: "In predictable times, such as we lived through in the 25 years between the Marshall Plan and the OPEC cartel, the fundamentals [of management] tend to be taken for granted."

22. For an interesting account of this genealogy, see Cornelis J. Lammers, "Transience and Persistence of Ideal Types in Organization Theory," *Research in the Sociology of Organizations,* 6 (1988): 203–224.

23. Drucker, *The Age of Discontinuity,* 272.

24. See Mary Parker Follett, *Dynamic Administration,* eds., Henry C. Metcalf and L. Urwick (London: Sir Isaac Pitman and Sons, 1940).

25. For a thorough account of the comings and goings of various management rhetorics, see Stephen Barley and Gideon Kunda, "The Cognitive Cage: Cycles of Control in Managerial Thought" (Cornell University Working Paper, 1990). Barley and Kunda posit that the history of management discourse is not linear but cyclical, with periods of "soft" normative discourse alternating with "hard" rational discourse in approximately thirty-year cycles.

26. See for example Elliott Jaques, "In Praise of Hierarchy," *Harvard Business Review,* 68 (January–February 1990): 127–133.

27. Although the role of hierarchical authority is consistently downplayed in rhetoric about the new ideal organization, the legitimacy of management's role is typically reaffirmed via two different types of rhetorical claims. The first is the claim that management is becoming more professional and that managerial practice is becoming less capricious, less arbitrary, less irrational, and more scientific, more consistent, and more rational. Thus management is characterized as becoming more and more a coherent body of scientific knowledge possessed by professional managers and less and less an intuitive set of ideas used by untrained managers.

The rhetorical claim that management is becoming more professional appears to be made more often during periods of growth and competitive success such as during the period up to the Great Depression and during the two decades of growth following World War II. During more gloomy periods, such as the depression era and the period following the oil shocks of the 1970s, when American firms experienced a competitive decline, a different rhetorical claim is made. Greater rhetorical emphasis is placed on managers as leaders, and management is seen as becoming more visionary, inspirational, and charismatic. The image of management in this rhetoric is no longer that of the calm, rational professional making plans and decisions to maximize growth and increase prosperity but that of a gritty, indomitable leader fighting fires to stem decline and chart a new path to renewed prosperity.

28. Peter F. Drucker, *People and Performance: The Best of Peter Drucker on Management* (London: Heinemann, 1977), 19.

29. For an interesting discussion of fads in the field of business ideas see Richard T. Pascale, *Managing on the Edge: How the Smartest Companies Use Conflict to Stay Ahead* (New York: Simon & Schuster, 1990). See also John A. Byrne, "Business Fads: What's In—and Out," *Business Week* (January 20, 1986): 53.

30. Karl Marx, "The Communist Manifesto," in Robert C. Tucker, ed., *The Marx-Engels Reader* (New York: W. W. Norton, 1972), 476.

31. An interesting attempt to reach a compromise on the question of whether the status of flux has changed in the transition from Marx's era to our own "post-modern" era can be found in Harvey, *The Condition of Post-Modernity*.

32. Stanley Fish, *Doing What Comes Naturally: Change, Rhetoric, and the Practice of Theory in Literary and Legal Studies* (Durham, N.C.: Duke University Press, 1989), 485. Of course, the view that management is a socially (and hence rhetorically) constructed field has been developed before. See for example W. Graham Astley, "Administrative Science as Socially Constructed Truth," *Administrative Science Quarterly*, 30 (1985): 497–513; and Dan Gowler and Karen Legge, "The Meaning of Management and the Management of Meaning: A View from Social Anthropology," in Michael J. Earl, ed., *Perspectives on Management: A Multidisciplinary Analysis* (New York: Oxford University Press, 1983): 197–233.

33. There is a considerable body of empirical evidence that suggests, to quote organizational theorists Davis and Luthans, "that the modern manager's world is a verbal, specifically, oral one." T. R. V. Davis and F. Luthans, "Managers in Action: A New Look at Their Behavior and Operating Modes," *Organizational Dynamics* (Summer 1980): 65; also see Richard L. Daft and John C. Wiginton, "Language and Organization," *Academy of Management Review*, 4 (1979): 179–191. The role of verbal communication in everyday management situations will be considered in further detail in Chapter 3.

34. Jay A. Conger, "Inspiring Others: The Language of Leadership," *Academy of Management Review*, 5 (1991): 32.

35. Jeffrey Pfeffer, *Managing with Power: Politics and Influence in Organizations* (Boston: Harvard Business School Press, 1992), 282–283.

36. Ibid., 283.

37. That it is the *use* of a concept that determines its meaning is an idea commonly associated with the philosopher Ludwig Wittgenstein. As Louis Pondy has written paraphrasing him: "The meaning of a word is *the set of ways in which*

it is used" (emphasis ours) Louis R. Pondy, "Leadership Is a Language Game," in Morgan W. McCall, Jr., and Michael M. Lombardo, eds., *Leadership: Where Else Can We Go?* (Durham, N.C.: Duke University Press, 1978), 93.

In making our claim about reading being an *active* rather than passive activity, we are also consciously following the lead of many recent literary and social theorists who have argued that reading is never simply a matter of "consuming" the written wisdom of an author. *Reading needs to be reframed as a creative activity*, one in which people are free to draw highly original conclusions about what any given text really says. In the words of the late French philosopher Michel de Certeau, the reader always "invents in texts something different from what they 'intended'. . . . He combines their fragments and creates something unknown in the space organized by their capacity for allowing an indefinite plurality of meanings." See "Reading as Poaching" in Michel de Certeau, *The Practice of Everyday Life*, tr. Steven Rendall (Berkeley: University of California Press, 1984), 165–176. The creative ways that managers use concepts they find in the world might also be seen as akin to the anthropologist Claude Lévi-Strauss's account of *"bricolage,"* a process by which people inventively make do with whatever assortment of concepts and theories they can combine toward a particular end. See Claude Lévi-Strauss, *The Savage Mind* (Chicago: University of Chicago Press, 1966).

38. This model of the relationship of action and imagination has been distilled from the work of philosopher Paul Ricoeur. According to Ricoeur, the "heuristic force" of imagination is in the

> capacity to open and unfold new dimensions of reality by means of our suspension of beliefs in an earlier description. . . . The first way human beings attempt to understand and master the "manifold" of the practical field is to give themselves a fictive representation of it. . . . Without imagination, there can be no action. It is indeed through the anticipatory imagination of acting that I "try out" different possible courses of action and that I play . . . with possible practices. . . . It is in the realm of the imaginary that I try out my power to act, that I measure the scope of "I can." (Paul Ricoeur, "Imagination in Discourse and in Action," in Kathleen Blamey and John B. Thompson, trs., *From Text to Action* [Evanston, Ill.: Northwestern University Press, 1991], 176–187).

39. Peter M. Senge, "The Leader's New Work: Building Learning Organizations," *Sloan Management Review,* 32 (Fall 1990): 9–10.

40. Quoted in Alex Taylor, "What Hath Roger Smith Wrought?," *Fortune* (September 25, 1989): 233. See also Maryann Keller, *Rude Awakening: The Rise, Fall, and Struggle for Recovery of General Motors* (New York: Morrow, 1989).

41. These examples are drawn from the letters to stockholders in the 1980 and 1981 General Motors annual reports.

42. General Motors Annual Report, 1987.

43. Letter to Shareholders, General Electric Annual Report, 1990.

44. General Electric Annual Report, 1989.

45. See Letter to Stockholders, General Motors Annual Report, 1981.

46. Conger, "Inspiring Others: The Language of Leadership," 39.

47. General Electric Annual Report, 1990.

48. For more on the use of these devices see B. R. Clark, *The Distinctive College: Antioch, Reed, Swarthmore* (Chicago: Aldine, 1970); John W. Meyer and Brian Rowan, "Institutional Organizations: Formal Structure as Myth and Ceremony," *American Journal of Sociology*, 83 (1977): 159–179; Philip Selznick, *Leadership in Administration: A Sociological Interpretation* (Berkeley: University of California Press, 1957, 1984); and Alan L. Wilkins, "The Creation of Company Cultures: The Role of Stories and Human Resource Systems," *Human Resource Management*, 23 (1984): 41–60.

49. See Joanne Martin and Melanie E. Powers, "Organizational Stories: More Vivid and Persuasive than Quantitative Data," in B. Staw, ed., *Psychological Foundations of Organizational Behavior* (Glenview, Ill.: Scott, Foresman, 1983), 161–168. According to Martin and Powers, stories are effective at "articulating through exemplars the philosophy of management and the policies which make the organization distinctive." On the story's role as bond between past and future, see Ricoeur, "Imagination in Discourse and in Action," 177: "The function of the project, turned toward the future, and that of the narrative, turned toward the past, [in imagination] exchange their schemata and their grids, as the project borrows the narrative's structuring power and the narrative receives the project's capacity for anticipating."

50. Tichy and Charan, "Speed, Simplicity, Self-Confidence: An Interview with Jack Welch," 113.

51. For a more detailed discussion of the role of ambiguity in creating effective rhetoric, see W. Graham Astley and Raymond F. Zammuto, "Organization Science, Managers, and Language Games," forthcoming in *Organization Studies*: "By avoiding empirical precision, linguistic ambiguity increases the conceptual appeal of a theory by increasing the range of empirical phenomena to which the theory's conceptual vocabulary may potentially refer." Astley and Zammuto in turn cite Murray S. Davis, "That's Classic! The Phenomenology and Rhetoric of Successful Social Science Theories," *Philosophy of Social Science*, 16 (1986): 296. Davis writes: "An ambiguous theory can appeal to different—even hostile—divisions of its audience, allowing each subgroup to interpret the theory in congenial, if mutually incompatible, ways."

52. See Pfeffer, *Managing with Power*, 289–290.

53. Vaughn Bryson, "Seven Essentials of Success," Eli Lilly videotape (1991).

54. Senge, "The Leader's New Work," 14.

CHAPTER 3: ACTION: THE REALITIES OF MANAGING

1. Among other sources, much of the perspective of this chapter is developed from the important work of Terry Winograd and Fernando Flores on management and everyday life as applied to the issue of computer design. See Terry Winograd and Fernando Flores, *Understanding Computers and Cognition* (Reading, Mass.: Addison-Wesley, 1986). They write: "The word 'management' conveys the sense of active concern with action, and especially with the securing of effective cooperative action" (Ibid., 151).

2. Karl E. Weick, *The Social Psychology of Organizing*, 2d ed. (New York: Random House, 1979), 34.

3. See Eric Leifer, *Actors as Observers: A Theory of Skill in Social Relationships* (New York: Garland, 1991).

4. A moment's thought suggests that this is unlikely. Because of what mathematicians call "combinatorial explosion," the number of possible outcomes reaches almost infinitely high after a few hypothetical rounds. Our point about robust action in chess should be differentiated from the discussion of Tom Peters and Bob Waterman in *In Search of Excellence*, where similar research about chess masters is used to document the importance of pattern-recognition in management. While we do not dispute the importance of pattern-recognition in management, we are here more concerned with the "forward-looking" aspects of managerial action. See Thomas J. Peters and Robert H. Waterman, Jr., *In Search of Excellence: Lessons from America's Best-Run Companies* (New York: Harper & Row, 1982), 66–67.

5. Kenneth Arrow, *The Limits of Organization* (New York: W. W. Norton, 1970), 29.

6. Geoffrey Love and Robert G. Eccles, "Compaq Computer Corporation," Case Study 9-491-011. Boston: Harvard Business School, 1990.

7. See Karen Hopper Wruck, "Sealed Air Corporation's Leveraged Recapitalization," Case Study 9-391-067. Boston: Harvard Business School, 1990, rev. 1991. Additional information on Sealed Air is taken from a presentation made by the firm's CFO, William Hickey, at the Harvard Business School on December 12, 1991.

8. Adapting from the earlier work of Henri Fayol, Luther Gulick coined the acronym POSDCORB, which quickly became the textbook model of the nature of management work. See L. H. Gulick, "Notes on the Theory of Organization," in L. H. Gulick and L. F. Urwick, eds., *Papers on the Science of Administration* (New York: Columbia University Press, 1937), 13. See also Henri Fayol, *General and Industrial Management* (New York: IEEE Press, 1984); and Stephen K. Blumberg, "Notes on the Art of Administration," *Midwest Review of Public Administration,* 14, no. 3 (September 1980): 191–199.

9. See Winograd and Flores, *Understanding Computers and Cognition*, 71. They explicitly use the philosophy of German philosopher Martin Heidegger to reach the same conclusion about human action and management, writing: "We do at times engage in conscious reflection and systematic thought, but these are secondary to the pre-reflective experience of being *thrown in a situation* in which we are always already acting. We are always engaged in acting within a situation, without the opportunity to fully disengage ourselves and function as detached observers" (emphasis ours).

10. In academia at large, the rhetoric of planned, rational action is certainly on the defensive these days. Building on the earlier work of philosophers such as Heidegger, recent developments in sociology, cognitive science, and artificial intelligence (a leading example being the work of Winograd and Flores) have begun to stress the inadequacy of models of action based on the notion of rational planning. In computer science in particular—a field that shares much in common with managerial science—there has been a bona fide paradigm shift

away from the rhetoric of planning to a new rhetoric of "situated action" as a way of thinking about the nature of intelligence. In addition to Winograd and Flores, see Philip Agre, *The Dynamic Structure of Everyday Life,* Ph.D. diss. in Computer Science, MIT, 1988, forthcoming from Cambridge University Press. Also, Pattie Maes, ed., *Designing Autonomous Agents: Theory and Practice from Biology to Engineering and Back* (Cambridge, Mass.: MIT Press, 1990); Rodney A. Brooks, "Planning Is Just a Way of Avoiding Figuring Out What to Do Next," MIT Artificial Intelligence Lab Working Paper 303, 1987.

11. Jane Hannaway, *Managers Managing: The Workings of an Administrative System* (New York: Oxford University Press, 1989), 39.

12. Ibid., 37. See also John P. Kotter, *The General Managers* (New York: Free Press, 1982).

13. Henry Mintzberg, *The Nature of Managerial Work* (New York: Harper & Row, 1973), 31. More recently, managers studied by Lee Sproull showed similar patterns. During the course of a day they engaged in fifty-eight different activities with an average duration of nine minutes. (See Lee S. Sproull, "The Nature of Managerial Attention," in L. S. Sproull, ed., *Advances in Information Processing in Organizations* [Greenwich, Conn.: JAI Press, 1984], 15. Interruptions also appear to be a natural part of the job. Rosemary Stewart found that her managers worked uninterrupted for one-half hour only nine times during the four weeks she studied them. See Rosemary Stewart, *Managers and Their Jobs* (London: Macmillan, 1967).

14. Mintzberg, *The Nature of Managerial Work*, 44 (emphasis ours). The importance managers attach to building and maintaining their network of contacts is also discussed in Kotter, *The General Managers*.

15. See Pondy, "Leadership Is a Language Game," in Morgan W. McCall, Jr., and Michael M. Lombardo, eds., *Leadership: Where Else Can We Go?* (Durham, N.C.: Duke University Press, 1978).

16. Mintzberg, *The Nature of Managerial Work*, 38.

17. The listed points are adapted from Winograd and Flores, *Understanding Computers and Cognition*, 34–35.

18. Although only selectively mentioned in Winograd and Flores, a wide variety of recent philosophers have explored the ways that language functions as a kind of action. In particular, the branch of philosophy known as speech act theory has sought to create a comprehensive theory of language that highlights its "performative" aspects—the ways that language "does things" to the world and to our perceptions of it. See for example J. L. Austin, *How to Do Things with Words* (Cambridge, Mass.: Harvard University Press, 1962), and John Searle, *Speech Acts: An Essay in the Philosophy of Language* (Cambridge, England: Cambridge University Press, 1969).

19. Winograd and Flores, *Understanding Computers and Cognition*, 147. See Peter G.W. Keen and Michael S. Scott-Morton, *Decision Support Systems: An Organizational Perspective* (Reading, Mass.: Addison–Wesley, 1978), 58.

20. See Alfred Schutz, "Acting and Planning," in Helmut R. Wagner, ed., *On Phenomenology and Social Relations* (Chicago: University of Chicago Press, 1970), 134: "As Professor John Dewey has pointed out, in our daily life we are largely preoccupied with the next step. Men stop and think only when the

sequence of doing is interrupted . . . ." A similar perspective is applied to artificial intelligence in Brooks, "Planning Is Just a Way of Avoiding Figuring Out What to Do Next."

21. Philip Selznick, "Preface to the California Edition," in *Leadership in Administration: A Sociological Interpretation* (Berkeley: University of California Press, 1957, 1984), vii. See also William James, *Pragmatism* (Indianapolis, Ind.: Hackett Publishing, 1981); and John Dewey, *The Essential Writings* (New York: Harper & Row, 1977).

22. The Amgen paradox is recounted in James D. Berkley and Nitin Nohria, "Amgen Inc.: Planning the Unplannable," Case Study N9-492-052. Boston: Harvard Business School, 1992.

23. See Frederick W. Taylor, *The Principles of Scientific Management* (New York: W. W. Norton, 1911, 1947).

24. For an interesting discussion of the hype surrounding the term *reengineering,* see Paul Hemp, "Preaching the Gospel," *Boston Globe* (June 30, 1992), p. 35.

25. Actually, there is a movement afoot in many companies to take account of individuals in a way that may initially seem radical: conducting "New Age" personality testing. Nevertheless, these tests—Are you left-brained or right-brained? Introverted or extroverted?—often fall back on simplistic distinctions that give organization members little more than a lot of buzzwords and a fixed sense of their own unique characteristics as a manager. The trend deserves to be taken seriously, however, if not so much for its distillation and appropriation of psychological theory as for its acknowledgment that (as will be developed in the next chapter) individuals need to be restored to the center of attention.

26. Weick, *The Social Psychology of Organizing,* 149–150.

27. See David A. Nadler, J. Richard Hackman, and Edward E. Lawler III, *Managing Organizational Behavior* (Boston: Little, Brown, 1979), 28–38. See also John W. Atkinson, "Motivational Determinants of Risk-taking Behavior," *Psychological Review,* 64 (November 1957): 359–372.

28. For one version of this dichotomy, see David C. McClelland, "The Urge to Achieve," in Michael T. Matteson and John M. Ivancevich, eds., *Management and Organizational Behavior Classics* (Homewood, Ill.: BPI Irwin, 1989): 392–401. (Reprinted from *THINK Magazine,* 32, no. 6 [November–December 1966]: 19–23.) "Most people in this world," stated McClelland, ". . . can be divided into two broad groups. There is that minority which is challenged by opportunity and willing to work hard to achieve something and the majority which really does not care all that much."

29. Weick, *The Social Psychology of Organizing,* 195.

30. Ibid., 245.

CHAPTER 4: IDENTITY: THE QUEST FOR THE PARTICULAR

1. Carol Heimer, "Doing Your Job and Helping Your Friends: Universalistic Norms about Particular Others in Networks," in Nitin Nohria and Robert

G. Eccles, eds., *Networks and Organizations* (Boston: Harvard Business School Press, 1992).

For the interested reader, a moment should be taken to differentiate our argument from the kind of particularism often attributed to the influential "Human Relations" school, which similarly argued that the techniques of personnel management should be geared around a consideration of "the whole worker." The human relations tradition forms an important backdrop for all contemporary theorizing about organizations, yet it is hardly without its problems. In fact, Herbert Marcuse made an argument for seeing the particularism of human relations approaches as an ideological weapon: by "translating" universal concerns (bad wages, bad working conditions, managerial oppression, and so forth) into "personal" ones, he argued, the human relations approach served essentially to suppress worker dissent. (See Herbert Marcuse, *One Dimensional Man* [Boston: Beacon Press, 1964], 108–114; the positions he criticizes can be found in F. J. Roethlisberger and William J. Dickson, *Management and the Worker* [Cambridge, Mass.: Harvard University Press, 1939], 590–604.) Clearly, such is not the brand of particularism we mean to advocate here. As we will argue, it is important to *respect* the collective identifications of others, rather than merely trying to explain them away.

2. For a somewhat hyperbolic argument about the unfairness of affirmative action policies that illustrates much of the contemporary backlash against them, see Dinesh D'Souza, *Illiberal Education: The Politics of Race and Sex on Campus* (New York: Free Press, 1991).

3. See Douglas McGregor, "The Human Side of Enterprise," *Management Review*, 46, no. 11 (November 1957): 22–28, 88–92.

4. Ibid., 23.

5. Ibid., 88.

6. Ibid., 89.

7. See William G. Ouchi, *Theory Z: How American Business Can Meet the Japanese Challenge* (Reading, Mass.: Addison-Wesley, 1981), which describes how certain American companies (Theory Z) have adopted Japanese management practices (Theory J), which make them more effective than the typical American company (Theory A). According to Ouchi, Theory Z companies use a model of human behavior that "suggests that involved workers are the key to increased productivity." Ouchi noted that Theory Z was very similar to Theory Y, with the former referring to a type of organization and the latter referring to a type of manager. (See Ouchi, *Theory Z*, 4.)

8. McGregor, "The Human Side of Enterprise," 88–89.

9. This view of motivation takes McGregor's Theory Y as its point of departure, but diverges from it in an important fashion. For McGregor, "motivation" has been misunderstood because it has been assumed to be a matter of applying a certain external force in order to extract work. See McGregor, "The Human Side of Enterprise," 88–89: "The motivation, the potential for development, the capacity for assuming responsibility, the readiness to direct behavior toward organizational goals are all present in people. Management does not put them there. It is a responsibility of management to make it possible for people to recognize and develop these human characteristics for themselves."

While we similarly stress the internal nature of motivation, we further add that the multiplicity of dimensions along which it typically occurs make it a poor way of framing the issue in the first place.

10. Sociologist Harrison White explains, "Psychologists are looking in the wrong place to find identity. Identity is created not inside but outside our bodily integuments." (See Harrison White, *Identity and Control: A Structural Theory of Social Action* [Princeton, N.J.: Princeton University Press, 1992.])

11. Hannah Arendt, *The Human Condition* (Chicago: University of Chicago Press, 1958), 179.

12. Ibid.

13. William Whiting, "Industrial Conduct and Leadership," *Harvard Business Review*, 1 (April 1923): 323.

14. See the work of Erik H. Erikson, especially *Childhood and Society*, 2d ed. (New York: W. W. Norton, 1965). The phrase "being in the world" is borrowed from the work of German philosopher Martin Heidegger; see his *Being and Time*, trs., John Macquarrie and Edward Robinson (New York: Harper & Row, 1962).

15. White, *Identity and Control*, 20–21.

16. As suggested above, the notion that individual identity is produced *out* of social networks is a compelling idea that is of much interest to sociologists, who have not always been satisfied with attempts to ground identity in psychological theory. See for example Chapter 2, "Networks from Identities," in White, *Identity and Control*.

17. Arendt, *The Human Condition*, 183–184.

18. For the major statement of how "social comparison" shapes identity, see Leon Festinger, "A Theory of Social Comparison Processes," *Human Relations*, 7 (1954): 117–140.

19. Ibid., 179–180.

20. Herbert Simon, "Organizations and Markets," *Journal of Economic Perspectives*, 5, no. 2 (Spring 1991): 34.

21. Ibid.

22. Peter Brill and Marshall W. Meyer, "Organizational Empowerment and Organizational Identification," unpublished manuscript, Wharton School, 1992. This paper contains a very good discussion about the meaning and bases of identification, and the relationship between identification and empowerment.

23. Eliot Freidson, *Professional Powers: A Study of the Institutionalization of Formal Knowledge* (Chicago: University of Chicago Press, 1986), 30.

24. Magali Sarfatti Larson, *The Rise of Professionalism: A Sociological Analysis* (Berkeley: University of California Press, 1977), x. See also Joseph A. Raelin, *The Clash of Cultures: Managers Managing Professionals* (Boston: Harvard Business School Press, 1985).

25. Amartya Sen, "Goals, Commitment, and Identity," *Journal of Law, Economics, and Organization*, 1 (Fall 1985): 348.

26. Much has been written on the peculiarly Western invention of "selfhood" as a concept. See for example Francis Barker, *The Tremulous Private Body: Essays in Subjection* (London: Methuen, 1984); for a different, more analytical approach see White, *Identity and Control*. The following section resonates with

much in Kenneth J. Gergen's recent book, *The Saturated Self: Dilemmas of Identity in Contemporary Life* (New York: Basic Books, 1991), although we confess to having encountered Gergen's book too late to make more use of it here.

27. See Max Weber, *The Protestant Ethic and the Spirit of Capitalism*, tr., Talcott Parsons (New York: Charles Scribner's Sons, 1958).

28. Lawrence Friedman, *The Republic of Choice: Law, Authority, and Culture* (Cambridge, Mass.: Harvard University Press, 1990), 18–50. The following discussion of American individualism draws heavily from Friedman's interesting and highly readable account.

29. See David Riesman, *The Lonely Crowd: A Study of the Changing American Character* (New Haven, Conn.: Yale University Press, 1950).

30. See William H. Whyte, Jr., *The Organization Man* (New York: Simon & Schuster, 1956).

31. See Christopher Lasch, *The Culture of Narcissism* (New York: W. W. Norton, 1979).

32. Friedman, *The Republic of Choice*, 33. Friedman's discussion of the changing nature of individualism draws heavily in turn from the important work of Robert Bellah et al., *Habits of the Heart: Individualism and Commitment in American Life* (Berkeley: University of California Press, 1985).

33. Friedman, *The Republic of Choice*, 26. Many contemporary observers are horrified as well, arguing that the range of choice in post-modern society serves to fragment the self and disrupt the social bond in general. See Steven Waldman, "The Tyranny of Choice," *The New Republic* (January 27, 1992): 22–25. For more on the question of post-modern identity, see Gergen, *The Saturated Self*; and Douglas Kellner, "Popular Culture and the Construction of Postmodern Identities," in Scott Lash and Jonathan Friedman, eds., *Modernity and Identity* (Cambridge, Mass.: Basil Blackwell, 1992): 141–177.

34. For some writers, it is this very disappearance of a master plan that is characteristic of contemporary, post-modern society; the argument is that Western society has by and large dispensed with the idea that there is a single, proper way to conduct one's life—or a single, proper way to conduct anything for that matter. In the words of the French philosopher Jean-Francois Lyotard, contemporary society features a "breaking up of the grand narratives" and (in a phrasing borrowed from Wittgenstein) their replacement by a "dissemination of language games." (See Jean-Francois Lyotard, *The Post-Modern Condition: A Report on Knowledge*, trs., Geoff Bennington and Brian Massumi [Minneapolis: University of Minnesota Press, 1984], 15–17.) Needless to say, there are interesting parallels between such an argument and the arguments we have been advancing about the place of rhetoric and robust action in management.

35. Anthony Giddens, *Modernity and Self-Identity: Self and Society in the Late Modern Age* (Stanford, Calif.: Stanford University Press, 1991), 14.

36. Peter F. Drucker, *The Age of Discontinuity: Guidelines to Our Changing Society* (New York: Harper & Row, 1968), 248.

37. Richard M. Merelman, *Making Something of Ourselves: On Culture and Politics in the United States* (Berkeley: University of California Press, 1984), 30.

38. A similar argument is made by Jean-Francois Lyotard who writes that "the old poles of attraction represented by nationalities, parties, professions,

institutions, and historical traditions are losing their attraction. And it does not look as though they will be replaced, at least not on their former scale" (Lyotard, *The Post-Modern Condition*, 14). For Lyotard too, the individual has become the primary social unit.

Some writers clearly mourn the waning of traditional social identifications and the new individualism that has resulted. Christopher Lasch's *The Culture of Narcissism* used the term *apotheosis of individualism* to dissect the way the "development of the self" had come—pathologically, in his view—to be the center of existence. (See Lasch, *The Culture of Narcissism*, 127–134.) Much the same argument is to be found in Daniel Bell's earlier, and more intellectually robust, *The Cultural Contradictions of Capitalism* (London: Heinemann, 1976).

39. The possibility that organizations are more loosely bounded than in the past helps explain the recent hysteria over "organizational culture" in both organizations and management literature. In an interesting sense, it is only when the cohesiveness of organizations becomes strained that rhetoric about this cohesiveness begins to proliferate. See Chapter 1, "The Limits of Cultural Vision," in Merelman, *Making Something of Ourselves*, 1–26.

40. See Brill and Meyer, "Organizational Empowerment and Organizational Identification." The data Brill and Meyer report in their working paper are proprietary and as of the writing of this book not available for release. The statistics they cite are based on data collected by Stanard & Company's SRA Attitude Survey. While the surveys are not formal random samples of the population, each one contains hundreds of thousands of respondents and so they can be assumed to be representative of American industry as a whole.

41. Rosabeth Moss Kanter, *When Giants Learn to Dance: Mastering the Challenge of Strategy, Management, and Careers in the 1990s* (New York: Simon & Schuster, 1989). The trend Kanter notes will be reinforced by the fact that the growth rates of jobs already classified as professional (such as scientists, health care professionals, and lawyers) as well as of others known for high turnover (such as sales and service) are higher than those of other occupations. See Table 3–7: The Changing Occupational Structure, 1984–2000, in William B. Johnston and Arnold H. Packer, *Workforce 2000: Work and Workers for the Twenty-First Century* (Indianapolis, Ind.: Hudson Institute, 1987), 97.

42. Even the most vocal supporters of lifetime employment, such as IBM, have backed off their earlier commitments in the face of these changes. Various attempts have been made to theorize (and hence rhetorically legitimate or even celebrate) the trend toward lateral rather than vertical careers. (A relatively early celebration of this style of career is to be found for example in Alvin Toffler, *Future Shock* [New York: Random House, 1970], 49–182.) In these "post-entrepreneurial careers," the term used by Kanter to describe them, a person can hold jobs in a given organization at several different points in time, interspersed with jobs in the organizations of customers, suppliers, competitors, and even her own venture. (See Kanter, *When Giants Learn to Dance*, 310–311.) Examples abound, some of which are highly publicized, of people who are today shaping careers of this nature. Yet exactly how widespread the practice is and how dominant it will become is difficult to determine.

43. Kanter also emphasizes the importance of reputation in the post-entrepreneurial careers cited above. See Kanter, *When Giants Learn to Dance*, 310–311.

44. Johnston and Packer, *Workforce 2000*, 95.

45. Ibid. The common misinterpretation of this "factoid" is that white males will only number 15% of the *total* workforce. While this could ostensibly happen, it is far away at current projections.

46. Thomas A. Stewart, "Gay in Corporate America: What It's Like, and How Business Attitudes Are Changing," *Fortune* (December 16, 1991): 42–56.

47. For an early framing of the problem that foreshadows some of our diagnosis here, see Chapter 21, "Is Personnel Management Bankrupt?" in Peter F. Drucker, *The Practice of Management* (Harper & Row, 1954): 273–288.

48. Heimer, "Doing Your Job and Helping Your Friends."

49. Ibid.

50. *Oxford American Dictionary*, Eugene Ehrlich et al., eds. (New York: Oxford University Press, 1980).

CHAPTER 5: STRATEGY AS A LANGUAGE GAME

1. Sun-Tzu, *The Art of War*, tr., Thomas Cleary (Boston: Shambhala, 1988).

2. The landmark statement of the "competitive advantage" perspective is to be found in Michael Porter, *Competitive Advantage: Creating and Sustaining Superior Performance* (New York: Free Press, 1985). For a fuller critique of the military analogy, see Karl E. Weick, *The Social Psychology of Organizing*, 2d ed. (New York: Random House, 1979), 49–51.

3. For an excellent exposition of this view based in the economic theory of industrial organization see Michael Porter, *Competitive Strategy: Techniques for Analyzing Industries and Competitors* (New York: Free Press, 1980).

4. The case for market share as the key to competitive advantage has been made by Robert D. Buzzell, Bradley T. Gale, and Ralph G.M. Sultan, "Market Share—A Key to Profitability," *Harvard Business Review*, 53 (January–February 1975): 97–106. A contrary position which reveals how elusive the competitive advantage issue can be is to be found in Carolyn Y. Woo and Arnold C. Cooper, "The Surprising Case for Low Market Share," *Harvard Business Review*, 60 (November–December 1982): 106–113.

5. The case for a portfolio approach to gain competitive advantage is well argued by Sidney Schoeffler, Robert D. Buzzell, and Donald F. Heany, "Impact of Strategic Planning on Profit Performance," *Harvard Business Review*, 52 (March–April 1974): 137–145. See also Philippe Haspeslagh, "Portfolio Planning: Uses and Limits," *Harvard Business Review*, 60 (January–February 1982): 58–74.

6. On this see Porter, *Competitive Advantage*; G. Bennett Stewart III, *The Quest for Value* (New York: Harper & Row, 1990); and Donald B. Ewaldz, "How Integrated Should Your Company Be?," *The Journal of Business Strategy* (July–August 1991): 52–55.

7. See C. K. Prahalad and Gary Hamel, "The Core Competence of the

Corporation," *Harvard Business Review,* 68 (May–June 1990): 79–91; and Pankaj Ghemawat, *Commitment: The Dynamic of Strategy* (New York: Free Press, 1991).

8. See Kenichi Ohmae, "Getting Back to Strategy," *Harvard Business Review,* 66 (November–December 1988): 149–156.

9. The importance of innovation has been stressed by Rosabeth Kanter, *The Change Masters: Innovations for Productivity in the American Corporation* (New York: Simon & Schuster, 1983); Richard Foster, *Innovation: The Attacker's Advantage* (New York: Summit, 1986); and most recently by Tom Peters, "Get Innovative or Get Dead (Part One)" *California Management Review* 33, no. 1 (1990): 9–26.

10. The most recent source of competitive advantage is seen to be in time or speed. See for example George Stalk, Jr., "Time—The Next Source of Competitive Advantage," *Harvard Business Review,* 66 (July–August 1988): 41–51; and Joseph L. Bower and Thomas M. Hout, "Fast-Cycle Capability for Competitive Power," *Harvard Business Review,* 66 (November–December 1988): 110–118.

11. Eileen Shapiro, personal communication.

12. The rhetorical nature of strategic language has received consideration before, although usually not in these terms. See Kenneth R. Andrews, *The Concept of Corporate Strategy,* 3rd ed. (Homewood, Ill.: Richard D. Irwin, 1987), 15–16: "Whether you wish to think of a view of the total corporation as its *vision,* or a statement of purpose as its *mission statement . . .* is up to you. The language for describing so central an activity as choice of purpose is infinitely varied. . . . In the meantime, remember that what you are doing has no meaning for yourself or others unless you can sense and convey to others what you are doing it for."

13. See Ludwig Wittgenstein, *Philosophical Investigations,* tr., G. E. M. Anscombe (Oxford: Basil Blackwell, 1974). The *Investigations*—written toward the end of Wittgenstein's life—forms a sharp break with his earlier work, which attempted to trace just the kind of logical view of thought and language he would later criticize. The notion of language games has since been used in various capacities in the management literature, most notably in Louis R. Pondy, "Leadership Is a Language Game," in Morgan W. McCall, Jr., and Michael M. Lombardo, eds., *Leadership: Where Else Can We Go?* (Durham, N.C.: Duke University Press, 1978).

14. Gary Hamel and C. K. Prahalad, "Strategic Intent," *Harvard Business Review,* 67 (May–June 1989): 63.

15. The entries in Table 5-1 are excerpted from Hamel and Prahalad, "Strategic Intent."

16. Prahalad and Hamel, "The Core Competence of the Corporation," 82.

17. Ibid., 79.

18. Ibid., 80.

19. John D.C. Roach, "From Strategic Planning to Strategic Performance: Closing the Achievement Gap," in Robert B. Lamb, ed., *Competitive Strategic Management* (Englewood Cliffs, N.J.: Prentice-Hall, 1984).

20. See Philip Selznick, *Leadership in Administration: A Sociological Interpretation* (Berkeley, Calif.: University of California Press, 1957); and Edith T. Penrose, *The Theory of the Growth of the Firm* (Oxford: Basil Blackwell, 1959).

21. See Andrews, *The Concept of Corporate Strategy* for the notion of corporate competence; Howard Stevenson, "Defining Corporate Strengths and Weaknesses," *Sloan Management Review* (Spring 1976): 51–68 for the related notion of corporate strengths and weaknesses; Charles W. Hofer and Dan E. Schendel, *Strategy Formulation: Analytical Concepts* (St. Paul, Minn.: West, 1978) and Michael A. Hitt and R. Duane Ireland, "Corporate Distinctive Competence and Firm Performance," *Decision Sciences*, 15 (1984): 324–349, for the notion of distinctive competence; S. A. Lippman and Richard P. Rumelt, "Uncertain Imitability: An Analysis of Inter-firm Differences in Efficiency Under Competition," *Bell Journal of Economics*, 13 (1982): 418–438 for the idea of inimitable assets; and Hiroyuki Itami, *Mobilizing Invisible Assets* (Cambridge, Mass.: Harvard University Press, 1987) for the idea of invisible assets. Even a cursory reading of these sources will clearly show how closely related these concepts are and how similar they are to Prahalad and Hamel's idea of core competence.

22. Pankaj Ghemawat, "Resources and Strategy: An IO Perspective" (Harvard Business School Working Paper, 1991). For a further discussion of the duality between the resource- and market-based views of the firm, see David J. Collis, "Organizational Capability as a Source of Profit" (Harvard Business School Working Paper 91-046, 1991); and Robert M. Grant, "The Resource-Based Theory of Competitive Advantage: Implications for Strategy Formulation," *California Management Review* (Spring 1991): 114–135.

23. George Stalk, Philip Evans, and Lawrence E. Shulman, "Competing on Capabilities: The New Rules of Corporate Strategy," *Harvard Business Review*, 70 (March–April 1992): 57–69.

24. Ibid., 66.

25. Prahalad and Hamel, "The Core Competence of the Corporation," 86.

26. For a discussion of how to define strategic business units, see Derek F. Abell, *Defining the Business: The Starting Point of Strategic Planning* (Englewood Cliffs, N.J.: Prentice-Hall, 1980); for the value chain.

27. James Brian Quinn, "Managing Strategies Incrementally," in Robert B. Lamb, ed., *Competitive Strategic Management* (Englewood Cliffs, N.J.: Prentice-Hall, 1984), 37–38.

28. Francis J. Aguilar and Richard Hamermesh, "General Electric: Strategic Position 1981," Case Study 9-381-174. Boston: Harvard Business School, 1981, 2–3. In McKinsey's definition, an SBU was defined as having "a unique set of competitors, a unique business mission, a competitor in external markets . . ., the ability to accomplish integrated strategic planning, and the ability to call the shots on the variables crucial to the success of the business."

29. Francis J. Aguilar, Richard Hamermesh, and Caroline Brainard, "General Electric: Reg Jones and Jack Welch," Case Study 9-391-144. Boston: Harvard Business School, 1991.

30. See Christopher A. Bartlett and V. S. Rangan, "Komatsu Ltd.," Case Study 9-385-277. Boston: Harvard Business School, 1985.

31. Prahalad and Hamel, "The Core Competence of the Corporation," 89.

32. See Aguilar, Hamermesh, and Brainard, "General Electric: Reg Jones and Jack Welch."

33. Ibid.

34. See Richard G. Hamermesh, *Making Strategy Work: How Senior Managers Produce Results* (New York: John Wiley, 1986), 21–22. Hamermesh's findings were later confirmed by Philippe Haspeslagh in a larger survey. He too found that managers used portfolio planning in a wide variety of ways, often improvising and adapting the technique to make it suit their particular needs. It is perhaps because of these virtues of being a legitimate and flexible tool for action that Haspeslagh estimated that a full 45% of the *Fortune* 500 companies had introduced the portfolio planning approach to some extent. (See Haspeslagh, "Portfolio Planning.")

35. Hamermesh, *Making Strategy Work,* 67.

36. The dangers of how the BCG matrix came to be used are discussed at length by Stuart St. P. Slatter, "Common Pitfalls in Using the BCG Product Portfolio Matrix," *London Business School Journal* (Winter 1980): 18–22. For one of the most provocative arguments about how the rote application of such models led to the decline of American competitiveness, see Robert H. Hayes and William J. Abernathy, "Managing Our Way to Economic Decline," *Harvard Business Review,* 58 (July–August 1980): 67–77. Also see Ronald Henkoff, "How to Plan for 1995," *Fortune* (December 31, 1990): 70–77.

37. Francis J. Aguilar, Richard G. Hamermesh, and Caroline Brainard, "General Electric, 1984," Case Study 9-385-315. Boston: Harvard Business School, 1985.

38. The path-dependence of strategy is most apparent from a reading of Penrose, *The Theory of the Growth of the Firm.*

39. Henry Mintzberg, "Crafting Strategy," *Harvard Business Review,* 65 (July–August 1987): 66.

40. Robert A. Burgelman, "Intra-Organizational Ecology of Strategy Making and Organizational Adaptation: Theory and Field Research," *Organization Science,* 2 (1991): 239–262. On this, see also Quinn, "Managing Strategies Incrementally," 36: "The processes used to generate major strategies are typically fragmentary and evolutionary with a high degree of intuitive content. Although one usually finds in these fragments some very refined pieces of formal analysis, overall strategies emerge as a series of conscious internal decisions blend and interact with changing external events to slowly mutate key managers' broad consensus about what patterns of action make sense for the future."

41. See Ghemawat, *Commitment.*

42. See Amar Bhide, "Hustle as Strategy," *Harvard Business Review,* 64 (September–October 1986): 59–65.

43. To make this point about strategy as a concept is to stay close to Wittgenstein's later ideas about language games and the very concept of language itself. For example, in the *Philosophical Investigations,* Wittgenstein poses the example of the concept of "games" and shows that the great variety of different kinds of games cannot be subsumed under a single, definable concept of what a game is. The concept is simply defined by practice—by the variety of different situations in which people use the word *game* to describe what they are doing. See section 66 in Wittgenstein, *Philosophical Investigations.* See also the discussion in Stanley Cavell's essay, "The Availability of Wittgenstein's Later Philosophy," in Stanley Cavell, ed., *Must We Mean What We Say?* (New York: Cambridge

University Press, 1976), 44–72. According to Cavell: "There is no one set of characteristics . . . which everything we call "games" shares. . . . Language has no essence" (Cavell, 50). Our argument here has certain parallels to what management theorist Louis Pondy has already argued about the nature of "leadership" as a concept—namely, that it is best seen as a language game that covers a "pastiche" of different practices rather than a single essence. See Pondy, "Leadership Is a Language Game."

44. Elizabeth Olmstead Teisberg, "Strategic Responses to Uncertainty" (Harvard Business School Working Paper, 1990).

45. Quinn, "Managing Strategies Incrementally," 40.

46. Per-Henrik Mansson, "Volnay's Veteran Vintner," *The Wine Spectator* (January 31, 1992), 30.

47. For a discussion of corporate identity, see Walter P. Marguiles, "Make the Most of Your Corporate Identity," *Harvard Business Review,* 55 (July–August 1977): 66–74. Also see Wally Olins, *Corporate Identity: Making Business Strategy Visible Through Design* (Boston: Harvard Business School, 1990).

48. Mats Alvesson, "Organization: From Substance to Image?," *Organization Studies,* 11 (1990): 373–394.

49. For the Johnson & Johnson story, see the case and video on the company's philosophy and culture prepared by Francis J. Aguilar and Arvind Bhambri, "Johnson & Johnson (A): Philosophy and Culture," Case Study 9-384-053 and video 9-884-525. Boston: Harvard Business School, 1984. For a more general discussion of the role that vision statements and the like play in building strong employee identification with a company's strategy see Terrence E. Deal and Anthony A. Kennedy, *Corporate Cultures: The Rites and Rituals of Corporate Life* (Reading, Mass.: Addison-Wesley, 1982).

50. The importance of focus and its performance implications have been studied at length by Cynthia Montgomery and Birger Wernerfelt. (See Montgomery and Wernerfelt, "Diversification, Ricardian Rents, and Tobin's q.," *Rand Journal of Economics,* 19 [Winter 1988]: 623–632.) Our own research has confirmed these findings. For a sample of conglomerates we found that their average ROE, ROA, and ROI for the period 1969–1988 were 12.5%, 2.79%, and 7.4%, respectively. For the S&P 500 for the same period, the average ROE, ROA, and ROI were 13.05%, 3.66%, and 8.01%. See Nitin Nohria and Robert G. Eccles, "Corporate Capability" (Harvard Business School Working Paper, 1991).

51. The idea of relatedness is discussed at length by Richard Rumelt, *Strategy, Structure, and Economic Performance* (Boston: Division of Research, Harvard Business School, 1974). The argument for synergies as a way of justifying expansion can be found in Rosabeth Moss Kanter, *When Giants Learn to Dance: Mastering the Challenge of Strategy, Management, and Careers in the 1990s* (New York: Simon & Schuster, 1989).

52. For other examples of conglomerates that manage to preserve a coherent identity (such as GE, TRW, and Raytheon), see Nohria and Eccles, "Corporate Capability."

53. Thomas J. Peters and Robert H. Waterman, Jr., *In Search of Excellence*

(New York: Harper & Row, 1982), 305. The original quote is from Sandra Salmans, "Demergering Britain's G.E.," *New York Times* (July 6, 1980): F7.

54. There are numerous ways in which companies are compared with each other that shape their reputations. An explicit attempt to judge the relative reputations of firms is to be found in *Fortune* magazine's annual Corporate Reputations survey which in 1990 covered 305 companies in 32 industry groups and ranked them in terms of reputations along the dimensions of management, quality, innovation, investment value, financial soundness, people development, social responsibility, and use of assets. For more, see Sarah Smith, "America's Most Admired Corporations," *Fortune* (January 29, 1990): 58–92.

55. The story of Roddick's store is told in Anita Roddick, *Body and Soul: Profits with Principles, The Amazing Success Story of Anita Roddick and the Body Shop* (New York: Crown, 1991).

CHAPTER 6: ON STRUCTURE AND STRUCTURING

1. See Paul R. Lawrence and Jay W. Lorsch, *Organization and Environment: Managing Differentiation and Integration* (Boston: Division of Research, Harvard Business School, 1967).

2. See Max Weber, *Economy and Society: An Outline of Interpretive Sociology*, vol. 2 (Berkeley: University of California Press, 1978).

3. Some of the most important early statements of the contingency theory perspective include Tom Burns and G. M. Stalker, *The Management of Innovation* (London: Tavistock, 1961); Lawrence and Lorsch, *Organization and Environment*; Charles Perrow, "A Framework for the Comparative Analysis of Organizations," *American Sociological Review*, 32, no. 2 (April 1967): 194–208; Arthur L. Stinchcombe, "Bureaucratic and Craft Administration of Production: A Comparative Study," *Administrative Science Quarterly*, 4 (September 1959): 168–187; and Joan Woodward, *Industrial Organization: Theory and Practice* (Oxford: Oxford University Press, 1965). Another excellent but later book in this tradition is Raymond E. Miles and Charles C. Snow, *Organizational Strategy, Structure, and Process* (New York: McGraw-Hill, 1978).

4. Elliott Jaques, "In Praise of Hierarchy," *Harvard Business Review*, 68 (January–February 1990): 127.

5. Jaques's opinion of these arguments is that "the theorists' belief that our changing world requires an alternative to hierarchical organization is simply wrong, and all their proposals are based on an inadequate understanding of not only hierarchy but also human nature" (Jaques, "In Praise of Hierarchy," 127).

6. Henry Mintzberg, "The Effective Organization: Forces and Forms," *Sloan Management Review*, 32, no. 2 (Winter 1991): 66. Although this article identifies five different organizational "forms," Mintzberg emphasizes that he is rethinking his own earlier work which emphasized "configuration" and "natural co-alignment" to take greater account of the need for organizations to "build their own unique solutions to problems" (Ibid., 54–55). While these unique solutions may combine characteristics of different forms, the metaphor Mintzberg uses (the LEGO™ toy) is still a design-oriented one.

7. James R. Houghton, "The Age of the Hierarchy Is Over," *New York Times* (September 24, 1989): Sec. 3, p. 3.

8. Ibid.

9. Ibid.

10. Ibid. For more on Corning, see Ashish Nanda and Christopher A. Bartlett, "Corning Incorporated: A Network of Alliances," Case Study 9-391-102. Boston: Harvard Business School, 1990; also see Keith H. Hammond, "Corning's Class Act: How Jamie Houghton Has Reinvented the Company," *Business Week* (May 13, 1991): 68–76.

11. For examples of the flurry of interest in the use of decentralization during the 1940s and 1950s, see: John Allen Murphy, "What's Behind Today's Trend Toward Decentralization," *Sales Management* (October 1, 1946): 37–39; John Allen Murphy, "How the Wheels Go Round under Decentralized Management," *Sales Management* (October 15, 1946): 50–58; John Allen Murphy, "How to Keep Your Product Alive, Your Management Alert?—Decentralization!," *Sales Management* (November 1, 1946): 50–57; Raymond Villers, "Control and Freedom in a Decentralized Company," *Harvard Business Review,* 32 (March–April 1954): 89–96; Perrin Stryker, "The Subtleties of Delegation," *Fortune* (March 1955): 90–97, 160–164; Waino W. Suojanen, "Leadership, Authority, and the Span of Control," *Advanced Management* (September 1957): 17–22; and Bennett E. Kline and Norman H. Martin, "Freedom, Authority, and Decentralization," *Harvard Business Review,* 36 (May–June 1958): 69–75.

12. Stryker, "The Subtleties of Delegation," 95 (italics in original).

13. A. A. Stambaugh, "Decentralization: The Key to the Future," *Dun's Review and Modern Industry* (September 1953): 53–54.

14. Writing more than fifty years ago, Chester Barnard observed that "one will hear repeatedly that you can't understand an organization or how it works from its organization chart, its charter, rules and regulations, nor from looking at or even watching its personnel." (Chester I. Barnard, *The Functions of the Executive* [Cambridge, Mass.: Harvard University Press, 1938, 1968], 121.)

15. See Alfred D. Chandler, Jr., *Strategy and Structure: Chapters in the History of the American Industrial Enterprise* (Cambridge, Mass.: MIT Press, 1962).

16. See Richard F. Vancil, *Decentralization: Managerial Ambiguity by Design* (Homewood, Ill.: Dow Jones–Irwin, 1979).

17. As we argue, terminological confusion between "decentralization" and "divisionalization" is better understood when one takes a rhetorical stance and recognizes that there is ultimately no "correct" definition for each. Nevertheless, providing such definitions is precisely what David Solomons attempted to do in his classic study, *Divisional Performance: Measurement and Control.* He began his book by addressing the confusion:

> The terms "divisionalization" and "decentralization" are sometimes used as if they were interchangeable. They are, however, not synonyms, for the devolution of authority to make decisions, which is the essence of decentralization, is often carried to considerable lengths in businesses which are not divisionalized. Such businesses may have widely dispersed plants, sales offices and research facilities, each the responsibility of its own manager who may be given

wide latitude as to how his operation is to be conducted. Divisionalization, however, adds to decentralization the concept of "delegated profit responsibility." (David Solomons, *Divisional Performance: Measurement and Control* [Homewood, Ill.: Richard D. Irwin, 1965], 3).

For Solomons, decentralization is a matter of dispersed decision making, divisionalization a matter of profit responsibility. By his definition, a divisionalized firm could be centralized along important dimensions—although he hardly discusses this possibility and instead focuses on the decentralization of decisions that accompany divisionalization. Somewhat ironically, however, he later commits the same fallacy he warns against when he describes a situation wherein each unit—purchasing, training, labor relations, traffic, accounting, and so forth—is a profit center as an instance of "complete decentralization" (Ibid., 14–15). Alas, such are the traps into which the best of us fall when we set out to discover the true meaning of management terminology.

18. Vancil, for example, found that decentralization was common even "in relatively homogeneous businesses with sales of $100 million or less," a finding that challenged Chandler's thesis that strategies of diversification are the cause of decentralized structures (Vancil, *Decentralization: Managerial Ambiguity by Design,* 3).

19. This definition was perhaps more common at mid-century when such geographic dispersion was first becoming widely evident. See for example Paul Meadows, "Post-Industrialism," *Technology Review,* 49 (December 1946): 101–103, 120, 122.

20. See Chandler, *Strategy and Structure.* In describing decentralization as a philosophy of management, Chandler refers to a paper written by Donaldson Brown in 1927 when he was an executive at General Motors. See Donaldson Brown, "Decentralized Operations and Responsibilities with Coordinated Control," *Annual Convention Series,* vol. 57 (New York: American Management Association, 1927).

21. For an example of this view, witness Peter Drucker's stereotype of the "command-and-control organization of today, with its emphasis on decentralization." (Peter F. Drucker, "The Coming of the New Organization," *Harvard Business Review,* 66 [January–February 1988]: 53.)

22. Charles Handy, *The Age of Unreason* (Boston: Harvard Business School Press, 1989), 118.

23. Ibid.

24. Again, this rather polemical statement follows in the footsteps of "ordinary language" theorists who, following Wittgenstein, argue that it is *practice* that determines meaning and not vice versa. See for example the discussion (already cited) in Louis R. Pondy, "Leadership Is a Language Game," in Morgan W. McCall, Jr., and Michael M. Lombardo, eds., *Leadership: Where Else Can We Go?* (Durham, N.C.: Duke University Press, 1978).

25. Lewis Carroll, *Alice's Adventures in Wonderland and Through the Looking-Glass* (Oxford: Oxford University Press, 1971), 190.

26. Carroll writes: " 'The question is,' said Humpty Dumpty, 'which is to be master—that's all.' " (Ibid).

27. Alfred P. Sloan, *My Years with General Motors* (Garden City, N.Y.: Doubleday, 1963), 53.

28. Ibid., 57.

29. Ibid., 58.

30. Ibid.

31. Other example of such explicit cycles might be seen in alternations between product and market structures, between function and product structures, between geography and product structures, and between functional and geographic structures.

32. Stanley M. Davis and Paul R. Lawrence, *Matrix* (Reading, Mass.: Addison-Wesley, 1977), xi.

33. Ibid.

34. Ibid.

35. For this argument, see C. K. Prahalad and Yves Doz, *The Multinational Mission: Balancing Local Demands and Global Vision* (New York: Free Press, 1987).

36. Christopher A. Bartlett and Sumantra Ghoshal, *Managing Across Borders: The Transnational Solution* (Boston: Harvard Business School Press, 1989), 32.

37. Ibid., 57.

38. Ibid., 59.

39. Ibid., 57.

40. On this, see Christopher A. Bartlett and Sumantra Ghoshal, "Matrix Management: Not a Structure, A Frame of Mind," *Harvard Business Review,* 68 (July–August 1991): 138–145.

41. Davis and Lawrence, *Matrix,* 18.

42. Bartlett and Ghoshal, *Managing Across Borders,* 57.

43. In the language of speech act theory, one could say that structural design concepts often have the characteristics of a "performative utterance"—that is, they are not so much descriptions of the world as they are ways of *acting upon it* through language. See J. L. Austin, *How to Do Things with Words* (Cambridge, Mass.: Harvard University Press, 1962). Austin's highly readable account is especially interesting for his treatment of what makes certain performatives situationally ineffectual, an issue related to our earlier discussion of Humpty Dumpty and managerial legitimacy. The adventurous may also consult the more radical French philosopher of language Jacques Derrida, who comments on Austin's distinction by noting that the performative "produces or transforms a situation" (Jacques Derrida, "Signature, Event, Context," in *Margins of Philosophy,* tr., A. Bass [Chicago: University of Chicago Press, 1982], 321).

44. James D. Berkley and Nitin Nohria, "Allen-Bradley's ICCG: Repositioning for the '90s," Case Study N9-491-066. Boston: Harvard Business School, 1990.

45. The virtues of teams have been extolled by none other than *Fortune* reporter Brian Dumaine, author of "The Bureaucracy Busters" article which began Chapter 2. In a recent *Fortune* cover story, he writes: "If superteams are working right, *mirabile dictu,* they manage themselves. No boss required. A superteam arranges schedules, sets profit targets, and—gulp—may even know everyone's salary. It has a say in hiring and firing team members as well as managers. It orders materials and equipment. It strokes customers, improves

quality, and, in some cases, devises strategy" (Brian Dumaine, "Who Needs a Boss?," *Fortune* [May 7, 1990]: 52). Of course, cross-functional activity is not really a new idea—it has figured prominently in the writings of such earlier management thinkers as Mary Parker Follett. See for example Follett's 1926 description of a factory with a system of "interlocked committees," a development she pointed to as "perhaps the most important trend in business organization" (Mary Parker Follett, "The Meaning of Responsibility in Business Management," in *Dynamic Administration* [London: Sir Isaac Pitman and Sons, 1941], 157.)

46. Chandler, *Strategy and Structure,* 161.

47. All information on Appex is from Julie Gladstone and Nitin Nohria, "Appex Corporation," Case Study 9-491-082. Boston: Harvard Business School, 1991.

48. We do not know which Japanese companies have used such a structure. In fact, when we have taught this case at the Harvard Business School we have had Japanese students remark that they were unaware of such a structure in Japanese companies. Perhaps Ghosh was engaging in the always-effective rhetorical technique of invoking Japanese management practices to legitimize an innovation.

49. The use of the term *division* for the Operations cost center illustrates the flexibility managers have in the terms they use to describe a structure. In other companies, the term *division* is reserved for units that are profit centers, i.e., which both earn revenues from external sales (versus internal transfers) and incur costs.

50. See John J. Gabarro, *The Dynamics of Taking Charge* (Boston: Harvard Business School Press, 1987).

51. A stimulating discussion of the "Ship of Theseus" and other such identity conundrums can be found in Eli Hirsch, *The Concept of Identity* (Oxford: Oxford University Press, 1981), esp. 68–71.

CHAPTER 7: TOWARD ROBUST PERFORMANCE MEASUREMENT

1. The classic example of this in the social sciences is to be found in the famed Hawthorne Experiments conducted at the Western Electric Company in the 1920s and 1930s. These experiments, which laid the groundwork for the emerging human relations school of management, showed that workers participating in experiments were acutely aware of being observed—and that their awareness of the situation had an enormous impact upon their productivity. See the discussion in George C. Homans, *Fatigue of Workers* (New York: Reinhold, 1941), 56–65.

2. For arguments about the problems with emphasizing accrual accounting measures see Michael T. Jacobs, *Short-Term America: The Causes and Cures of Our Business Myopia* (Boston: Harvard Business School Press, 1991); H. Thomas Johnson and Robert S. Kaplan, *Relevance Lost: The Rise and Fall of Management*

Accounting (Boston: Harvard Business School Press, 1987); Dana Wechsler Linden, "Lies of the Bottom Line," *Forbes* (November 12, 1990): 106–112; Donald A. Curtis, "The Modern American Accounting System: Does It Really Measure Corporate Performance?," *FE: The Magazine for Financial Executives*, 1, no. 1 (1985): 58–62; and Donald A. Curtis, *Management Rediscovered: How Companies Can Escape the Numbers* (Homewood, Ill.: Dow Jones–Irwin, 1990). For arguments in favor of focusing on cash as the key performance measure see Yuji Ijiri, "Cash-Flow Accounting and Its Structure," *Journal of Accounting, Auditing, and Finance*, 1, no. 4 (1978): 331–348; and Yuji Ijiri, "Recovery Rate and Cash Flow Accounting," *Financial Executive*, 48 (March 1980): 54–60. For a critique of cash flow as a performance measure see D. A. Egginton, "In Defence of Profit Measurement: Some Limitations of Cash Flow and Value Added as Performance Measures for External Reporting," *Accounting and Business Research*, 14, no. 54 (Spring 1984): 99–111.

3. Data on Sealed Air Corporation are taken from Karen Hopper Wruck, "Sealed Air Corporation's Leveraged Recapitalization," Case Study 9-391-067. Boston: Harvard Business School, rev. 1991; and from a presentation made by the company's CFO, William Hickey, at the Harvard Business School on December 12, 1991.

4. Robert N. Anthony and James S. Reece, *Accounting Principles*, 6th ed. (Homewood, Ill.: Richard D. Irwin, 1989), 13–14.

5. Ibid.

6. Ibid.

7. James G. March, "Ambiguity and Accounting: The Elusive Link between Information and Decision Making," *Accounting, Organizations, and Society*, 12, no. 2 (1987): 165.

8. See Richard F. Vancil, *Decentralization: Managerial Ambiguity by Design* (Homewood, Ill.: Dow Jones-Irwin, 1978); Robert S. Kaplan, *Advanced Management Accounting* (Englewood Cliffs, N.J.: Prentice-Hall, 1982); Robert G. Eccles, *The Transfer Pricing Problem: A Theory for Practice* (Lexington, Mass.: Lexington Books, 1985); and Robert G. Eccles and Dwight B. Crane, *Doing Deals: Investment Banks at Work* (Boston: Harvard Business School Press, 1988).

9. See Richard F. Vancil, "What Kind of Management Control Do You Need?," *Harvard Business Review*, 51 (March–April 1973): 75–86. Vancil argued that strategy and structure must be taken into consideration when determining which performance measure is best and thus what kind of responsibility center an organizational unit should be.

10. Peter F. Drucker, "The Coming of the New Organization," *Harvard Business Review*, 66 (January–February 1988): 50 (emphasis ours).

11. For some traditional but thoughtful discussions of these issues see Vancil, *Decentralization: Managerial Ambiguity by Design;* and Kenneth A. Merchant, *Rewarding Results: Motivating Profit Center Managers* (Boston: Harvard Business School Press, 1989).

12. See David A. Garvin, "How the Baldrige Award Really Works," *Harvard Business Review*, 6 (November–December 1991): 80–95.

13. Brian M. Cook, "In Search of Six Sigma: 99.9997% Defect Free," *Industry Week* (October 1, 1990): 60–65.

14. Lloyd Dobyns and Clare Crawford-Mason, *Quality or Else: The Revolution in World Business* (Boston: Houghton Mifflin, 1991), 138.

15. T. J. Rodgers, "No Excuses Management," *Harvard Business Review,* 68 (July–August 1990): 85.

16. Ibid. See also Richard Brandt, "The Bad Boy of Silicon Valley: Meet T. J. Rodgers, CEO of Cypress Semiconductor," *Business Week* (December 9, 1991): 64–70.

17. See Nitin Nohria and Cynthia Cook, "Hill, Holliday, Connors, Cosmopulos, Inc. Advertising (A)," Case Study 9-491-016. Boston: Harvard Business School, rev. 1991.

18. Robert G. Eccles, "The Performance Measurement Manifesto," *Harvard Business Review,* 69 (January–February 1991): 131.

19. For some examples of arguments for nonfinancial measures see Robert Bittlestone, "Executive Information and Strategic Control," text of address on October 1, 1990, at London Conference, *Executive Information for the Finance Function* (London: Metapraxis, 1990); Robert Malchione, "Making Performance Measurements Perform," *Perspective* (Boston: The Boston Consulting Group, 1991); "Performance Measurement: Impact on Competitive Performance," *Outlook, Industrial Competitiveness,* 6, no. 4 (Boston: Harbor Research, no date); Robert S. Kaplan and David P. Norton, "The Balanced Scorecard—Measures That Drive Performance," *Harvard Business Review,* 70 (January–February 1992): 71–79; and Ray Stata, "Organizational Learning—The Key to Management Innovation," *Sloan Management Review,* 30, no. 3 (Spring 1989): 63–74.

20. Johnson and Kaplan, *Relevance Lost: The Rise and Fall of Management Accounting,* 259.

21. Ibid., 125. We should emphasize that even today—despite the emphasis often placed by senior management on accounting-based performance measures—managers continue to supplement accounting-based measures with other types of information in making decisions. See for example Sharon M. McKinnon and William J. Bruns, Jr., *The Information Mosaic* (Boston: Harvard Business School Press, 1992).

22. See Ronald G. Greenwood, *Managerial Decentralization* (Lexington, Mass.: Lexington Books, 1974).

23. S. A. Spencer, "The Dark at the Top of the Stairs: What Higher Management Needs from Information Systems," *Management Review,* 51 (July 1962): 4–12. Spencer listed the number of calls made, the speed of service, the on-time delivery performance record, the level of quality, the frequency and nature of complaints, share of market position, productivity, absenteeism, waste, remakes, and parts turnover as examples of measures that should be used to supplement financial ones.

24. See McKinnon and Bruns, *The Information Mosaic.*

25. Marshall W. Meyer, "The Performance Paradox" (Wharton School Department of Management Working Paper, undated).

26. See William J. Bruns, Jr., and F. Warren McFarlan, "Information Technology Puts Power in Control Systems," *Harvard Business Review,* 65 (September–October 1987): 89–94.

27. Data on Crompton Greaves are taken from Nitin Nohria and Julie A.

Gladstone, "Crompton Greaves Ltd.," Case Study 9-491-074. Boston: Harvard Business School, 1990.

28. For a good discussion of many of the issues involved in linking rewards to performance see Merchant, *Rewarding Results: Motivating Profit Center Managers.*

29. For a discussion of some of the pitfalls in managing by the numbers see Thomas A. Stewart, "Why Budgets Are Bad for Business," *Fortune* (June 4, 1990): 179–190. A useful analysis of why budgeting is so problematic in most companies can also be found in M. Edgar Barrett and LeRoy B. Fraser III, "Conflicting Roles in Budgeting in Operations," *Harvard Business Review,* 55 (July–August 1977): 137–146. The authors show the conflicts that emerge when a budget is simultaneously used for planning, evaluation, and motivational purposes.

CHAPTER 8: MAKING THE KNOWLEDGE SYSTEM WORK

1. Joseph L. Badaracco, Jr., *The Knowledge Link: How Firms Compete Through Strategic Alliances* (Boston: Harvard Business School Press, 1991), 27. Badaracco's book presents an interesting argument about the causes and extent of the growth of knowledge in contemporary society. See also Chapter 3, "The Dimensions of Knowledge and Technology," in Daniel Bell, *The Coming of Post-Industrial Society* (New York: Basic Books, 1973), 165–266.

2. Robert D. Calkins, "Objectives of Business Education," *Harvard Business Review,* 25 (Autumn 1946): 47.

3. In fact, it is tempting to see the steady accumulation of managerial knowledge as one of the central features of modern society. Governments, armies, schools, and other institutions have all depended on this constant accumulation of managerial technique as a means of consolidating power and building social legitimacy. The question of exactly how institutions have developed "power/knowledge" was central to the work of the late French historian Michel Foucault. See for example his *Discipline and Punish: The Birth of the Prison* (New York: Vintage Books, 1979) and *Power/Knowledge: Selected Interviews and Other Writings* (New York: Pantheon Books, 1980).

4. Chris Argyris, Robert Putnam, and Diana McLain Smith, *Action Science: Concepts, Methods, and Skills for Research and Intervention* (San Francisco: Jossey-Bass, 1985), 36.

5. Ibid., 80–81. In his theory of action science, Argyris distinguishes between what he calls "espoused theory"—what people say their theory of action is—and "theory-in-use," which is the theory actually implicit in the person's actions.

6. For Argyris and others, "action science"—by this and other names such as "intervention theory"—is about generating useful knowledge about organizations through making "interventions" on them in the form of efforts to create "organizational change."

7. An interesting case where theory clearly preceded practice has been documented in Alfred D. Chandler, Jr., *Strategy and Structure: Chapters in the History*

of the American Industrial Enterprise (Cambridge, Mass.: MIT Press, 1962). As we touched on in Chapter 6, Chandler shows how General Motors, Du Pont, Standard Oil of New Jersey, and Sears independently yet almost simultaneously groped their way to the invention of the multidivisional form based on separate profit centers out of the large functional structures which predominated in the 1910s and 1920s. Just as interestingly, several decades went by before this new structure received any kind of formal academic exposition.

8. The exact criteria that determine good formal research are open to loud debate, and have been for some time. For two varied approaches to this problem in the management literature, see W. Graham Astley and Raymond F. Zammuto, "Organization Science, Managers, and Language Games," forthcoming in *Organization Studies*; and Samuel B. Bacharach, "Organizational Theories: Some Criteria for Evaluation," *Academy of Management Review*, 14 (1989): 496–515. For more directly philosophical approaches to the issue (which have tended lately to stress the lack of any firm criteria for defining "good science"), see Thomas Kuhn, *The Structure of Scientific Revolutions*, 2d. ed. (Chicago: University of Chicago Press, 1970); and, for an avowedly anarchist approach, Paul K. Feyerabend, *Against Method* (New York: Verso, 1988).

9. See John A. Byrne, "Is Research in the Ivory Tower 'Fuzzy, Irrelevant, Pretentious'?," *Business Week* (October 19, 1990): 62–66.

10. Lyman W. Porter and Lawrence E. McKibbin, *Management Education and Development: Drift or Thrust into the 21st Century?* (New York: McGraw-Hill, 1988), 170.

11. Ibid., 180. For other discussions of the limited utility of formal research to managers, see John S. Fielden and Jean D. Gibbons, "Merit Myopia and Business School Faculty Publications," *Business Horizons* (March–April 1991): 8–12; Alan Deutschman, "The Trouble with MBAs," *Fortune* (July 29, 1991): 67–79; Benjamin M. Oviatt and Warren D. Miller, "Irrelevance, Intransigence, and Business Professors," *The Academy of Management Executive*, 3 (1989): 304–312; Janice M. Beyer and Harrison M. Trice, "The Utilization Process: A Conceptual Framework and Synthesis of Empirical Findings," *Administrative Science Quarterly*, 27 (1982): 591–622; Paul Shrivastava and Ian I. Mitroff, "Enhancing Organizational Research Utilization: The Role of Decision Makers' Assumptions," *Academy of Management Review*, 9 (1984): 18–26; and Kenneth W. Thomas and Walter G. Tymon, Jr., "Necessary Properties of Relevant Research: Lessons from Recent Criticisms of the Organizational Sciences," *Academy of Management Review*, 7 (1982): 345–352.

12. The Ford Foundation report was written by Robert Aaron Gordon and James Edwin Howell, *Higher Education for Business* (New York: Columbia University Press, 1959); the Carnegie report by Frank C. Pierson et al., *The Education of American Businessmen: A Study of University-College Programs in Business Administration* (New York: McGraw-Hill, 1959). As the reader might well expect, the reports emphasized external forces as creating pressures for change. Gordon and Howell for instance note: "The need for competent, imaginative, and responsible business leadership is greater than ever before; the need becomes more urgent as business grows ever more complex and as the environment with

which it has to cope continues to change at an accelerating tempo" (Gordon and Howell, *Higher Education for Business,* 4).

13. Pierson et al., *The Education of American Businessmen,* 313.

14. Ibid., 353.

15. Commission on Admission to Graduate Management Education, *Leadership for a Changing World: The Future Role of Graduate Management Education* (Los Angeles: Graduate Management Admission Council, 1990), 20. This report similarly noted: "The leadership of management schools will be tested as never before by the massive changes taking place in the environment today" (Ibid., 2). The three changes cited by the report as most important are technological change, globalization, and demographic diversity.

16. S.A.M. Committee on Relations with Colleges and Universities, Society for the Advancement of Management, *Management Education: A Report on the Survey Among Business and Educational Leaders* (New York: Society for the Advancement of Management, 1948), 3. Interestingly enough, educators did not voice a similar concern.

17. Seen through Feyerabend's account of what makes for good science, the sloppy and anarchistic research methodology of managers is actually much closer to the way real scientific progress happens than we might think. See *Against Method,* where the author argues that "theoretical anarchism is more humanitarian and more likely to encourage progress than its law-and-order alternatives," adding later that most accounts of the scientific method give "an inadequate account of the past development of science and are liable to hinder science in the future" (Feyerabend, *Against Method,* 9, 163–164).

18. Eileen C. Shapiro, *How Corporate Truths Become Competitive Traps* (New York: John Wiley, 1991), xi.

19. Obviously these categories are not mutually exclusive. Stories imply models, diagrams imply frameworks, and so forth. But knowledge is often captured in a particular form of rhetoric that embodies its other elements.

20. Book writing by CEOs—often accomplished with the help of ghost writers—has become a popular pastime. The most successful has been Lee Iacocca, whose book with William Novak, *Iacocca: An Autobiography* (New York: Bantam Books. 1984) was the number one best-seller in 1984 and 1985 with 1,055,000 and 1,520,000 copies, respectively.

21. Christopher Knowlton, "The Buying Binge in Business Books," *Fortune* (February 13, 1989): 101–103.

22. See David F. Hawkins, "Empire Glass Company (A)," Case Study 109-043. Boston: Harvard Business School, 1964.

23. Thomas J. Peters and Robert H. Waterman, Jr., *In Search of Excellence* (New York: Harper & Row, 1982), 3–26.

24. Richard T. Pascale, *Managing on the Edge: How the Smartest Companies Use Conflict to Stay Ahead* (New York: Simon & Schuster, 1990), 16–17.

25. Michelle Clayman, "In Search of Excellence: The Investor's Viewpoint," *Financial Analysts Journal* (May–June 1987): 56.

26. Ibid., 54.

27. Ibid., 59, 62.

28. See Peters and Waterman, *In Search of Excellence,* 156, 292.

29. Leslie Brokaw, "Books That Transform Companies," *INC* (July 1991): 34 (emphasis in original).

30. The problem this natural linguistic ambiguity creates for doing scientific research is enormous. Without a clear and common definition of a term such as *empowerment,* it is impossible to determine what contributes to empowerment and what detracts from it, or even to measure whether it has increased or decreased over time. As we suggested in Chapter 6, the same difficulty exists with concepts like "decentralization," "formality of structure," and "degree of authority." Studies by Richard F. Vancil (see *Decentralization: Managerial Ambiguity by Design* [Homewood, Ill.: Dow-Jones-Irwin, 1978]) and the Aston Group, for example, did not have much success in establishing clear relationships about what variables determine particular structural characteristics. (For reviews of the work of the Aston Group, see Sergio E. Mindlin and Howard E. Aldrich, "Interorganizational Dependence: A Review of the Concept and a Reexamination of the Findings of the Aston Group," *Administrative Science Quarterly,* 20 [September 1975]: 382–392; and Howard E. Aldrich, "Technology and Organizational Structure: A Reexamination of the Findings of the Aston Group," *Administrative Science Quarterly,* 17 [March 1972]: 26–43.) Establishing such relationships in the social sciences is notoriously difficult. Consider, for example, the enormous efforts that have gone into determining exactly what I.Q. tests measure and the controversies that still rage about their potential racial and ethnic biases.

In organizations, a related problem with conducting such formal research is that managers always have their own values, opinions, and agendas; they bring their own "baggage" to the research situation and will often respond accordingly. Consider a hypothetical investigation into the prevalence of empowerment in organizations. Without really knowing what a researcher means by empowerment, a manager may tailor her answers according to how much she is concerned about confidentiality—especially if the CEO has been talking about how empowered the middle managers are. She may be reluctant to say she doesn't feel empowered for fear of being labeled as someone who doesn't have what it takes to be empowered. Or she may respond negatively in the hopes of sending a message to top management about the inadequacy of their commitment to the cause.

31. In an interesting form of institutional self-examination using a tool developed for managers, Oviatt and Miller use Michael Porter's five-forces framework to explain why business professors resist attempts to make their research more pertinent to managers. See Oviatt and Miller, "Irrelevance, Intransigence, and Business Professors," 304.

CHAPTER 9: PUTTING CHANGE IN PERSPECTIVE

1. On this, see for example James G. March, "Footnotes to Organizational Change," *Administrative Science Quarterly,* 26 (1981): 563: "Organizations are continually changing, routinely, easily and responsively." March notes that studies

on implementing change indicate "not that organizations are rigid and inflexible," but instead, "that they are impressively imaginative."

2. For a good discussion of the ideology of change in Western intellectual history, see Roland N. Stromberg, *European Intellectual History Since 1789,* 5th ed. (Englewood Cliffs, N.J.: Prentice-Hall, 1990): esp. 139–140.

3. For an explanation of this perspective and its application to organizations, see Connie J.G. Gersick, "Revolutionary Change Theories: A Multilevel Exploration of the Punctuated Equilibrium Paradigm," *Academy of Management Review,* 16 (1991): 10–36. Along similar lines, Michael Tushman and Elaine Romanelli describe organizations as passing through reorientations, which they describe as "relatively short periods of discontinuous change where strategies, power, structure, and systems are fundamentally transformed towards a new basis of alignment" (Michael L. Tushman and Elaine Romanelli, "Organizational Evolution: A Metamorphosis Model of Convergence and Reorientation," in L. L. Cummings and Barry M. Staw, eds., *Research in Organizational Behavior,* vol. 7 [Greenwich, Conn.: JAI Press, 1985], 173). See also Michael L. Tushman, William H. Newman, and Elaine Romanelli, "Convergence and Upheaval: Managing the Unsteady Pace of Organizational Evolution," *California Management Review* (Fall 1986): 29–44; and Larry E. Greiner, "Evolution and Revolution As Organizations Grow," *Harvard Business Review,* 50 (July–August 1972): 37–46.

As Gersick discusses, punctuated equilibrium models currently enjoy wide popularity in a number of disciplines. For a related approach to biology, see Stephen Jay Gould, *The Panda's Thumb* (New York: W. W. Norton, 1980); to the scientific method, see Thomas Kuhn, *The Structure of Scientific Revolutions,* 2d ed. (Chicago: University of Chicago Press, 1970); and to the world in general in a "grand theory," Ilya Prigogine and Isabelle Stengers, *Order Out of Chaos: Man's New Dialogue with Nature* (New York: Bantam Books, 1984).

4. The communications theorist James Beniger puts this attitude in some perspective, noting that since the 1950s we have constantly been told that "one or the other social transformation is now in progress" (James R. Beniger, *The Control Revolution: Technological and Economic Origins of the Information Society* [Cambridge, Mass.: Harvard University Press, 1986], 2).

5. See Peter F. Drucker, "The Coming of the New Organization," *Harvard Business Review,* 66 (January–February 1988): 45–53.

6. See Shoshana Zuboff, *In the Age of the Smart Machine: The Future of Work and Power* (New York: Basic Books, 1988).

7. Charles Handy, *The Age of Unreason* (Boston: Harvard Business School Press, 1990), 17.

8. As Beniger rightly observes, important changes in society "do not result from single discrete events, despite the best efforts of later historians (or contemporary observers) to associate the changes with such events" (Beniger, *The Control Revolution,* 2). Our position on historical change has also been informed by Michel Foucault. See Michel Foucault, *The Archeology of Knowledge,* tr., A. M. Sheridan Smith (New York: Pantheon Books, 1972).

9. See for example the preface in Zuboff, *In the Age of the Smart Machine,* xi–xv.

10. Like politics, the word *power* too often gets a bad rap. Jeffrey Pfeffer attempts to right this by defining power "as the potential ability to influence behavior, to change the course of events, to overcome resistance, and to get people to do things that they would not otherwise do" (Jeffrey Pfeffer, *Managing with Power: Politics and Influence in Organizations* [Boston: Harvard Business School Press, 1992], 30). Pfeffer's book shows how the ability to use and understand power is crucial to effective management.

11. In their classic book *A Behavioral Theory of the Firm,* Richard A. Cyert and James D. March suggested: "Let us view the organization as a coalition. It is a coalition of individuals, some of them organized into sub-coalitions" (Richard A. Cyert and James D. March, *A Behavioral Theory of the Firm* [Englewood Cliffs, N.J.: Prentice-Hall, 1963], 27). For more on how such coalitions work, see also Charles Perrow, *Complex Organizations: A Critical Essay* (Glenview, Ill.: Scott, Foresman, 1972); and Pfeffer, *Managing with Power.*

12. Handy, *The Age of Unreason,* 3.

13. Eric M. Leifer and Harrison C. White, "Wheeling and Annealing: Federal and Multidivisional Control," Chapter 13 in James F. Short, ed., *The Social Fabric: Dimensions and Issues* (Beverly Hills: Sage Publications, 1986): 223–240.

14. Jane Linder and Robert G. Eccles, "Hercules Incorporated: Anatomy of a Vision," Case Study 9-186-305. Boston: Harvard Business School, 1985.

15. March, "Footnotes to Organizational Change," 563.

16. Robert H. Schaffer and Harvey A. Thomson, "Successful Change Programs Begin with Results," *Harvard Business Review,* 70 (January–February 1992): 80.

17. Ibid., 82.

18. Michael Beer, Russell A. Eisenstat, and Bert Spector, *The Critical Path to Corporate Renewal* (Boston: Harvard Business School Press, 1990), 39.

19. Ibid., 23.

20. Ibid., 39–40.

21. Data for this example are taken from a series of Harvard Business School cases prepared by Todd Jick. See Todd Jick, "Bob Galvin and Motorola, Inc. (A)," Case Study 9-487-062, rev. March 1989; "Bob Galvin and Motorola, Inc. (B)," Case Study 9-487-063, 1987; and "Bob Galvin and Motorola, Inc. (C)," Case Study 9-487-064, 1987. All from Boston: Harvard Business School.

22. This assessment appears in Jick's own teaching note for the Motorola case series: "What makes the case particularly provocative is that Galvin's actions are so unlike the textbook description of how to lead change" (Todd Jick, "Bob Galvin and Motorola, Inc. (A) (B) (C)," Teaching Note 5-491-100. [Boston: Harvard Business School]).

23. Jick, "Bob Galvin and Motorola, Inc. (A)," 8.

24. The consultant was Robert Schaffer, co-author of the *Harvard Business Review* article cited in Note 16 above.

25. Jick, "Bob Galvin and Motorola, Inc. (B)," 2.

26. Jick, "Bob Galvin and Motorola, Inc. (C)," 1.

27. Leifer and White, "Wheeling and Annealing," 238.

28. Ibid.

29. Ibid., 239.

30. Ibid., 240.

31. Leifer and White observe: "Knowing where to encourage system 'crystallization' may thus be the paramount skill of the very top" (Ibid., 239).

32. Jick, "Bob Galvin and Motorola (A)," 9.

33. For the argument that managers should emphasize measurable short-term performance goals in their change program methodologies (an approach that we ourselves resist), see Schaffer and Thomson, "Successful Change Programs Begin with Results."

BIBLIOGRAPHY

I. HUMANITIES

Arendt, Hannah. *The Human Condition.* Chicago: University of Chicago Press, 1958.

Aristotle. *On Rhetoric.* Tr. and ed., George Kennedy. New York: Oxford University Press, 1991.

Austin, J. L. *How to Do Things with Words.* Cambridge, Mass.: Harvard University Press, 1962.

Barker, Francis. *The Tremulous Private Body: Essays in Subjection.* London: Methuen, 1984.

Baumeister, Roy F. *Identity: Cultural Change and the Struggle for Self.* New York: Oxford University Press, 1986.

Bell, Daniel. *The Cultural Contradictions of Capitalism.* London: Heinemann, 1976.

Bellah, Robert et al. *Habits of the Heart: Individualism and Commitment in American Life.* Berkeley: University of California Press, 1985.

Booth, Wayne. *The Rhetoric of Fiction.* Chicago: University of Chicago Press, 1961.

———. "The Revival of Rhetoric." In Martin Steinmann, ed., *New Rhetorics.* New York: Scribner's. 1967.

Carroll, Lewis. *Alice's Adventures in Wonderland and Through the Looking-Glass.* Oxford: Oxford University Press, 1971.

Cavell, Stanley. *Must We Mean What We Say?* New York: Cambridge University Press, 1976.

de Certeau, Michel. *The Practice of Everyday Life.* Tr., Steven Rendall. Berkeley: University of California Press, 1984.

Derrida, Jacques. "Signature, Event, Context." In *Margins of Philosophy,* A. Bass, tr. Chicago: University of Chicago Press, 1982.

Dewey, John. *The Essential Writings.* New York: Harper & Row, 1977.

D'Souza, Dinesh. *Illiberal Education: The Politics of Race and Sex on Campus.* New York: Free Press, 1991.

Ehninger, Douglas. "On Systems of Rhetoric." *Philosophy and Rhetoric,* 1 (1968): 131–144.

Feyerabend, Paul K. *Against Method*. New York: Verso, 1988.

Fish, Stanley. "Rhetoric." In *Doing What Comes Naturally: Change, Rhetoric, and the Practice of Theory in Literary and Legal Studies*. Durham, N.C.: Duke University Press, 1989.

Foucault, Michel. *The Archeology of Knowledge*. Tr., A.M. Sheridan Smith. New York: Pantheon Books, 1972.

———. *Discipline and Punish: The Birth of the Prison*. Ed. and tr., Colin Gordon. New York: Vintage Books, 1979.

———. *Power/Knowledge: Selected Interviews and Other Writings*. New York: Pantheon Books, 1980.

Friedman, Lawrence. *The Republic of Choice: Law, Authority, and Culture*. Cambridge, Mass.: Harvard University Press, 1990.

Gross, Alan G. *The Rhetoric of Science*. Cambridge, Mass.: Harvard University Press, 1990.

Harvey, David. *The Condition of Post-Modernity*. Cambridge, Mass.: Basil Blackwell, 1989.

Heidegger, Martin. *Being and Time*. Trs., John Macquarrie and Edward Robinson. New York: Harper & Row, 1962.

Hirsch, Eli. *The Concept of Identity*. Oxford: Oxford University Press, 1981.

James, William. *Pragmatism*. Indianapolis, Ind.: Hackett Publishing, 1981.

Kellner, Douglas. "Popular Culture and the Construction of Postmodern Identities." In Scott Lash and Jonathan Friedman, eds., *Modernity and Identity*. Cambridge, Mass.: Basil Blackwell, 1992: 141–177.

Kennedy, George A. "Prooemion." In *Aristotle: On Rhetoric*. New York: Oxford University Press, 1991.

Lasch, Christopher. *The Culture of Narcissism*. New York: W. W. Norton, 1979.

Lévi-Strauss, Claude. *The Savage Mind*. Chicago: University of Chicago Press, 1966.

Lyotard, Jean-Francois. *The Post-Modern Condition: A Report on Knowledge*. Trs., Geoff Bennington and Brian Massumi. Minneapolis: University of Minnesota Press, 1984.

Marcuse, Herbert. *One Dimensional Man*. Boston: Beacon Press, 1964.

Marx, Karl. "The Communist Manifesto." In Robert C. Tucker, ed., *The Marx-Engels Reader*. New York: W. W. Norton, 1972.

McCloskey, Donald N. *The Rhetoric of Economics*. Milwaukee: University of Wisconsin Press, 1985.

Merelman, Richard M. *Making Something of Ourselves: On Culture and Politics in the United States*. Berkeley: University of California Press, 1984.

Perelman, Chaim and L. Olbrechts-Tyteca. *The New Rhetoric: A Treatise on Argumentation.* Trs., John Wilkinson and Purcell Weaver. Notre Dame, Ind.: University of Notre Dame Press, 1958, 1971.

Plato. *Plato: The Collected Dialogues,* Edith Hamilton and Huntington Cairns, eds. Princeton, N.J.: Princeton University Press, 1961.

Polanyi, Michael. *Knowing and Being: Essays by Michael Polanyi,* Marjorie Green, ed. Chicago: University of Chicago Press, 1969.

Putnam, Hilary. *The Many Faces of Realism.* LaSalle, Ill.: Open Court, 1987.

Ricoeur, Paul. "Imagination in Discourse and in Action." In *From Text to Action.* Trs., Kathleen Blamey and John B. Thompson. Evanston, Ill.: Northwestern University Press, 1991: 176–187.

Rorty, Richard. *The Linguistic Turn.* Chicago: University of Chicago Press, 1967.

————. *Philosophy and the Mirror of Nature.* Princeton, N.J.: Princeton University Press, 1979.

Searle, John. *Speech Acts: An Essay in the Philosophy of Language.* Cambridge, England: Cambridge University Press, 1969.

Stromberg, Roland N. *European Intellectual History Since 1789,* 5th ed. Englewood Cliffs, N.J.: Prentice-Hall, 1990.

Sun-Tzu. (6th century B.C.) *The Art of War.* Tr., Thomas Cleary. Boston: Shambhala, 1988.

Toffler, Alvin. *Future Shock.* New York: Random House, 1970.

Waldman, Steven. "The Tyranny of Choice." *The New Republic* (January 27, 1992): 22–25.

Weber, Max. *The Protestant Ethic and the Spirit of Capitalism.* Tr., Talcott Parsons. New York: Charles Scribner's Sons, 1958.

Wittgenstein, Ludwig. *Philosophical Investigations.* Tr., G. E. M. Anscombe. Oxford: Basil Blackwell, 1974.

Wölfflin, Heinrich. *Principles of Art History: The Problem of the Development of Style in Later Art.* Tr., M.D. Hottinger. New York: Dover, 1932.

II. SOCIAL, COGNITIVE, AND PHYSICAL SCIENCES

Agre, Philip. *The Dynamic Structure of Everyday Life.* Ph.D. diss. in Computer Science, MIT, 1988. Cambridge University Press (forthcoming).

Arrow, Kenneth. *The Limits of Organization.* New York: W. W. Norton, 1970.

Atkinson, John W. "Motivational Determinants of Risk-taking Behavior." *Psychological Review,* 64 (November 1957): 359–372.

Bell, Daniel. *The Coming of Post-Industrial Society*. New York: Basic Books, 1973.

Beniger, James R. *The Control Revolution: Technological and Economic Origins of the Information Society*. Cambridge, Mass.: Harvard University Press, 1986.

Brooks, Rodney A. "Planning Is Just a Way of Avoiding Figuring Out What to Do Next." MIT Artificial Intelligence Lab Working Paper 303, 1987.

Clark, B. R. *The Distinctive College: Antioch, Reed, Swarthmore*. Chicago: Aldine, 1970.

Davis, Murray S. "That's Classic! The Phenomenology and Rhetoric of Successful Social Science Theories." *Philosophy of Social Science*, 16 (1986): 285–301.

Erikson, Erik H. *Childhood and Society*, 2d ed. New York: W. W. Norton, 1965.

Festinger, Leon. "A Theory of Social Comparison Processes." *Human Relations*, 7 (1954): 117–140.

Freidson, Eliot. *Professional Powers: A Study of the Institutionalization of Formal Knowledge*. Chicago: University of Chicago Press, 1986.

Gergen, Kenneth J. *The Saturated Self: Dilemmas of Identity in Contemporary Life*. New York: Basic Books, 1991.

Giddens, Anthony. *Modernity and Self-Identity: Self and Society in the Late Modern Age*. Stanford, Calif.: Stanford University Press, 1991.

Gould, Stephen Jay. *The Panda's Thumb*. New York: W. W. Norton, 1980.

Johnston, William B. and Arnold H. Packer. *Workforce 2000: Work and Workers for the Twenty-first Century*. Indianapolis, Ind.: Hudson Institute, 1987.

Kuhn, Thomas. *The Structure of Scientific Revolutions*, 2d ed. Chicago: University of Chicago Press, 1970.

Lammers, Cornelis J. "Transience and Persistence of Ideal Types in Organization Theory." *Research in the Sociology of Organizations*, 6 (1988): 203–224.

Larson, Magali Sarfatti. *The Rise of Professionalism: A Sociological Analysis*. Berkeley: University of California Press, 1977.

Leifer, Eric. *Actors as Observers: A Theory of Skill in Social Relationships*. New York: Garland, 1991.

Leifer, Eric M. and Harrison C. White. "Wheeling and Annealing: Federal and Multidivisional Control." In James F. Short, ed., *The Social Fabric: Dimensions and Issues*. Beverly Hills: Sage Publications, 1986: 223–240.

Lippman, S. A. and Richard P. Rumelt. "Uncertain Imitability: An

Analysis of Inter-firm Differences in Efficiency Under Competition." *Bell Journal of Economics,* 13 (1982): 418–438.

Maes, Pattie, ed. *Designing Autonomous Agents: Theory and Practice from Biology to Engineering and Back.* Cambridge, Mass.: MIT Press, 1990.

McClelland, David C. "The Urge to Achieve." In Michael T. Matteson and John M. Ivancevich, eds., *Management and Organizational Behavior Classics.* Homewood, Ill.: BPI Irwin, 1989: 392–401. Reprinted from *THINK Magazine,* 32, no. 6 (November–December 1966): 19–23.

Meyer, John W. and Brian Rowan. "Institutional Organizations: Formal Structure as Myth and Ceremony." *American Journal of Sociology,* 83 (1977): 159–179.

Penrose, Edith T. *The Theory of the Growth of the Firm.* Oxford: Basil Blackwell, 1959.

Perrow, Charles. "A Framework for the Comparative Analysis of Organizations." *American Sociological Review,* 32, no. 2 (April 1967): 194–208.

———. *Complex Organizations: A Critical Essay.* Glenview, Ill.: Scott, Foresman, 1972.

———. *Organizational Analysis: A Sociological View.* London: Tavistock, 1974.

Piore, Michael J., and Charles E. Sabel. *The Second Industrial Divide: Possibilities for Prosperity.* New York: Basic Books, 1984.

Prigogine, Ilya and Isabelle Stengers. *Order Out of Chaos: Man's New Dialogue with Nature.* New York: Bantam Books, 1984.

Riesman, David. *The Lonely Crowd: A Study of the Changing American Character.* New Haven, Conn.: Yale University Press, 1950.

Schutz, Alfred. "Acting and Planning." In Helmut R. Wagner, ed., *On Phenomenology and Social Relations.* Chicago: University of Chicago Press, 1970.

Selznick, Philip. *Leadership in Administration: A Sociological Interpretation.* Berkeley: University of California Press, 1957, 1984.

Sen, Amartya. "Goals, Commitment, and Identity." *Journal of Law, Economics, and Organization,* 1 (Fall 1985): 341–355.

Silverman, David. *The Theory of Organizations: A Sociological Framework.* New York: Basic Books, 1971.

Simon, Herbert. "Organizations and Markets." *Journal of Economic Perspectives,* 5, no. 2 (Spring 1991): 34–38.

Sproule, J. Michael. "The New Managerial Rhetoric and the Old Criticism." *Quarterly Journal of Speech,* 74 (1988): 468–486.

Stinchcombe, Arthur L. "Bureaucratic and Craft Administration of Production: A Comparative Study." *Administrative Science Quarterly,* 4 (September 1959): 168–187.

Weber, Max. *Economy and Society: An Outline of Interpretive Sociology*, vol. 2. Berkeley: University of California Press, 1978.

White, Harrison. *Identity and Control: A Structural Theory of Social Action*. Princeton, N.J.: Princeton University Press, 1992.

Winograd, Terry and Fernando Flores. *Understanding Computers and Cognition*. Reading, Mass.: Addison-Wesley, 1986.

Woodward, Joan. *Industrial Organization: Theory and Practice*. Oxford: Oxford University Press, 1965.

Zuboff, Shoshana. *In the Age of the Smart Machine: The Future of Work and Power*. New York: Basic Books, 1988.

III. MANAGEMENT

Abell, Derek F. *Defining the Business: The Starting Point of Strategic Planning*. Englewood Cliffs, N.J.: Prentice-Hall, 1980.

Aldrich, Howard E. "Technology and Organizational Structure: A Reexamination of the Findings of the Aston Group." *Administrative Science Quarterly*, 17 (March 1972): 26–43.

Alvesson, Mats. "Organization: From Substance to Image?" *Organization Studies*, 11 (1990): 373–394.

Andrews, Kenneth R. *The Concept of Corporate Strategy*, 3d ed. Homewood, Ill.: Richard D. Irwin, 1987.

Ansoff, H. Igor. "The Firm of the Future." *Harvard Business Review*, 43 (September–October 1965): 162–167.

Anthony, Robert N. and James S. Reece. *Accounting Principles*, 6th ed. Homewood, Ill.: Richard D. Irwin, 1989.

Applegate, Lynda M., James I. Cash, Jr., and D. Quinn Mills. "Information Technology and Tomorrow's Manager." *Harvard Business Review*, 66 (November–December 1988): 130–131.

Argyris, Chris, Robert Putnam, and Diana McLain Smith. *Action Science: Concepts, Methods, and Skills for Research and Intervention*. San Francisco: Jossey-Bass, 1985.

Argyris, Chris and Donald Schön. *Organizational Learning: A Theory of Action Perspective*. Reading, Mass.: Addison-Wesley, 1978.

Astley, W. Graham. "Administrative Science as Socially Constructed Truth." *Administrative Science Quarterly*, 30 (1985): 497–513.

Astley, W. Graham and Raymond F. Zammuto. "Organization Science, Managers, and Language Games." *Organization Studies* (forthcoming).

Bacharach, Samuel B. "Organizational Theories: Some Criteria for Evaluation." *Academy of Management Review*, 14 (1989): 496–515.

HARVARD BUSINESS SCHOOL PRESS, BOSTON, MA 02163

Thank you for your interest in this book. We would like to know more about our readers.
Please take a moment to complete and return this card.

Book Title/Author _____

Purchased at _____

Comments: _____

☐ **Please send me a FREE Harvard Business School Press book catalog.**

I am interested in the following subject areas:

☐ Accounting/Control ☐ Marketing/Sales ☐ International Business
☐ Finance ☐ Human Resource Mgt. ☐ Business and the Public Sector
☐ Manufacturing/Operations Mgt. ☐ Information Technology ☐ Business History
☐ Services Management ☐ General Mgt./Business Policy ☐ Other:

☐ **I am interested in teaching materials for:** ☐ Academic classroom use ☐ Corporate training

☐ **Please send me *Harvard Business Review* subscription information.**

My Name _____

My Job Title/Industry _____

Company's Name _____

Street Address _____

City _____ State _____ Zip _____ Country _____

Telephone Number _____ FAX Number _____

This is my ☐ Home Address ☐ Business Address

For information on quantity discounts of ten or more books, please call Frank Tamoshunas at (617) 495-6198.

Harvard Business School Press
Boston, Massachusetts 02163

BUSINESS REPLY MAIL
FIRST CLASS MAIL   PERMIT NO. 2725   BOSTON, MA

POSTAGE WILL BE PAID BY ADDRESSEE:

Harvard Business School Press

230-Western

60 Harvard Way

Boston, MA 02163-9903

HBS

PRESS

Badaracco, Joseph L., Jr. *The Knowledge Link: How Firms Compete Through Strategic Alliances*. Boston: Harvard Business School Press, 1991.

Barley, Stephen and Gideon Kunda. "The Cognitive Cage: Cycles of Control in Managerial Thought." Cornell University Working Paper, 1990.

Barnard, Chester I. *The Functions of the Executive*. Cambridge, Mass.: Harvard University Press, 1938, 1968.

Barrett, M. Edgar and LeRoy B. Fraser III. "Conflicting Roles in Budgeting in Operations." *Harvard Business Review*, 55 (July–August 1977): 137–146.

Bartlett, Christopher A. and Sumantra Ghoshal. *Managing Across Borders: The Transnational Solution*. Boston: Harvard Business School Press, 1989.

———. "Matrix Management: Not a Structure, A Frame of Mind." *Harvard Business Review*, 68 (July–August 1991): 138–145.

Beer, Michael, Russell A. Eisenstat, and Bert Spector. *The Critical Path to Corporate Renewal*. Boston: Harvard Business School Press, 1990.

Bennis, Warren. *Why Leaders Can't Lead: The Unconscious Conspiracy Continues*. San Francisco: Jossey-Bass, 1989.

Beyer, Janice M. and Harrison M. Trice. "The Utilization Process: A Conceptual Framework and Synthesis of Empirical Findings." *Administrative Science Quarterly*, 27 (1982): 591–622.

Bhide, Amar. "Hustle as Strategy." *Harvard Business Review*, 64 (September–October 1986): 59–65.

Bittlestone, Robert. "Executive Information and Strategic Control." Address text from London Conference, *Executive Information for the Finance Function*. London: Metapraxis, 1990.

Blumberg, Stephen K. "Notes on the Art of Administration." *Midwest Review of Public Administration*, 14, no. 3 (September 1980): 191–199.

Bower, Joseph L. and Thomas M. Hout. "Fast Cycle Capability for Competitive Power." *Harvard Business Review*, 66 (November–December 1988): 110–118.

Brill, Peter and Marshall W. Meyer. "Organizational Empowerment and Organizational Identification." Unpublished manuscript, Wharton School, 1992.

Brown, Donaldson. "Decentralized Operations and Responsibilities with Coordinated Control." *Annual Convention Series*, vol. 57. New York: American Management Association, 1927.

Bruns, William J. and F. Warren McFarlan. "Information Technology Puts Power in Control Systems." *Harvard Business Review*, 65 (September–October 1987): 89–94.

Burgelman, Robert A. "Intra-Organizational Ecology of Strategy Making and Organizational Adaptation: Theory and Field Research." *Organization Science,* 2 (1991): 239–262.

Burns, Tom and G. M. Stalker. *The Management of Innovation.* London: Tavistock, 1961.

Buzzell, Robert D., Bradley T. Gale, and Ralph G. M. Sultan. "Market Share—A Key to Profitability." *Harvard Business Review,* 53 (January–February 1975): 97–106.

Calkins, Robert D. "Objectives of Business Education." *Harvard Business Review,* 25 (Autumn 1946): 46–57.

Chandler, Alfred D., Jr. *Strategy and Structure: Chapters in the History of the American Industrial Enterprise.* Cambridge, Mass.: MIT Press, 1962.

———. *The Visible Hand: The Managerial Revolution in American Business.* Cambridge, Mass.: Harvard University Press, 1977.

Collis, David J. "Organizational Capability as a Source of Profit." Harvard Business School Working Paper 91-046, 1991.

Commission on Admission to Graduate Management Education. *Leadership for a Changing World: The Future Role of Graduate Management Education.* Los Angeles: Graduate Management Admission Council, 1990.

Conger, Jay A. "Inspiring Others: The Language of Leadership." *The Academy of Management Executive,* 5 (1991): 31–45.

Cordiner, Ralph J. *New Frontiers for Professional Managers.* New York: McGraw-Hill, 1956.

Curtis, Donald A. "The Modern American Accounting System: Does It Really Measure Corporate Performance?" *FE: The Magazine for Financial Executives* 1, no. 1 (1985): 58–62.

———. *Management Rediscovered: How Companies Can Escape the Numbers.* Homewood, Ill.: Dow Jones–Irwin, 1990.

Cyert, Richard A. and James D. March. *A Behavioral Theory of the Firm.* Englewood Cliffs, N.J.: Prentice-Hall, 1963.

Daft, Richard L. and John C. Wiginton. "Language and Organization." *Academy of Management Review,* 4 (1979): 179–191.

Davenport, Thomas A. and James E. Short. "The New Industrial Engineering: Information Technology and Business Process Redesign." *Sloan Management Review,* 31, no. 4 (Summer 1990): 11–27.

Davis, Stanley M. *Future Perfect.* Reading, Mass.: Addison-Wesley, 1987.

Davis, Stan and Bill Davidson. *2020 Vision: Transform Your Business to Succeed in Tomorrow's Economy.* New York: Simon & Schuster, 1991.

Davis, Stanley M. and Paul R. Lawrence. *Matrix.* Reading, Mass.: Addison-Wesley, 1977.

Davis, T. R. V. and F. Luthans. "Managers in Action: A New Look at Their Behavior and Operating Modes." *Organizational Dynamics* (Summer 1980): 64–80.

Deal, Terrence E. and Anthony A. Kennedy. *Corporate Cultures: The Rites and Rituals of Corporate Life.* Reading, Mass.: Addison-Wesley, 1982.

Dobyns, Lloyd and Clare Crawford-Mason. *Quality or Else: The Revolution in World Business.* Boston: Houghton Mifflin, 1991.

Drucker, Peter F. *The Practice of Management.* New York: Harper & Row, 1954.

———. *Landmarks of Tomorrow.* New York: Harper, 1959.

———. "Long Range Planning: Challenge to Management Science." *Management Science,* 5 (1959): 238–239.

———. *The Age of Discontinuity: Guidelines to Our Changing Society.* New York: Harper & Row, 1968.

———. *People and Performance: The Best of Peter Drucker on Management.* London: Heinemann, 1977.

———. *Managing in Turbulent Times.* New York: Harper & Row, 1980.

———. "The Coming of the New Organization." *Harvard Business Review,* 66 (January–February 1988): 45–53.

Eccles, Robert G. *The Transfer Pricing Problem: A Theory for Practice.* Lexington, Mass.: Lexington Books, 1985.

———. "The Performance Measurement Manifesto." *Harvard Business Review,* 69 (January–February 1991): 131–137.

Eccles, Robert G. and Dwight B. Crane. *Doing Deals: Investment Banks at Work.* Boston: Harvard Business School Press, 1988.

Eccles, Robert G. and Nitin Nohria. "The Post-Structuralist Organization." Harvard Business School Working Paper, 1991.

Egginton, D. A. "In Defence of Profit Measurement: Some Limitations of Cash Flow and Value Added as Performance Measures for External Reporting." *Accounting and Business Research,* 14, no. 54 (Spring 1984): 99–111.

Ewaldz, Donald B. "How Integrated Should Your Company Be?" *The Journal of Business Strategy* (July–August 1991): 52–55.

Fayol, Henri. *General and Industrial Management.* New York: IEEE Press, 1916, 1984.

Feigenbaum, Armand. "Total Quality Control." *Harvard Business Review,* 34 (November–December 1956): 93–101.

Fielden, John S. and Jean D. Gibbons. "Merit Myopia and Business School Faculty Publications." *Business Horizons* (March–April 1991): 8–12.

Follett, Mary Parker. *Dynamic Administration: The Collected Papers of Mary Parker Follett,* Henry C. Metcalf and L. Urwick, eds. London: Sir Isaac Pitman and Sons, 1941.

Foster, Richard. *Innovation: The Attacker's Advantage*. New York: Summit, 1986.

Freeman, Frank H. "Books That Mean Business: The Management Best Sellers." *Academy of Management Review*, 10 (1984): 345–350.

Gabarro, John J. *The Dynamics of Taking Charge*. Boston: Harvard Business School Press, 1987.

Garvin, David A. "How the Baldrige Award Really Works." *Harvard Business Review*, 69 (November–December 1991): 80–95.

Gersick, Connie J. G. "Revolutionary Change Theories: A Multilevel Exploration of the Punctuated Equilibrium Paradigm." *Academy of Management Review*, 16 (1991): 10–36.

Ghemawat, Pankaj. "Resources and Strategy: An IO Perspective." Harvard Business School Working Paper, 1991.

———. *Commitment: The Dynamic of Strategy*. New York: Free Press, 1991.

Gordon, Robert Aaron and James Edwin Howell. *Higher Education for Business*. New York: Columbia University Press, 1959.

Gowler, Dan and Karen Legge. "The Meaning of Management and the Management of Meaning: A View from Social Anthropology." In Michael J. Earl, ed., *Perspectives on Management: A Multidisciplinary Analysis*. New York: Oxford University Press, 1983: 197–233.

Grant, Robert M. "The Resource-Based Theory of Competitive Advantage: Implications for Strategy Formulation." *California Management Review* (Spring 1991): 114–135.

Greenwood, Ronald G. *Managerial Decentralization*. Lexington, Mass.: Lexington Books, 1974.

Greiner, Larry E. "Evolution and Revolution As Organizations Grow." *Harvard Business Review*, 50 (July–August 1972): 37–46.

Gulick, L. H. "Notes on the Theory of Organization." In L. H. Gulick and L. F. Urwick, eds., *Papers on the Science of Administration*. New York: Columbia University Press, 1937: 1–46.

Hamel, Gary and C. K. Prahalad. "Strategic Intent." *Harvard Business Review*, 67 (May–June 1989): 63–76.

Hammer, Michael. "Reengineering Work: Don't Automate, Obliterate." *Harvard Business Review*, 66 (July–August 1990): 104–112.

Hamermesh, Richard G. *Making Strategy Work: How Senior Managers Produce Results*. New York: John Wiley, 1986.

Handy, Charles. *The Age of Unreason*. Boston: Harvard Business School Press, 1990.

Hannaway, Jane. *Managers Managing: The Workings of an Administrative System*. New York: Oxford University Press, 1989.

Haspeslagh, Philippe. "Portfolio Planning: Uses and Limits." *Harvard Business Review*, 60 (January–February 1982): 58–74.

Hayes, Robert H. and William J. Abernathy. "Managing Our Way to

Economic Decline." *Harvard Business Review*, 58 (July–August 1980): 67–77.

Heimer, Carol. "Doing Your Job and Helping Your Friends: Universalistic Norms about Particular Others in Networks." In Nitin Nohria and Robert G. Eccles, eds., *Networks and Organizations*. Boston: Harvard Business School Press, 1992.

Hitt, Michael A. and R. Duane Ireland. "Corporate Distinctive Competence and Firm Performance." *Decision Sciences*, 15 (1984): 324–349.

Hofer, Charles W. and Dan E. Schendel. *Strategy Formulation: Analytical Concepts*. St. Paul, Minn.: West, 1978.

Homans, George C. *Fatigue of Workers*. New York: Reinhold, 1941.

Hopper, Max D. "Rattling SABRE—New Ways to Compete on Information." *Harvard Business Review*, 68 (May–June 1990): 118–125.

Ijiri, Yuji. "Cash-Flow Accounting and Its Structure." *Journal of Accounting, Auditing, and Finance*, 1, no. 4 (1978): 331–348.

———. "Recovery Rate and Cash Flow Accounting." *Financial Executive*, 48, no. 3 (March 1980): 54–60.

Itami, Hiroyuki. *Mobilizing Invisible Assets*. Cambridge, Mass.: Harvard University Press, 1987.

Jacobs, Michael T. *Short-Term America: The Causes and Cures of Our Business Myopia*. Boston: Harvard Business School Press, 1991.

Jaques, Elliott. "In Praise of Hierarchy." *Harvard Business Review*, 68 (January–February 1990): 127–133.

Jensen, Michael C. "Agency Costs of Free Cash Flow: Corporate Finances and Takeovers." *American Economic Review*, 76 (May 1986): 323–329.

———. "Active Investors, LBOs, and the Privatization of Bankruptcy." *Journal of Applied Corporate Finance*, 2, no. 1 (Spring 1989): 35–44.

———. "The Eclipse of the Public Corporation." *Harvard Business Review*, 67 (September–October 1989): 61–74.

Jensen, Michael C. and William M. Meckling. "Theory of the Firm: Managerial Behavior, Agency Costs and Ownership Structure." *Journal of Financial Economics*, 3 (1976): 305–360.

Johnson, H. Thomas and Robert S. Kaplan. *Relevance Lost: The Rise and Fall of Management Accounting*. Boston: Harvard Business School Press, 1987.

Kanter, Rosabeth. *The Change Masters: Innovations for Productivity in the American Corporation*. New York: Simon & Schuster, 1983.

———. *When Giants Learn to Dance: Mastering the Challenge of Strategy, Management, and Careers in the 1990s*. New York: Simon & Schuster, 1989.

Kaplan, Robert S. *Advanced Management Accounting*. Englewood Cliffs, N.J.: Prentice-Hall, 1982.

Kaplan, Robert S. and David P. Norton. "The Balanced Scorecard—

Measures That Drive Performance." *Harvard Business Review,* 70 (January–February 1992): 71–79.

Katz, Robert L. "Toward a More Effective Enterprise." *Harvard Business Review,* 38 (September–October 1960): 80–102.

Keen, Peter G.W. and Michael S. Scott-Morton. *Decision Support Systems: An Organizational Perspective.* Reading, Mass.: Addison-Wesley, 1978.

Keller, Maryann. *Rude Awakening: The Rise, Fall, and Struggle for Recovery of General Motors.* New York: Morrow, 1989.

Kline, Bennett E. and Norman H. Martin. "Freedom, Authority, and Decentralization." *Harvard Business Review,* 36 (May–June 1958): 69–75.

Kotter, John P. *The General Managers.* New York: Free Press, 1982.

———. *A Force for Change: How Leadership Differs from Management.* New York: Free Press, 1990.

Kotter, John P. and James L. Heskett. *Corporate Culture and Performance.* New York: Free Press, 1992.

Lawrence, Paul R. and Jay W. Lorsch. *Organization and Environment: Managing Differentiation and Integration.* Boston: Division of Research, Harvard Business School, 1967.

Likert, Rensis. "Measuring Organizational Performance." *Harvard Business Review,* 36 (March–April 1958): 41–50.

March, James G. "Footnotes to Organizational Change." *Administrative Science Quarterly,* 26 (1981): 563–577.

———. "Ambiguity and Accounting: The Elusive Link between Information and Decision Making." *Accounting, Organizations, and Society,* 12, no. 2 (1987): 153–168.

Marguiles, Walter P. "Make the Most of Your Corporate Identity." *Harvard Business Review,* 55 (July–August 1977): 66–74.

Martin, Joanne and Melanie E. Powers. "Organizational Stories: More Vivid and Persuasive than Quantitative Data." In B. Staw, ed., *Psychological Foundations of Organizational Behavior.* Glenview, Ill.: Scott, Foresman, 1983, 161–168.

McGregor, Douglas. "The Human Side of Enterprise." *Management Review,* 6, no. 11 (November 1957): 22–28, 88–92.

———. *The Human Side of Enterprise.* New York: McGraw-Hill, 1965.

McKinnon, Sharon M. and William J. Bruns, Jr. *The Information Mosaic.* Boston: Harvard Business School Press, 1992.

Meadows, Paul. "Post-Industrialism." *Technology Review,* 49 (December 1946): 101–103, 120, and 122.

Merchant, Kenneth A. *Rewarding Results: Motivating Profit Center Managers.* Boston: Harvard Business School Press, 1989.

Meyer, Marshall W. "The Performance Paradox." Wharton School, Department of Management Working Paper, undated.

Miles, Raymond E. and Charles C. Snow. *Organizational Strategy, Structure, and Process.* New York: McGraw-Hill, 1978.

Miller, Danny and Peter H. Friesen. *Organizations: A Quantum View.* Englewood Cliffs, N.J.: Prentice-Hall, 1984.

Miller, J. A. "Contingency Theory, Values, and Change." *Human Relations,* 31, no. 10 (October 1978): 885–904.

Mindlin, Sergio E. and Howard E. Aldrich. "Interorganizational Dependence: A Review of the Concept and a Reexamination of the Findings of the Aston Group." *Administrative Science Quarterly,* 20 (September 1975): 382–392.

Mintzberg, Henry. *The Nature of Managerial Work.* New York: Harper & Row, 1973.

———. "Crafting Strategy." *Harvard Business Review,* 65 (July–August 1987): 66–75.

———. "The Effective Organization: Forces and Forms." *Sloan Management Review,* 32, no. 2 (Winter 1991): 54–67.

Mohrman, Susan A. and Thomas Cummings. "Self-Designing Organizations: Toward Implementing Quality of Worklife Innovations." In R. Woodman and W. Pasmore, eds., *Research in Organizational Change and Development,* vol. 1. Greenwich, Conn.: JAI Press, 1987: 275–310.

Montgomery, Cynthia and Birger Wernerfelt. "Diversification, Ricardian Rents, and Tobin's q." *Rand Journal of Economics,* 19 (Winter 1988): 623–632.

Nadler, David A., J. Richard Hackman, and Edward Lawler III. *Managing Organizational Behavior.* Boston: Little, Brown, 1979.

Nohria, Nitin and Robert G. Eccles. "Corporate Capability." Harvard Business School Working Paper, 1991.

Ohmae, Kenichi. "Getting Back to Strategy." *Harvard Business Review,* 66 (November–December 1988): 149–156.

———. "Managing in a Borderless World." *Harvard Business Review,* 67 (May–June 1989): 152–161.

Olins, Wally. *Corporate Identity: Making Business Strategy Visible Through Design.* Boston: Harvard Business School Press, 1990.

Ouchi, William G. *Theory Z: How American Business Can Meet the Japanese Challenge.* Reading, Mass.: Addison-Wesley, 1981.

Oviatt, Benjamin M. and Warren D. Miller. "Irrelevance, Intransigence, and Business Professors." *The Academy of Management Executive,* 3 (1989): 304–312.

Pascale, Richard T. *Managing on the Edge: How the Smartest Companies Use Conflict to Stay Ahead.* New York: Simon & Schuster, 1990.

Pascale, Richard and Anthony Athos. *The Art of Japanese Management: Applications for American Executives.* New York: Simon & Schuster, 1981.

"Performance Measurement: Impact on Competitive Performance." *Outlook, Industrial Competitiveness,* 6, no. 4. Boston: Harbor Research, undated.

Peters, Tom. "Get Innovative or Get Dead (Part One)." *California Management Review,* 33, no. 1 (1990): 9–26.

———. "Get Innovative or Get Dead (Part Two)." *California Management Review,* 33, no. 2 (1990): 9–23.

Peters, Thomas J. and Robert H. Waterman, Jr. *In Search of Excellence: Lessons from America's Best-Run Companies.* New York: Harper & Row, 1982.

Pfeffer, Jeffrey. *Managing with Power: Politics and Influence in Organizations.* Boston: Harvard Business School Press, 1992.

Pierson, Frank C. et al. *The Education of American Businessmen: A Study of University-College Programs in Business Administration.* New York: McGraw-Hill, 1959.

Pondy, Louis R. "Leadership Is a Language Game." In Morgan W. McCall, Jr., and Michael M. Lombardo, eds., *Leadership: Where Else Can We Go?* Durham, N.C.: Duke University Press, 1978.

Porter, Lyman W. and Lawrence E. McKibbin. *Management Education and Development: Drift or Thrust into the 21st Century?* New York: McGraw-Hill, 1988.

Porter, Michael. *Competitive Strategy: Techniques for Analyzing Industries and Competitors.* New York: Free Press, 1980.

———. *Competitive Advantage: Creating and Sustaining Superior Performance.* New York: Free Press, 1985.

Prahalad, C. K. and Yves Doz. *The Multinational Mission: Balancing Local Demands and Global Vision.* New York: Free Press, 1987.

Prahalad, C. K. and Gary Hamel. "The Core Competence of the Corporation." *Harvard Business Review,* 68 (May–June 1990): 79–91.

Quinn, James Brian. "Managing Strategies Incrementally." In Robert B. Lamb, ed., *Competitive Strategic Management.* Englewood Cliffs, N.J.: Prentice-Hall, 1984: 35–61.

Raelin, Joseph A. *The Clash of Cultures: Managers Managing Professionals.* Boston: Harvard Business School Press, 1985.

Reece, James S. and William R. Cool. "Measuring Investment Center Performance." *Harvard Business Review,* 56 (May–June 1978): 26–40.

Roach, John D.C. "From Strategic Planning to Strategic Performance: Closing the Achievement Gap." In Robert B. Lamb, ed., *Competitive Strategic Management.* Englewood Cliffs, N.J.: Prentice-Hall, 1984: 209–222.

Roddick, Anita. *Body and Soul: Profits with Principles, The Amazing Success Story of Anita Roddick and the Body Shop.* New York: Crown, 1991.

Roethlisberger, F. J. and William J. Dickson. *Management and the Worker.* Cambridge, Mass.: Harvard University Press, 1939.

Rodgers, T. J. "No Excuses Management." *Harvard Business Review,* 68 (July–August 1990): 84–98.

Rumelt, Richard. *Strategy, Structure, and Economic Performance.* Boston: Division of Research, Harvard Business School, 1974.

S.A.M. Committee on Relations with Colleges and Universities, Society for the Advancement of Management. *Management Education; A Report on the Survey Among Business and Educational Leaders.* New York: Society for the Advancement of Management, 1948.

Schaffer, Robert H. and Harvey A. Thomson. "Successful Change Programs Begin with Results." *Harvard Business Review,* 70 (January–February 1992): 80–89.

Schoeffler, Sidney, Robert D. Buzzell, and Donald F. Heany. "Impact of Strategic Planning on Profit Performance." *Harvard Business Review,* 52 (March–April 1974): 137–145.

Senge, Peter M. "The Leader's New Work: Building Learning Organizations." *Sloan Management Review,* 32 (Fall 1990): 7–23.

Shapiro, Eileen. *How Corporate Truths Become Competitive Traps.* New York: John Wiley, 1991.

Shrivastava, Paul and Ian I. Mitroff. "Enhancing Organizational Research Utilization: The Role of Decision Makers' Assumptions." *Academy of Management Review,* 9 (1984): 18–26.

Slatter, Stuart St. P. "Common Pitfalls in Using the BCG Product Portfolio Matrix." *London Business School Journal* (Winter 1980): 18–22.

Sloan, Alfred P. *My Years with General Motors.* Garden City, N.Y.: Doubleday, 1963.

Solomons, David. *Divisional Performance: Measurement and Control.* Homewood, Ill.: Richard D. Irwin, 1965.

Spencer, S. A. "The Dark at the Top of the Stairs: What Higher Management Needs from Information Systems." *Management Review,* 51 (July 1962): 4–12.

Sproull, Lee S. "The Nature of Managerial Attention." In L. S. Sproull, ed., *Advances in Information Processing in Organizations.* Greenwich, Conn.: JAI Press, 1984: 9–27.

Stalk, George, Jr. "Time—The Next Source of Competitive Advantage." *Harvard Business Review,* 66 (July–August 1988): 41–51.

Stalk, George, Philip Evans, and Lawrence E. Shulman. "Competing on Capabilities: The New Rules of Corporate Strategy." *Harvard Business Review,* 70 (March–April 1992): 57–69.

Stambaugh, A. A. "Decentralization: The Key to the Future." *Dun's Review and Modern Industry* (September 1953): 53–54.

Stata, Ray. "Organizational Learning—The Key to Management Innovation." *Sloan Management Review,* 30, no. 3 (Spring 1989): 63–74.

Stevenson, Howard. "Defining Corporate Strengths and Weaknesses." *Sloan Management Review* (Spring 1976): 51–68.

Stevenson, Howard H., Michael J. Roberts, and H. Irving Grousbeck. *New Business Ventures and the Entrepreneur.* Homewood, Ill.: Richard D. Irwin, 1989.

Stewart, G. Bennett III. *The Quest for Value.* New York: Harper & Row, 1990.

Stewart, Rosemary. *Managers and Their Jobs.* London: Macmillan, 1967.

Suojanen, Waino W. "Leadership, Authority, and the Span of Control." *Advanced Management* (September 1957): 17–22.

Taylor, Frederick W. *The Principles of Scientific Management.* New York: W. W. Norton, 1911, 1947.

Teisberg, Elizabeth Olmstead. "Strategic Responses to Uncertainty." Harvard Business School Working Paper, 1990.

Thomas, Kenneth W. and Walter G. Tymon, Jr. "Necessary Properties of Relevant Research: Lessons from Recent Criticisms of the Organizational Sciences." *Academy of Management Review,* 7 (1982): 345–352.

Tichy, Noel and Ram Charan. "Speed, Simplicity, Self-Confidence: An Interview with Jack Welch." *Harvard Business Review,* 67 (September–October 1989): 112–120.

Toffler, Alvin. *The Adaptive Corporation.* London: Pan Books, 1985.

Tushman, Michael L., William H. Newman, and Elaine Romanelli. "Convergence and Upheaval: Managing the Unsteady Pace of Organizational Evolution." *California Management Review* (Fall 1986): 29–44.

Tushman, Michael L. and Elaine Romanelli. "Organizational Evolution: A Metamorphosis Model of Convergence and Reorientation." In L. L. Cummings and Barry M. Staw, eds., *Research in Organizational Behavior,* vol. 7. Greenwich, Conn.: JAI Press, 1985.

Vancil, Richard F. "What Kind of Management Control Do You Need?" *Harvard Business Review,* 51 (March–April 1973): 75–86.

———. *Decentralization: Managerial Ambiguity by Design.* Homewood, Ill.: Dow Jones–Irwin, 1979.

Villers, Raymond. "Control and Freedom in a Decentralized Company." *Harvard Business Review,* 32 (March–April 1954): 89–96.

Weick, Karl. *The Social Psychology of Organizing,* 2d ed. New York: Random House, 1979.

Whiting, William. "Industrial Conduct and Leadership." *Harvard Business Review,* 1 (April 1923): 322–330.

Whyte, William H. Jr. *The Organization Man.* New York: Simon & Schuster, 1956.

Wilkins, Alan L. "The Creation of Company Cultures: The Role of Stories and Human Resource Systems." *Human Resource Management,* 23 (1984): 41–60.

Woo, Carolyn Y. and Arnold C. Cooper. "The Surprising Case for Low Market Share." *Harvard Business Review,* 60 (November–December 1982): 106–113.

IV. BUSINESS PRESS

Brandt, Richard. "The Bad Boy of Silicon Valley: Meet T. J. Rodgers, CEO of Cypress Semiconductor." *Business Week* (December 9, 1991): 64–70.

Brokaw, Leslie. "Books That Transform Companies." *INC* (July 1991): 35–36.

Byrne, John A. "Business Fads: What's In—and Out." *Business Week* (January 20, 1986): 53.

———. "Is Research in the Ivory Tower 'Fuzzy, Irrelevant, Pretentious'?" *Business Week* (October 19, 1990): 62–66.

Clayman, Michelle. "In Search of Excellence: The Investor's Viewpoint." *Financial Analysts Journal* (May–June 1987): 54–63.

Cook, Brian M. "In Search of Six Sigma: 99.9997% Defect Free." *Industry Week* (October 1, 1990): 60–65.

Deutschman, Alan. "The Trouble with MBAs." *Fortune* (July 29, 1991): 67–79.

Dumaine, Brian. "Who Needs a Boss?" *Fortune* (May 7, 1990): 52–60.

———. "The Bureaucracy Busters." *Fortune* (June 17, 1991): 36–50.

Faltermayer, Edmund. "The Deal Decade: Verdict of the 80s." *Fortune* (August 26, 1991): 58–70.

Freedman, David. "The Myth of Strategic I.S." *CIO* (July 1991): 42–48.

Hammond, Keith H. "Corning's Class Act: How Jamie Houghton Has Reinvented the Company." *Business Week* (May 13, 1991): 68–76.

Hemp, Paul. "Preaching the Gospel." *Boston Globe* (June 30, 1992): 35.

Henkoff, Ronald. "How to Plan for 1995." *Fortune* (December 31, 1990): 70–77.

Houghton, James R. "The Age of the Hierarchy Is Over." *New York Times* (September 24, 1989): Sec. 3, p. 3.

Iacocca, Lee. *Iacocca: An Autobiography.* With William Novak. New York: Bantam Books, 1984.

"Is Anybody Listening?" *Fortune* (September 1950): 176.

Knowlton, Christopher. "The Buying Binge in Business Books." *Fortune* (February 13, 1989): 101–103.

Langstaff, Peggy. "Success Stories: Business Books That Lead to the Top." *Publishers Weekly* (August 9, 1991): 15–23.

Linden, Dana Wechsler. "Lies of the Bottom Line." *Forbes* (November 12, 1990): 106–112.

Main, Jeremy. "Manufacturing the Right Way." *Fortune* (May 21, 1990): 54–64.

Malchione, Robert. "Making Performance Measurements Perform." *Perspective*. Boston: The Boston Consulting Group, 1991.

Mansson, Per-Henrik. "Volnay's Veteran Vintner." *The Wine Spectator* (January 31, 1992): 30.

Murphy, John Allen. "What's Behind Today's Trend Toward Decentralization." *Sales Management* (October 1, 1946): 37–39.

———. "How the Wheels Go Round under Decentralized Management." *Sales Management* (October 15, 1946): 50–58.

———. "How to Keep Your Product Alive, Your Management Alert? —Decentralization!" *Sales Management* (November 1, 1946): 50–57.

Naisbitt, John. *Megatrends: Ten New Directions Transforming Our Lives.* New York: Warner Books, 1982.

Neff, Robert. "Can Tokyo Keep the Nikkei from Going Through the Floor?" *Business Week* (March 2, 1992): 34.

Newman, George. "The Absolute Measure of Corporate Excellence." *Across the Board,* 28, no. 10 (October 1991): 10–12.

Price, George R. "How to Speed Up Invention." *Fortune* (November 1956): 150.

Salmans, Sandra. "Demergering Britain's G.E." *New York Times* (July 6, 1980): F7.

Smith, Sarah. "America's Most Admired Corporations." *Fortune* (January 29, 1990): 58–92.

Stewart, Thomas A. "Why Budgets Are Bad for Business." *Fortune* (June 4, 1990): 179–190.

———. "GE Keeps Those Ideas Coming." *Fortune* (August 12, 1991): 40–49.

———. "Gay in Corporate America." *Fortune* (December 16, 1991): 42–56.

Stryker, Perrin. "The Subtleties of Delegation." *Fortune* (March 1955): 90–97, 160–164.

Taylor, Alex. "What Hath Roger Smith Wrought?" *Fortune* (September 25, 1989): 233–236.

Treece, James B. "Is Another Smith Headed for the Top at GM?" *Business Week* (March 26, 1990): 78, 80.

Verity, John W. and Gary McWilliams. "Is It Time to Junk the Way You Use Computers?" *Business Week* (July 22, 1991): 66–69.

Ways, Max. "Tomorrow's Management: A More Adventurous Life in a Free-Form Corporation." *Fortune* (July 1, 1966): 84–87, 148–150.

Weber, Jonathan. "The Productivity Paradox: Computer Revolution Fails to Light Fire Under Output." *Los Angeles Times* (March 8, 1992): D1, D13.

Welch, Jack. "Management for the Nineties." General Electric Executive Speech Reprint, 1988.

White, Joseph B. "GM's Problems Have Overtaken Stempel's Go-slow Approach." *The Wall Street Journal* (December 16, 1991): Sec. B, p. B1.

V. CASE STUDIES

Aguilar, Francis J. and Arvind Bhambri. "Johnson & Johnson (A): Philosophy and Culture." Case Study 9-384-053, Video 9-884-525. Boston: Harvard Business School, 1984.

Aguilar, Francis J. and Richard G. Hamermesh. "General Electric: Strategic Position 1981." Case Study 9-381-174. Boston: Harvard Business School, 1981.

Aguilar, Francis J., Richard G. Hamermesh, and Caroline Brainard. "General Electric, 1984." Case Study 9-385-315. Boston: Harvard Business School, 1985.

———. "General Electric: Reg Jones and Jack Welch." Case Study 9-391-144. Boston: Harvard Business School, 1991.

Bartlett, Christopher A., Kenton Elderkin, and Krista McQuade. "The Body Shop International." Case Study 9-392-032. Boston: Harvard Business School, 1991.

Bartlett, Christopher A. and V. S. Rangan. "Komatsu Ltd." Case Study 9-385-277. Boston: Harvard Business School, 1985.

Bartlett, Christopher A. and Michael Y. Yoshino. "Corning Glass Works." Case Study 9-381-160. Boston: Harvard Business School, 1981.

Berkley, James D. and Nitin Nohria. "Amgen Inc.: Planning the Unplannable." Case Study N9-492-052. Boston: Harvard Business School, 1992.

———. "Allen-Bradley's ICCG: Repositioning for the '90s." Case Study N9-491-066. Boston: Harvard Business School, 1990.

Elderkin, Kenton W. and Christopher A. Bartlett. "General Electric: Jack Welch's Second Wave." Case Study 9-391-248. Boston: Harvard Business School, 1991.

Gladstone, Julie and Nitin Nohria. "Appex Corporation." Case Study 9-491-082. Boston: Harvard Business School, 1991.

Hawkins, David F. "Empire Glass Company (A)." Case Study 109-043. Boston: Harvard Business School, 1964.

Jick, Todd. "Bob Galvin and Motorola, Inc. (A)." Case Study 9-487-062, rev. March 1989; "Bob Galvin and Motorola, Inc. (B)." Case Study 9-487-063; "Bob Galvin and Motorola, Inc. (C)." Case Study 4-487-064. Boston: Harvard Business School, 1987.

————. "Bob Galvin and Motorola, Inc. (A) (B) (C)." Teaching Note 4-491-100. Boston: Harvard Business School, 1991.

Linder, Jane and Robert G. Eccles. "Hercules Incorporated: Anatomy of a Vision." Case Study 9-186-305. Boston: Harvard Business School, 1985.

Love, Geoffrey and Robert G. Eccles. "Compaq Computer Corporation." Case Study 9-491-011. Boston: Harvard Business School, 1990, rev. 1991.

Nanda, Ashish and Christopher A. Bartlett. "Corning Incorporated: A Network of Alliances." Case Study 9-391-102. Boston: Harvard Business School, 1990.

Nohria, Nitin and Cynthia Cook. "Hill, Holliday, Connors, Cosmopulos, Inc. Advertising (A)." Case Study 9-491-016. Boston: Harvard Business School, rev. 1991.

Nohria, Nitin and Julie A. Gladstone. "Crompton Greaves Ltd." Case Study 9-491-074. Boston: Harvard Business School, 1990.

Wruck, Karen Hopper. "Sealed Air Corporation's Leveraged Recapitalization." Case Study 9-391-067. Boston: Harvard Business School, rev. 1991.

INDEX

ABOUT THE AUTHORS

Robert G. Eccles is president of Advisory Capital Partners, Inc. (ACP), a firm that invests in and advises medium-sized firms. The integrative financial, strategic, and organizational advisory services provided by ACP are focused on implementing growth plans that are funded by an equity capital investment. ACP makes these investments as a minority partner, allowing incumbent management to retain control. In working with its clients, ACP focuses on the basics of management and does not rely on the latest academic and consulting fads and buzzwords. Prior to becoming president of ACP, Dr. Eccles was a professor at Harvard Business School where he served on the faculty for 14 years. When he left Harvard he was chairman of the Organizational Behavior/Human Resource Management area. Dr. Eccles received two S.B. degrees from MIT in mathematics and humanities/social science and A.M. and Ph.D. degrees in sociology from Harvard.

Nitin Nohria is an associate professor of Business Administration at the Harvard Business School. He finished his undergraduate work in chemical engineering at the Indian Institute of Technology, Bombay in 1984 and then received a Ph.D. in management from the Sloan School of Management at the Massachusetts Institute of Technology in 1988. His research and teaching interests are primarily in the area of organization structure and change. He is the editor (with Robert G. Eccles) of *Networks in Organizations,* for which he also wrote several chapters.

James D. Berkley recently completed a two-year position as research associate in organizational behavior at the Harvard Business School. Prior to coming to Harvard, he studied literature and philosophy at Williams College, where he received his B.A. in 1990. In addition to his work on organizations, Berkley has also written on such topics as virtual reality and contemporary American culture, and was a participant at the 1991 Cyberspace conference in Santa Cruz, California.